FAMILY VIOLENCE AND THE WOMEN'S MOVEMENT
The Conceptual Politics of Struggle

Feminists have always perceived wife abuse as just one of many manifestations of the unequal division of power between men and women. But as public awareness of the issue grew, government agencies began to take the issue over. They redefined wife-battering as a social problem for which professional and legislative responses were appropriate solutions. They ignored its connection to more fundamental questions of male power.

Gillian Walker systematically and empirically examines the process by which the issue of wife-battering was taken away from feminists and the women being abused. She has combined her own first-hand experiences as a feminist activist with a careful analysis of documents and with interviews of participants in various federal and provincial conferences and hearings. From this she shows how the experience of wife abuse became defined as part of the broader issue of family violence.

The women who together started and shaped the transition-house movement today find their status changed. They are directed away from political action. Instead they are expected only to provide services in crisis shelters, increasingly monitored and under-funded, part of a broader network of services to 'troubled families.' Meanwhile, society fails to address the question of gender inequality as the root cause of wife-battering.

Walker's analysis of the conceptual processes involved in naming an 'issue' and defining a 'social problem' offers insights into the politics of social action generally. It speaks to the struggles of all grassroots activists.

GILLIAN A. WALKER is Associate Professor, Carleton School of Social Work, Carleton University. She is co-editor of *Community Organization and the Canadian State*, and author, with P. Susan Penfold, of *Women and the Psychiatric Paradox*.

GILLIAN A. WALKER

FAMILY VIOLENCE
and the Women's Movement:

The Conceptual Politics of Struggle

UNIVERSITY OF TORONTO PRESS
Toronto Buffalo London

© University of Toronto Press 1990
Toronto Buffalo London
Printed in Canada

ISBN 0-8020-2740-7 (cloth)
ISBN 0-8020-6782-X (paper)

Canadian Cataloguing in Publication Data

Walker, Gillian A.
    Family violence and the women's movement

    Includes bibliographical references.
    ISBN 0-8020-2740-7 (bound) ISBN 0-8020-6782-X (pbk.)

    1. Wife abuse – Political aspects. 2. Feminism.
    I. Title.

HV6626.W34 1990   362.82'92   C90-094195-2

This book has been published with the help of a grant from the
Social Science Federation of Canada, using funds provided by the
Social Sciences and Humanities Research Council of Canada.

Contents

ACKNOWLEDGMENTS vii

1 The Women's Movement and the Relations of Ruling / 3

2 The Entry Point: Raising the Issue of 'Wife-Battering' / 21

3 Translating the Issue to the Purview of the State / 36

4 Documents as Organizers / 57

5 Discourse as Dilemma / 73

6 The Concept of Violence / 95

7 Particularizing the General / 111

8 Hearing the Issue / 133

9 Negotiating the Elements / 152

10 Reporting for Action / 168

11 Action and Reaction / 194

12 Conceptual Practices and the Relations of Ruling / 207

NOTES 221

REFERENCES 241

INDEX 251

Acknowledgments

It has become something of a truism to state that no piece of work is the achievement of the author alone. Nevertheless, in the case of this book it must be said once more. The intellectual keystone of this work is the method of analysis developed by Dorothy E. Smith. I want, first and foremost, to acknowledge her importance to me as a teacher, scholar, and friend. Taking up her approach in my work has involved me in a journey in which I have had many companions, all of whom have contributed to it over the years. Alison Griffith, Adele Mueller, Marie Campbell, Roxana Ng, Himani Bannerji, Ann Manicom, and Alice DeWolff have been particularly influential in this enterprise, both as scholars and as friends, as have Nancy Jackson, who made helpful comments on an earlier draft, and George Smith, who provided an important part of the data and offered advice and technical assistance. My friends among the students, staff, and faculty in the departments of Adult Education and Sociology at the Ontario Institute for Studies in Education have been a constant source of support and stimulation. Brenda Parris, Trudy Don, Richard Johnston, and many others shared their experience, expertise, and time with me most generously. Various important practical forms of friendship and support came from Val and Tony Hotchkiss, Sue Findlay, Gill Bryan, Trudy Cowan, and other friends in Toronto and Brantford.

The roots of this work are in Vancouver, and I want to acknowledge the contribution of colleagues, family, and friends there who have encouraged and supported me throughout its completion. My women's group – Joann Robertson, Sue Penfold, Susie Innes, and Ingrid Pacey – the women who founded the Battered Women's Support Services Collective and members of the Women's Research Centre, especially Jan

Barnsley, Gene Errington, Debra Lewis, Ajax Quimby, Holly Prince, and Frances Wasserlein; colleagues at the Women Students' Office at the University of British Columbia; along with my sons and many other dear friends – all deserve my gratitude and thanks.

Colleagues and friends at Carleton University, in the School of Social Work there, and in the Ottawa community have cheered me on and often taken up the slack for me as I struggled to finish this book. Their encouragement and concern were an important part of my being able to do so. Beth Mairs and Valerie Watson provided me with valuable research assistance and material, and I have also drawn on the work of Pamela Johnson, Trish Crowe, and Milada Selucky. I would like to thank Kathleen Rockhill, James Draper, Patricia Morgan, Alan Thomas, and Sheila Neysmith for the thoughtful and interesting questions they raised at the dissertation stage of this project. These questions proved most helpful in clarifying a number of issues and added to my understanding of the topic.

My parents, Beatrice and Paddy Bagnall, have been a loving and constant source of emotional and economic support throughout the years. There is no way to express adequately the debt of gratitude and love I owe to them.

I was also fortunate the receive financial aid for two years from the Doctoral Fellowship Program of the Social Sciences and Humanities Research Council.

Finally, I thank Karen Dunbar for the almost superhuman effort she put into transforming many drafts of my work into a readable manuscript. Her patience and skill were a crucial part of the enterprise, as was the care taken by Iris Taylor in producing it in a revised form. The revision process benefited from the support of Roland Lecomte, Director of the School of Social Work, and Marilyn Marshall, Dean of Social Sciences, at Carleton University. Virgil Duff, the editorial staff, and the readers for the University of Toronto Press and the Social Science Federation of Canada have given me encouragement and help in the publication process. The index was prepared with skill and enthusiasm by Sheryl Adam, in Vancouver.

I thank you all; any praise is yours, the faults are my own.

FAMILY VIOLENCE AND THE WOMEN'S MOVEMENT
The Conceptual Politics of Struggle

1 The Women's Movement and the Relations of Ruling

The 1980s have been described as the decade in which the major issue for feminists – in Canada, the United States, and Britain, at least – has been the relations between women and 'the state.'[1] The previous decade or so was one of intense political activity as women continued to identify further aspects of their oppression and organized a broad range of projects designed to combat the worst excesses in an effort to move forward towards liberation. The specific conjunction of the development of the women's movement and the political structures of government in Canada has produced a situation whereby much of the activity of the women's movement has been directed towards or funded by the state.[2]

Recent considerations of the implications of the way in which the struggle for women's liberation has been focused by its relation to the state have arisen from the recognition that there are problems with reliance on the state when it comes to achieving major or long-term changes in women's subordinate status. A change in government, with its attendant changes in policy and strategies; economic restraint and cut-backs in government spending; the rise of the group calling itself REAL. Women and its demands for government funding based on its being representative of large numbers of non-feminist or anti-feminist women; and the lack of real change in women's economic status – all have contributed to a sense of the need to review and reconsider feminist strategies and assess progress so far.[3]

In the last few years feminists have organized a number of events designed to explore and evaluate the relation of women, in general, and the women's movement, in particular, to the state – however we may define that term. Women have shared their knowledge and experience as state workers and as recipients of state services in discussion and study groups and in formal and informal organizations. Workshops and sessions at academic conferences have addressed the topic.[4] A conference on women and the state held in Toronto in 1987 focused exclusively on finding ways to describe, analyse, and develop strategies in relation to an understanding of the nature of state procedures and practices; the conference was designed to make sense of women's experience as workers, activists, consumers, and providers of state services. Numerous books and articles by established feminists have also appeared, in Canada and elsewhere, reviewing the progress of the movement's initiatives and assessing future directions and possibilities for the liberation of women.[5]

This book takes as its starting-point this process of questioning, reviewing, and assessing. It developed out of exploration and discussion of the contradictions that I and my friends and colleagues have experienced between our commitment as feminist activists and our situation as professionals: educators, academics, therapists, social workers, and so on. Examining those experiences from our standpoint as women and as feminists has led to an understanding of the position that professionals occupy in the management of people's lives on behalf of a ruling apparatus; that is, the network of institutions and activities, including those of the state, whereby power is exercised and our society organized, administered, and ruled. The terms 'ruling,' 'ruling relations' and 'ruling apparatus' are used throughout this book to designate those institutional forms that actually organize, regulate, and control society through state administration, legislative processes, the management process, business and industry, professional organizations, and the textually mediated discourses of science, culture, technology, news and so on.[6] As feminists work to define and evaluate the relationship between women, the women's movement, and the relations of ruling, it is increasingly evident that one-dimensional views of a monolithic state apparatus are not adequate to the task.

KNOWLEDGE AND THE WOMEN'S MOVEMENT

To recognize and understand the operation of the state as a feature of the relations of ruling is of crucial importance to feminists as professionals, activists, and women struggling to manage their lives and the lives of their children. Professional ideology teaches us that, as professionals, we are outside the state, neutral, objective, and self-regulating. Feminism teaches us that professional practices are oppressive and biased.[7] They arise from, and operate in relation to, an objectified body of knowledge arising in the work processes of formal organizations and institutions interconnected by a range of discourses. The rise of a welfare-state apparatus has meant that more and more of us are employed directly by institutions as professionals, bureaucrats, and service and clerical workers. Women must also turn to the state for services such as health care, social-security payments, unemployment insurance, housing, and education. Feminists in Canada have found various levels of government the predominant sources of funding for their organizations and programs. Under these circumstances, we have to look at what we do as professionals, activists, and women in general, and see how our activities are part of the way in which social relations are brought into being and reproduced. We must also come to see how the state is articulated to these activities, as a part of how ruling is accomplished.

This necessity has led, in part, to feminists taking up a particular critique of the way in which the practical activities that constitute knowledge operate in relation to the work of the women's movement.[9] The book assembles and analyses the details of a process of organizing and struggling for change around what feminists have identified as a 'women's issue' – that of the plight of women whose husbands or male intimates beat, brutalize, and otherwise abuse them. The struggle has been called by various commentators, particularly in the United States, 'the Battered Women's Movement' or 'the Shelter Movement.'[10] These writers have described the rise, progress, continuation, or decline of such a movement in various terms, most notably as a process of co-optation, institutionalization, and state appropriation that has been sometimes more and sometimes less successfully struggled against.[11] While there appear to be many similarities in the development and disposition of this 'issue' in the United States, in Canada, and in a number of European countries, the relation of the movement to the state appears to differ according to the particular conjunction of the broader women's movement, the existing formal party political configurations, and the organizational forms of the particular state.

The events and processes assembled in this book, however, are not brought together in an attempt to write a history of the Battered Women's Movement in Canada or of its successes and failures to date.[12]

Neither do I endeavour to identify the characteristics of a social movement as a framework for tracing a process of co-optation.[13] Nor is it my intention to produce an elaboration of existing theories of the state. Rather, I have set out to do something different: to trace the process whereby wife-beating came to be seen as an issue in the first place; to look at how the work of the women's movement succeded in placing it in the public sphere of action and concern; and to analyse the ways in which the outcomes to date relate to the organizing and mobilizing initiatives taken by activists. Achieving these goals requires an examination of the struggle against those seeking to claim the issue in terms of their professional mandate, and the ways in which the issue has been translated to the purview of the state. This study does so in a very specific way, focusing on local events in order to uncover the particulars of the struggle and the conceptual underpinnings that make sense of seemingly contradictory outcomes. It identifies the operation of an aspect of ruling relations; the analysis reveals a layered and many-levelled web of negotiated relations in which ideological constructs play a co-ordinating role.

My argument, then, is concerned with what can be learned from such an analysis, not only about specific and local events but also about the broader processes of knowledge and power whereby issues are transformed from political concerns (using 'political' here in the sense of the feminist maxim of 'personal as political') into social problems. Once such a transformation has taken place, administrative, professional, and institutional responses, rather than changes in political structures, are seen to be appropriate solutions. This transformation process is, I argue, one of absorption and control of the struggles undertaken by the women's movement. Such an analysis addresses the dilemmas and contradictions of feminist practice.

SHAPING SOCIAL PROBLEMS

In her important 1981 article on the state's shaping of social problems, Morgan points to a significant lacuna in the analysis undertaken by those working to understand the nature and practices of the state.[14] She outlines two major analytic positions: one, she suggests, studies the processes engaged in by popular movements that demand expanded services while treating the state as a set of apparatuses; the other examines social interventions of the welfare state in such a way that we learn nothing of the struggles that have taken place and had an impact on both the form and the content of such interventions. Morgan suggests that the failure of analysts to examine the state as a set of social relations, determined by capitalist interests and shaped by successful organizing to change social life, leaves us with an analytic gap. This gap 'prevents us from understanding the nature of grassroots movement failures or co-optation, and thus keeps us on a treadmill of ineffective organizing.'[15]

Building on Morgan's point, Ng poses a series of questions within the quest for a framework for analysis that would address the gap identified by Morgan. She suggests that raising the question 'How does the state serve to reproduce capitalist social relations ... as a practical matter, in everyday life?' presents us with 'a more fundamental epistemological issue about the analyses of the state and class in contemporary societies.'[16] This question, in turn, leads to one concerning the relationship between analyses of 'macro' processes, such as those done by Marxist theorists, and 'micro' analyses, done by ethnomethodologists. It also leads to an examination of the relationship between formal organizations and procedures and our own practices. It means asking ourselves how we, as members of society, 'participate in the processes which maintain and reproduce our own oppression and the oppression of others.'[17] It means developing a framework that can help us 'analyse our own activities and evaluate our own actions, so that ... as intellectuals committed to social justice, and as community activists committed to social change ... we can act more effectively; so that we won't work on the "wrong" side.'[18]

Ng's study of the provision of employment placement services to immigrant women uncovers ways in which the class character of the state is reproduced when a grass-roots agency is forced to use bureaucratic and professional methods of working. These bureaucratic and professional practices are identified by Morgan as forming the lineaments of a 'social problem apparatus' charged with 'managing the more problematic aspects of capitalist social relations: mental health, deviance, violence and crime.'[19] Ng examines the actual work practices imposed by interaction with the state; processes of funding, management, and evaluation of grass-roots projects, themselves designed to remedy some of the most blatant inequalities of access in the capitalist labour process. In the case that Ng documents, the difficulties examined are those experienced by immigrant women, and the process she traces reveals the impact of state funding provisos on those working to change this aspect of women's subordinate position.[20]

Meuller, in her study of the 'women in development' discourse, displays a different aspect, that of the contradictions that develop for feminist academics and professionals entering into particular relations of ruling. In this instance, research and thinking are reformulated in such a way that they become vehicles whereby Third World women are constructed as a recognizable object for interventions by the development agencies of advanced capitalist societies.[21]

My work deals with another facet of the interaction between the state and the women's movement, but one that must be seen within the same framework – that of the organization of social relations linking the local and everyday activities and practices of people with the general and abstracted procedures of ruling and administering the particular form of society in which we live. I focus on the ideological features of social organization and take up the method advanced by Smith[22] from the work of Marx and Engels,[23] which analyses ideological structures and the social construction of documentary forms of reality.

SOCIAL STRUCTURES AND RULING RELATIONS

Society as we know it is not random but organized, ordered, and governed, with varying degrees of efficiency perhaps, but nonetheless structured. The form of ruling goes beyond formal government and the notably coercive apparatus of law and order. Under such a regime, as opposed to overtly totalitarian ones, we are not ruled on a day-to-day basis by terror but by ideological procedures – ways of thinking, understanding, and acting – that enlist us in our own ordering. Ideological procedures are a feature of the way our society is governed. They form part of the work of a ruling apparatus comprising a complex of relations, including the state, the managerial and administrative processes, education, the professions, the media, and so on, that organize and control contemporary capitalist society.[24] These are ruling relations in that they can be identified as the dominant mode of an exercise of power that involves the continual transcription of the local and particular actualities of our lives into abstracted and generalized forms. Ruling, in this context, identifies a network of institutional and organizational practices, as well as the discourses in texts that interpenetrate the multiple sites of power.[25]

Marx and Engels suggest that, in every era, the ideas of the ruling class are the ruling ideas; the class that is the ruling material force in a society is also its ruling intellectual force. Ruling ideas are the expression of the dominant material relationships. Those who rule, as a class, do so as, among other things, thinkers, producers of ideas, and regulators of ideas.[26] In our time, as Schreader points out: 'The practice of ruling also extends beyond the simple legitimization of ruling class ideas and activities, for it involves the social construction of reality. It is here that the professions fit in. The professions are intimately involved in the social construction of reality; both in the production of knowledge and also through their professional practices with individuals.'[27]

Although in various ways those who rule strive to maintain what Gramsci has characterized as ideological hegemony,[28] the process by which social reality is constructed results in there being considerable discrepancy and disjunction between the ideological forms provided for us to understand our world and our direct experience of our situation in that world.[29] These gaps and disjunctions have, under particular historic considerations and in certain sites, allowed for the voicing of 'counter-hegemonic' ideas and the taking of action by those who feel that they are not being governed by their own best interests.

The work of feminist critics over the last decade or so has made it clear that what has been seen as a matter of class is also a matter of gender. The forms of thought through which we come to know about ourselves and the society in which we live originate in positions of dominance that have hitherto been held, almost invariably, by men. They constitute a view of the world from those positions, positions from which women have been virtually excluded.[30]

Though the occasional woman has been admitted to a special position of dominance, it has been as an individual, an exception and not as a representative of her sex. When women are considered in specific instances and in relation to the development of 'women's' professions, such as social work, nursing, and teaching, it can be seen that those women who have occupied dominant positions have done so in relation to their class and, where they have been held to represent their sex, it has been in very specific and controlled ways that direct the nature or restrict the impact of their work. Thus, historically, women have been prohibited from full participation in the public arena where power is exercised through courses of action organized as ideological practices.

It is a disservice to us as women and to our understanding of the structuring, ordering, and ruling of society, however, to regard ourselves as having been merely passive victims of historical processes controlled by a conspiracy of men. We need, instead, to analyse and understand women's differing relation to the capitalist enterprise and our active participation in the everyday production and reproduction of that relation.[31] As women again struggle to enter the public area on our own terms, the processes of exclusion are being transformed into ones that absorb, appropriate, and reorganize our work.

This book is concerned with the conceptual practices used by professionals (researchers, practitioners, academics, policy makers) to provide us with ways of understanding and organizing our experiences of the world. Beyond this concern, the book examines the location of these practices in the ruling relations of society, and, in particular, how such conceptual practices come to be an integral part of the political process involved in that ruling relation. I take my entry point and focus the dilemmas and contradictions that women face as feminists when they seek to enter the political process in order to redress difficulties and dangers in their lives.

IDEOLOGICAL PRACTICES

Two interrelated aspects need to be taken into account in considering ideological practices. One is the dynamic, changing nature of capitalism; the other is the increasingly abstract modes of organization and administration that have evolved with the changing forms.

Here is how Smith describes the first aspect: 'Capitalism as a mode of production is essentially a dynamic system of change. It changes the material bases of our lives, the organization of our work, and our social relations, in a continual active process of which all of us are part ... We have to deal with these [changes] in whatever way we can. The mechanisms enforcing stability, the control processes of the society – laws, administration, the professions taking up the problems of individuals – these have the job of responding to such changes.'[32]

One of the ways in which responses must be made is through the development of appropriate language with which to realize the abstracted mode of ruling. As Smith states: 'As professionals, government, and corporate apparatuses become consolidated as a ruling apparatus, forms of action in words and symbols become fully differentiated. Language is constituted as a discrete mode of action.'[33] It is part of the job of professionals, including academics, in 'taking up the problems of individuals,' to engage in an active process of defining issues 'to accord with organizational practices and bring [them] within the appropriate professional jurisdictions.'[34]

Concepts are not constructed randomly or accidentally but are actual work processes in the production of knowledge. In themselves, concepts provide for particular courses of action. Understood in this way, concepts can be seen to do more than name a phenomenon. They are part of a social relation (used here to signify an ongoing and concerted course of action) that organizes the particular phenomena in specific ways and provides for response to what has been thus identified. To call what happens to women at the hands of their husbands or boy friends an instance of 'family violence' or 'spouse abuse,' 'wife-battering,' 'interspousal violent episodes' or 'domestic disputes' is to enter the actual experience into a set of conceptual practices and bureaucratic processes that do a particular kind of work. It is not, therefore, a 'cosmetic quibble' when feminists draw attention to the implications of the terminology involved.[35] 'Domestic disputes' and 'domestics,' for example, are terms that originate in police work and denote a bureaucratic category that designates the type of report and the priority of response of the police to reported incidents. The domestic dispute category covers any disturbance between persons related by blood, marriage, or household or neighbourhood proximity. This locates the problem within the legal system for which the Criminal Code and policies concerning its administration provide the organizational basis for policing practices with regard to law enforcement, peacekeeping, and the maintenance of order.[36]

When concepts do more than describe or name a situation and actually remove what people say and do from the social relations in which events take place – they become part of the construction of ideology. The practical actions, activities, and locations that connect up social relations are stripped away and dropped out of the conceptual form to be replaced by connectives that account for experience in terms of theory and discourse.

INSTITUTIONAL ETHNOGRAPHY

Smith has provided a distinctive method of analysis designed to explicate the complex relationship between the way an experience is shaped and the organizational forms that give it meaning. The method, which she has called an 'institutional ethnography,' provides 'an ethnography of the social relations which articulate members of society to the institutional and administrative relations through which this society is ruled and managed.'[37] The object of an institutional ethnography is to situate the problem to be studied in the 'real world' of practical, everyday activities, the 'lived relations' of a class society. The method identifies some of the components as interrelated, interlocking, and interdependent but not infinite. The social organization is complex but not mystical; it can be known.

Such a method, then, requires concepts and categories to be explicated in terms of their capacity to enter into and further organizational courses of action. When examining a problem, therefore, it is important to recognize that there is an 'intimate and interactive link between understanding and definition [of a problem] ... and the institution charged with its resolution.'[38] This generalizing relation in the making provides the analytic framework of this book. I trace and explicate the constitution of concepts such as wife-battering and family violence, and their location in the ideological practices that form the work processes of the women's movement, professional bodies mandated to deal with 'social problems,' and state policy makers who must organize, order and govern in such a way as to resolve or ameliorate the difficulties thus posed.

INSTITUTIONAL RELATIONS

This entry point is distinctively different from those of methods of enquiry that start within the discursive frameworks. Such frameworks are already developed for our understanding by theorists working with the tools of social science or by administrative procedures that organize our activities. Indeed, this entry point renders visible and calls into question those practices normally taken for granted in institutional procedures. Here I am using 'institution' and 'institutional' as Smith does:

to identify a complex of relations forming part of the ruling apparatus, organized around a distinctive function – education, health care, law, etc. In contrast to such concepts as bureaucracy, 'institution' does not define a determinate form of social organization, but rather the intersection and co-ordination of more than one relational mode of the ruling apparatus. Characteristically, state agencies are tied in with professional forms of organization, and both are interpenetrated by relations of discourse of more than one order ... Integral to the co-ordinating process are ideologies systematically developed to provide categories and concepts expressing the relation of local courses of action to the institutional function ... and providing a currency or currencies enabling interchange between different specialized parts of the complex.[39]

Such an understanding of 'institution' is particularly useful for this study. It provides a way to grasp the complexities of a process that concerns a multiplicity of groups, agencies, organizations, departments, and individuals, and offers a schema in which we 'might imagine institutions as nodes or knots in the relations of the ruling apparatus to class, co-ordinating multiple strands of action into a functional complex.'[40]

ETHNOGRAPHY AS ENTRY POINT

In addition, the notion of ethnography, Smith suggests, commits us 'to an exploration, description and analysis of such a complex of relations, not conceived in the abstract but from the entry point of some particular people or a particular person whose everyday world of working is organized thereby.'[41]

In this case, the entry point is the work of the women's movement in making visible the plight of women beaten and abused by their mates. Specifically, I have focused on the dilemmas and contradictions I experienced in working on the issue, as a feminist with professional training and activist commitments, with other feminists in Vancouver and across Canada. This experience provides an entry point to a generalizing process that sets in place a particular organizing framework for the later activities of the Ontario Association of Interval and Transition Houses in pressuring politicians to take up the issue. How it was taken up as part of the procedures of the Standing Committee on Social Development of the Ontario Legislature and what the outcome of the subsequent hearings provide for as a course of action form the subject of the second half of the book.

The interplay between the consciousness developing in the women's movement and the Ontario hearings can be captured in an ethnography that provides the basis for an analysis of experiences, records, texts, and transcripts. These demonstrate how the issue was taken up and translated to the purview of the state in such events as a national consultation organized by the Canadian Advisory Council on the Status of Women (CACSW), in documents in which a women's movement position began to be articulated in general terms, and finally in the federal government hearings that immediately preceded and greatly influenced those held in Ontario.

My argument is based on a close reading and analysis of the Hansard verbatim transcripts of the Ontario hearing; background documents consisting of written submissions, academic literature, a film, some internal correspondence between the committee's staff and members; and interviews with a few key participants in the procedure. I have also made extensive use of material from my own records, documents and texts from both policy and academic discourses, and my experience as a participant in earlier events. These data provide the lineaments of the process of conceptual co-ordination being organized by the interactions and frameworks under examination.

We see from this entry point a concerted process that leads to a particular co-ordination of institutional practices. Here, we can make use of Smith's discovery that such co-ordination is 'mediated ideologically.'[42] We can see that the categories and concepts that concern us, such as 'battered wife' and 'family violence,' 'express the relation of members' actual practices – their work – to the institutional function.'[43] Thus the events described in the following chapters can be understood more fully when we come to examine the differing institutional locations of, for instance, the protagonists on the United Way Task Force on Family Violence in Vancouver, or the participants in the federal government consultation in Ottawa in 1980. We will see that family violence has a particular relation to the work of professionals, particularly social workers, as does domestic violence to the work of the police: 'Institutional ideologies are acquired by members as methods of analyzing experiences located in the work processes of institutions. Professional training in particular teaches people how to recycle the actualities of their experience into the forms in which it is recognizable within institutional discourse.'[44]

These forms, however, are not generally recognized as such but are given, by the very 'objective' processes of their production, the status of information or 'fact.' In this way they are severed from 'their necessary anchorage in an economy of material conditions, time and effort.'[45] Indeed, Smith suggests that the work processes of actual individuals are specifically obscured and thus: 'The categories and concepts of ideologies substitute for actual relations, actual practices, work processes and organization and the practical knowledge and reasoning of actual individuals, the expressions of a textually mediated discourse.'[46]

THE CASE IN POINT

In April 1987, the government of Ontario announced its commitment to 'stem the tide of family violence in Ontario' by increasing government spending in the area by more than $7 million. The Ontario Association of Interval and Transition Houses (OAITH), the organization that represents almost all the shelter and related services in the province, praised the government for its recognition of the expertise of women working in interval and transition houses. It did not, however, celebrate the announcement as a victory and vindication for years of organizing, lobbying, serving on committees, appearing before government hearings, and so on. In fact, OAITH noted that only $300,000 had been provided for shelter expansion, and that this would not meet the demand for services anticipated in response to the government's proposed public- and professional-awareness campaign.[47]

The Ontario government's 1987 initiatives, part of a succession, continued to address the problem of family violence but did so in ways that have not made fundamental changes in the overall situation of women, beaten or not. In fact, in the case of family violence, the proposed measures fell far short of what women's groups had demanded. Most of the funding allotments have gone to the provision of services to victims of family violence by a range of traditional agencies and institutions. Feminist organizations have become just a small section of those whose service delivery is acknowledged and funded. This situation has prompted further questioning within the Transition House Movement as the inadequacy of ever-increasing social-service approaches and the need for large-scale political change have become more evident. Although the events being examined in this book took place in the late 1970s and early 1980s, in various parts of Canada and elsewhere, they provided a basis for the kinds of re-evaluation that are taking place today. To understand how the work of women in this area has come to be directed towards the provision of refuge and shelter sevices and the lobbying of government requires an examination of the development of the issue and the generalizing relations in which it has been transformed from its earier manifestations as a passionate political organizing focus.

The first part of this book describes and analyses the initial stages of the process, from its roots in local activities to its translation to the purview of the state. The events that provide the material for analysis in the second part of this book occurred in Ontario in 1982. The Standing Committee on Social Policy Development of the Ontario Legislature, in response to pressure from women's groups, considered the issue of family violence, focusing on wife-battering. A report and recommendations came before the legislature in December of that year and provided the basis for a series of government initiatives early in 1983. This process can be diagrammed as:

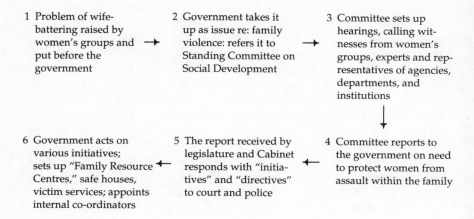

1 Problem of wife-battering raised by women's groups and put before the government →

2 Government takes it up as issue re: family violence: refers it to Standing Committee on Social Development →

3 Committee sets up hearings, calling witnesses from women's groups, experts and representatives of agencies, departments, and institutions ↓

6 Government acts on various initiatives; sets up "Family Resource Centres," safe houses, victim services; appoints internal co-ordinators ←

5 The report received by legislature and Cabinet responds with "initiatives" and "directives" to court and police ←

4 Committee reports to the government on need to protect women from assault within the family

Examining the particulars of this process in some detail shows a series of negotiations and transformations in which input from the particpants had an impact on the internal structuring of the state in relation to its procedures and departmental prerogatives. The impact was, however, limited and contained by the very way in which the issue was raised, formulated, negotiated, and co-ordinated through the work of the standing committee and its witnesses.

In the process of analysing these events, however, the focus of the book isolates for examination a political process of control that shapes and develops 'issues' and lodges them in the administrative procedures for ordering, organizing, and ruling contemporary society. Particularly, it takes up the process of institutional articulation and absorption that concepts, as ways of thinking, naming, and knowing, co-ordinate and make possible. This approach has allowed me to develop a framework that delineates the process in several stages. These stages loosely correspond both to the temporal sequence of events and to the ideological aspects in which the struggle for control and action were played out. Thus I am able to show the generalizing relation being put in place. In such a way, it is possible to see what is going on when issues that seemingly come out of 'nowhere' are linked up with structures where there is the possibility of getting something done to address them.

THE PROCESS OF ABSORPTION

The struggle I have described here can be characterized as having taken place in three stages, though capturing the ongoing and many-levelled process in this seemingly static way is, of course, a device and must be taken as such. The first stage involves the efforts of the women's movement to make the situation of women being beaten by their menfolk visible and actionable, an initially inchoate struggle for recognition. It denotes the women's movement's struggle to define a 'women's issue' in the face of professional concern to remove it from the political 'movement' context and organization, in order to provide services to 'troubled families.' The second stage marks the resulting struggle within the women's movement as the work of getting something done about 'the issue' is translated to and generalized within the purview of the state. Feminists strive to formulate an account of the problem, providing both an analysis of its roots and a basis for strategies upon which to act in realtion to increasing state involvement. The third stage traces a concerted effort on the part of movement activists, service providers, and others in various professional fields, in the enterprise of getting particular aspects of the ruling apparatus to respond properly to the needs of battered women. It marks a transformation and reorganization of the relations of the women's movement to the issue and to the agencies and institutions of the state. This book itself takes its place at the beginning of a possible fourth stage, one of dissatisfaction and strategic re-examination, provoked by the outcomes of this enterprise.

The temporal nature of these stages can be counterposed with an equally empirical conceptual mapping of the process in question. Concepts, when understood and analysed as practices of thinking and ordering, can be seen to do more than merely name or mark phenomena. Such practices construct events as phenomena as such and, at the same time, provide for courses of action to be taken; they perform this function of co-ordination in quite concrete ways.

The first stage of the process under examination shows how 'the issue' is created as such at the local level when the climate and space provided by the women's movement make a place where women can begin to admit that their husbands beat or otherwise ill-treat them. This situation becomes the main concern of transition houses and other types of women's centres that offer accommodation, although they may initially have been set up for and used by women who, for a variety of reasons, were homeless. Feminist professionals whose work brings them into contact with women's lives also begin to speak out about what they see and hear.[48] This stage of making women's plight public and refusing to accept it as a private problem draws attention to the magnitude of the issue and puts it in the public arena at the local level. Insistence on providing shelter and support, organized to embody feminist principles of consciousness raising, collectivity, and respect for women's own strength and power to make decisions, also puts activists in the position of having to talk about it in ways that name and validate the situation as legitimate for funding and intervention purposes. Those working in the area adopt terminology that demonstrates a co-ordinating capacity around which support services can be organized along feminist lines, changes can be demanded in policy, laws and administrative practices, and a discourse formulated. Concepts such as wife-battering, wife abuse, and battered women, initially developed as an extension of the already existing discourse on child abuse, form a basis for entering the public arena and are embraced as such.

These were the forms in which the situation was made visible and actionable as a 'women's issue' through the organization work and political activism of the women's movement. The conceptual terms, however, were often already determined by their location in a different discourse, that of professional providers of social services and makers of social policy. The latter are the members of what Morgan identifies as the 'social problem apparatus' whose job it is to manage the problems of individuals in individual ways.[49] Professionals apprised of the situation of women being beaten and abused were confronted with a new population for intervention and management. The solution, from their location in the ruling apparatus, was to absorb the issue into existing areas of concern where it could be treated as the problem of individual women in individual families – a problem of marital difficulties, family dynamics, and pathology – or as of secondary concern to the already formulated problem of child abuse. Women's movement activists struggled with professionals for control of the terms in which the issue was to be recognized and acted upon.

In the situation being examined here, the struggle becomes one of contestation over whose knowledge will define the situation, who is to be held to be to blame, and what kind of action will be taken by whom. It breaks down into a struggle between professionals who are the 'experts' mandated to deal with problems in terms of individuals and families, and women's groups who are attempting to develop solutions that dispute male domination through the use of violence and challenge the organization and structuring of family relations. The professional definition of the issue as family violence is a conceptual framework that provides for dealing with a range of problems in which violence is used by family members – such as child abuse, incest, spouse abuse, and elder abuse.

In the second stage, action concerning 'the issue' takes place both among and within women's groups and in the more public arena of policy-setting interactions with professionals and government. It becomes a struggle for a level of conceptual co-ordination that will allow for what feminists can accept as a more appropriate response from various aspects of the ruling social-problem apparatus. Particular strategies for getting the issue taken up within the jurisdiction and responsibility of particular institutions require the development of conceptual approaches that perform the necessary co-ordinating functions. Thus, for example, use of the particular term 'wife assault' references the criminal-justice system and a 'law and order' analysis in a way that 'wife abuse' fails to do, since assault is an offence under the Criminal Code. This is a stage in which the concept is worked on, mediated, negotiated, and struggled over in various arenas of conflict until some degree of conceptual coherence is achieved.

In the third stage, the struggle for feminists becomes one of ensuring that the definition of 'the issue,' to be lodged in the social-problem apparatus, recognizes and contains a proper understanding of the situation and needs of women assaulted by the men with whom they have intimate relationships. Thus, members of the women's movement who work with 'the issue' are committed to making their voice heard in the various forums in which 'the issue' is taken up locally and nationally: professional task forces, committees, and government hearings and commissions. Working on this enterprise requires women's movement representatives to develop professionalized definitions and practices in order to claim expertise and puts in place a form of conceptual co-ordination of the issue for the purpose of ensuring government response.

The processes of conceptual co-ordination reorganize the relations of government, professionals, and activists. The characteristics of the conceptual framework achieved allow for a variety of services to battered women to be put in place within different agencies and institutions at the local level. The organizations that women have pioneered, such as transition and interval houses, come to be seen as just one of a possible range of social services providing emergency shelter and relief to women with no other resource. Funding and policy measures put increasing pressure on such shelters to operate in a traditional institutional manner, and new shelters, crisis centres, and programs are funded with no requirement that feminist methods or principles be integral to their operation. Services are provided at various levels to individual women and men in an attempt to control men's violent behaviour, but the fundamental organization of the family and society identified by the women's movement as structuring women's oppression remains unchallenged. Women's movement organizations become linked to specific institutional sites as their work takes up the differentiated positions that grow out of and contribute to the conceptual frameworks developed. They take on more traditional and increasingly professionalized organizational forms as lobby groups, or service providers, while others work within bureaucratic structures in attempts to effect change.

THE ORGANIZATION OF THE BOOK

The first part of the book (chapters 2 to 6) traces the stages of the generalizing process set out in chapter 1. In this part, I identify the ideological practices and discursive frameworks that both demonstrate and organize the process. Chapters 2 and 3 describe a series of events that took place in Vancouver, Ottawa, and elsewhere, in which the processes can be seen in operation in the work of women's groups, professionals, agencies, and institutions. As the local process is translated to the federal level, a transition in the nature of the work takes place, and the first stage identified is translated into the second. Chapters 4, 5, and 6 examine documentary, discursive, and conceptual procedures through which the issue of wife-battering is formulated and moved forward into the purview of the state. The third stage in the process is to be seen in the development of concerted positions among representatives of women's groups, professionals, academics, agencies, and so on. These are fed back into the social-problem apparatus through such mechanisms as the public hearings held by the Ontario Legislature's Standing Committee on Social Develoment. The work of this committee and its witnesses provides focus for chapters 7 to 10. The concluding chapters examine the outcomes in both local and general terms and return us to the central organizing dilemma of the women's movement in Canada.

2 The Entry Point: Raising the Issue of 'Wife-Battering'

This chapter describes the struggle for recognition and control of the issue of wife-battering between women's movement activists and professionals whose work places them within what Morgan designates as the 'social problem apparatus.'[1] It also looks at some of the struggles involved in trying to develop a concerted analysis that would make the issue actionable in general terms. It is not a comparative study of the ways in which the women's movement here and elsewhere has taken action to confront wife-battering. Nor is it an attempt to come up with an adequate definition of the phenomenon as we have come to understand it. It is, rather, an account of how that particular aspect of women's experience of oppression gets put forward as an 'issue.' The process of conceptual co-ordination necessary to obtain resources and recognition both shapes and is shaped through the terminology involved.

It is also important to me, in working as a feminist, to understand the experiences of women in this society and the role of the women's movement in working for changes in the subordinated position of all women. This concern is not an abstract one but one that arises from my own experience as a woman and from a political commitment to feminist goals. Taking that experience as a starting-point makes sense both in terms of content and as a method of inquiry. I have access, via my own experience and the analytic work done by me and other women involved in the events, to the specifics of a historical process that sets up and illuminates the way in which what happens at the local level becomes part of the general and systematic organization of ruling relations. These events are directly connected or linked, through the work of the women's movement across the country and the involvement and interaction of professional agencies and government departments in that work, to the events in Ontario that provide material for analysis of the later stage of the generalizing process as the issue is absorbed by parts of the ruling apparatus.

The experience and the work of the women's movement provides an entry point that is grounded in the local everyday world and its exigencies, not in the academic discourse and conceptual realm, which is the customary place from which social-science enterprises begin. This analysis did not emerge from a conventional review of 'the literature' and definition of conceptual tools. Instead, I show here, and in subsequent chapters, how the concepts come to be constructed and defined. The academic discourse and 'the literature' is, itself, part of a political process with implications that go beyond the bounds of studying what is known to examine how it is we come to know it. This chapter sketches in aspects of this process, identified in the introduction as the first stage, as it can be seen in action, in the construction of an issue as such, the struggle for control of what is to be funded (and where), and the work involved in finding ways to put in place some understanding that would have the capacity to co-ordinate institutional responses.

VANCOUVER, EARLY 1970S

The early 1970s saw women in Vancouver, as elsewhere, organizing around a number of areas of concern to women. In particular, those involved in the Women's Place (a drop-in centre and central focus for many women's activities in the community) and the Vancouver Status of Women office (a group set up to co-ordinate women's needs for information and support and to monitor the government and pressure it to implement the recommendations of the Royal Commission on the Status of Women) were increasingly aware of the difficulties faced by women who needed to get out of situations where they were having 'marital difficulties.' These difficulties, it transpired (sometimes at a considerably later date), often included being beaten by their husbands or common-law partners. Concern that something be done about this and other housing problems faced by women led to the opening of Vancouver Transition House in 1973. Houses were being set up in Toronto, in the United States, and in Europe during the early 1970s, but, in fact, we knew little about each other's activities at the time.

The idea of such a house was greeted with a range of reactions, from enthusiasm in the women's community to lack of support and downright opposition from some people.[2] Existing institutions and agencies denied or explained away situations that might justify women leaving their homes, or accused feminists of breaking up the family by supplying an alternative. One of the women involved in the close to two years of organizing and lobbying it took to get the house open described a public forum held at the time: 'We were accused of trying to break up the family. They said – "the women ask for it." There was a reluctance to support a Transition House. And men would get up and admit it and say "no Transition House in my neighbourhood or my wife will leave me and go there." It was a very emotional meeting!'[3]

The house was immediately filled with women and their children escaping from beatings and brutality or other forms of abuse by husbands or boy-friends. Although the house was set up to address the broader issue of short-term housing for women and children, women who were in physical danger, especially those with children, soon became a priority. Women working to set up, staff, and maintain the house came to realize that women's experience of physical and psychological harm within their homes and in their most intimate relationships was widespread. As women spoke out about their experiences and took action by fleeing to women's shelters in Vancouver, other parts of Canada, and elsewhere, angry and outraged accounts began to appear in feminist newsletters and papers. The mainstream media, both locally and nationally, found the subject newsworthy and published articles and reports on the subject.[4] Our 'issue' was identified as one of women being beaten, abused, battered, and killed.

My own involvement in working with the women at Transition House began in 1974 as part of my practical training in a Master of Social Work program. I faced a dilemma in rejecting traditional professional approaches to 'treating clients' and wanted to find a way to work with women as a woman and from a feminist position. I tried to use my experience as an activist as a basis for organizing a program to provide follow-up support for women leaving Transition House. [Women often returned to abusive husbands at the end of their stay or after a period of trying to manage alone with their children, and this seemed to me to be an area where support groups could be useful.] My suggestion was considered by Transition House workers because of my activist affiliations and, although the program never fully materialized, I spent time with the staff collective and with women in the house, talking to them about their experiences and ways to make changes in their circumstances. After this initial contact, I was personally committed to working with what was rapidly being recognized as a vital women's issue – that of 'wife-beating' or 'battered' women. The tensions and contradictions between my professional status and my activist orientation are a crucial feature of my experience. They provide an entry point to my subsequent analytic work and a theme that runs throughout this book.

THE DEVELOPMENT OF AN 'ISSUE'

Over the next five years or so, a number of events crystallized the issue as one of major concern to women and a focus for the organizing activities of women's movement activists. A similar process had been taking place in other parts of Canada, the United States, and Britain. In Vancouver, part of this process can be recaptured from experience and materials produced at this time. Women working in Transition House and other feminist organizations needed to be able to describe and account for what was happening in a way that would go beyond raising public concern to evoking substantial response from a variety of agencies and institutions with the means and resources to do something to change the situation. At this point there was no specified term that identified the emergent issue; 'wife-beating,' '-wife abuse,' 'battered women,' and 'battered wives' were used interchangeably, and apparently unproblematically, to name, make visible, and assert the need for action.

What happened next was not a particularly linear or sequential process; rather it represents a number of parallel, contingent, sometimes connected or overlapping events in which the players were involved in various degrees and in different capacities. I will simply highlight a few instances that particularly affected me or about which I have information. The thread that unites the different pieces is that of putting together a particular understanding of the abuse being discovered and participating in the development of an analysis of it as a women's issue. This was a practical concern; in order to proceed to do something from the standpoint of women and within a feminist framework of analysis, something more than a 'Band-aid' approach to women in crisis and danger was obviously necessary. Women needed extensive protection and ultimately men had to be made to stop beating them. Feminists recognized that the work must progress from consciousness-raising about the existence and nature of the experience to political action aimed at changing the structures of society that perpetuated it.

The first step in such a process was one of working out how we, as feminists, would identify and analyse the violence men use against their partners – its causes, circumstances, and effects – in order to mobilize our energy and formulate aims and strategies that would lead to solutions. Those of us involved in the attempt to delineate the issue were located in a variety of situations. Some were Transition House workers who were hired, in Vancouver at least, on the basis of life experience and concern rather than any professional qualifications. Others were connected with a variety of women's groups that addressed a number of concerns, ranging from information and referral to crisis services and resources. A number of us were professionally trained and disillusioned with institutional approaches. Some saw women's problems in their daily work but lacked the mandate and resources to provide the solutions indicated by feminist approaches. Others had sought professional training in the hope of making an impact within institutions on behalf of women. We found little to help us gain a better understanding of the situation and less to enable us to change it. Our endeavour became one of developing the necessary analysis for ourselves, without any sense of the history of women's campaigns and struggles through the centuries against husbands' brutal treatment of their wives.

The issue became a topic for workshops at women's conferences, for classes and term papers in women's studies courses, and for a master's paper in the School of Social Work (which stimulated media interest and an article in a cross-Canada Sunday colour supplement). Published material was eagerly sought out; the publication of Pizzey's *Scream Quietly or the Neighbours Will Hear* in 1974 provided a written account of the founding of the first refuge in Britain. Pizzey used the words of women and children who contacted her or came to the shelter in order to evoke a vivid picture of the lives of fear, torment, and hopelessness that women were leading. Our outrage grew; we learned from women's experiences, and from attempts to find ways to support them in making changes in their circumstances, that institutional responses were punitive, victim-blaming, or, more commonly, denial or disbelief, a minimizing of women's injuries and a refusal to intervene even in life-threatening circumstances. Particularly brutal instances of beatings, torture, and murder that began to be publicized in the Vancouver press contributed to an increasing climate of public awareness, which in turn reinforced women's claims that the police, the courts, the social services, the medical profession, and the church were not responding effectively to women's plight. State agencies at both the provincial and the federal levels began to provide funding for various forms of research and programming; community and social-service agencies took the opportunity to extend their mandate to the newly identified 'area' of concern.

THE UNITED WAY OF GREATER VANCOUVER
STUDY ON WIFE-BATTERING

In 1975–6, the Vancouver United Way Organization's committee on social policy and research commissioned a pilot survey of incidences of wife-battering and research into police response to 'domestic disturbance' calls. The women in the feminist community who were concerned with various forms of violence against women were not impressed with the report, titled *Wife Battering: A Review and Preliminary Enquiry into Local Incidence, Needs and Resources*, which resulted from the pilot study.[5] The report did not appear to provide any useful way of understanding the problem, and though supportive of transition houses in a general way, its theoretical base rested on studies by social scientists from the United States. These studies approached the problem within a framework of general violence and violence within the family and did not seem relevant to our local concerns. The report's focus on supporting the family unit and comments on the danger to children of a man-hating transition-house environment alerted feminists to the underlying conservatism of the views it contained. Despite its joint authorship by two women, its timeliness, and its apparent significance in naming the issue as a public and professional concern, the report offended women from the women's movement by using academic material from the United States to present the basis for a professional framework for intervention in the form of treatment for family members. The report caused considerable stir in the professional community, however, since it was an indictment of professional practice for its failure to recognize and treat what was identified as a serious social problem.

The research into policing practice was presented in another report, *The Social Service Role of the Police: Domestic Crisis Intervention*, which dealt with wife-beating but effectively hid it 'under the inclusive category "domestic crisis," which police use in their work ... thus shifting from the feminists' terms and definition of the issue to a professional frame.'[6] The language of both reports masked who does what to whom under such euphemisms as 'domestic dispute,' 'husband–wife fights,' and 'violent outbreaks between spouses.'[7] Both these reports took as their starting-point not women's experience of having been beaten and abused, but the theory and practice of social science and the administration of law. They produced information and recommendations designed to further the work of professionals in the social-service and legal systems and incorporate into it the newly raised issue of wife-battering. The analysis of battering as a form of family or domestic violence provided a link with the existing discourse on child abuse, which was already under the jurisdiction of the social service, medical, and legal professions. The reports signalled a reorganization and delineation of the issue, changing it from a general feminist critique of professionalism and active work with women who were beaten, to a struggle on terrain carved out by the United Way in its capacity as mediator between the community and the state.[8]

SYMPOSIUM ON FAMILY VIOLENCE

United Way involvement progressed a stage farther in 1977 when this organization obtained funding from the federal Department of Health and Welfare to mount a major local conference to follow up on issues raised in the reports and bring the subject of wife-battering to the attention of public and professionals alike. At this point, the professionals on the planning committee for the proposed symposium used the concept of family violence, already developed in the academic work that had formed the basis of the research reports, to add child abuse and neglect to the symposium agenda.[9] Children were already a mandated target for protective services; a more general category, family violence, made it possible to add women to a broader definition of violence in the family. Professional concerns with wife-battering and child abuse were brought together and mediated by the initiatives of the United Way and its planning committee; Murray Straus, a U.S. academic and leading exponent of the family-violence position, was invited to be the keynote speaker.[10]

A representative of the women's groups who took part in the planning committee for the symposium saw the process as one where key decisions had already been made (presumably by United Way staff) and the framework set before the committee began its work. This is how she described it: 'They said, "We're going to have this symposium; we have the money to do it; these are the terms of reference ... Help us plan it." ... It was announced at the first meeting, I think, that Murray Straus would be there. He was the expert! ... We didn't try to change [the term]

Family Violence as already decided. We were trying to get a feminist perspective into it and we thought we could do that.'[11]

Already, at this early stage, the situation was being organized by the activities of the United Way into one which 'interest groups' were to be represented to ensure a balanced and objective approach. Women's groups were put in a position of participating in order to have their voices heard or refusing to take part and thus allowing the issue to be taken over and reconceptualized to conform to professional formulations.

Women's groups' representatives were concerned from the outset that there wasn't enough representation from feminist organizations on the symposium planning committee or the program. The whole issue was finally exposed and polarized at the symposium itself, in a lunch-time speech by Gene Errington, who had held an ombuds position in the Status of Women organization, had been one of the founding committee of Transition House, and was in other ways a high-profile member of the women's movement community. She took an impassioned position against the approach, language, and implications of Straus's keynote presentation and the orientation of the symposium, citing actual and horrifying examples of women's experience that showed the reality masked by the gender-neutral 'objective' theories held by academics and professionals.[12]

The speech caused a powerful and emotional reaction that polarized participants, but at the same time opened up ground for more decisive input from women, both those who worked with Transition House and other women's organizations and those who had themselves been battered. This influence can be seen in the broad range of recommendations developed by the symposium, which include child care, job training, and establishment of transition and interim 'second stage' housing. Transition House workers also recommended that something be done about men who batter, mindful of the fact that many women return to violent husbands and are anxious that the men should get treatment and help. Despite the obvious input from feminists in the final outcome, however, perhaps the most significant legacy from the symposium was the exposure of the political nature of the contradiction between the position and analyses of grass-roots women's activists and women who had been beaten themselves and the academic discourse being presented as expert knowledge by the professionals and social scientists who made up the bulk of the symposium program. The work of the symposium and its published proceedings entrenched the framework for considering wife-battering as a subset of family violence in a way that was to have ongoing implications for the work of activists and professionals alike.

THE TASK FORCE ON FAMILY VIOLENCE

The United Way immediately acted on one of the recommendations by striking a task force to be responsible for their implementation. Its members included representatives from a number of women's groups as well as from agencies and government departments.[13] The task force was organized into working groups, one of which, the one on wife-battering, formed three committees under its aegis during the lifetime of the task force. The committees worked on immigrant families, support groups for men, and, later, support groups for women, which was where I became involved. By the time the task force had been in operation for most of the first year of its two-year mandate, women's group representatives had become increasingly angered by the emphasis on public and professional education about family violence (i.e., child abuse and wife-battering) and the provision of therapy groups for men who batter. This last focus had become something of a *cause célèbre* for the task force and the United Way. It was picked up by the media as the first of its kind, and the men running it were invited to appear on talk shows, on national television, and on conference panels. These leaders were social workers and psychologists who had developed the modest program with the help of an academic in the field of professional education. They became, as a result of the publicity, instant experts in a whole new field of intervention: the treatment of 'battering men.'

It was at this point that Gene Errington, whose speech who had caused such turmoil at the symposium, insisted on joining the task force and

took over the chairing of the working group on wife-battering. She vigorously protested the lack of work being done on behalf of women and asked me to join the working group to form support groups for women who were being or had been beaten. I was not able to do this but agreed, instead, to use my activist experience and professional training as a basis to explore ways of working with women to set up a support-group program. I enlisted Joann Robertson, who shared my experience in developing this kind of group process. The program we designed offered information, practical aid, and consciousness-raising activities for women who were trying either to rebuild their lives after being battered or to survive in a situation where they were being beaten.

The idea was to provide support and training so that the women who participated in the program could eventually run effective groups for themselves and other battered women. Our professional status gave us credibility with the task force, which accepted the proposed program, but throughout its operation the working group had to struggle to gain for the program the level of importance accorded to men's treatment groups.

From the start, we were concerned that such support groups not be seen as an adequate solution in themselves and also that they not be used as an adjunct to the men's groups. Since we could not offer the women protection and recognized that the men's groups could not act as an actual restraint on the men participating, we were anxious that men not be allowed to use the groups as evidence of good intentions and leverage to persuade their partners to return home. We attempted to work co-operatively with the men's group leaders to cement a common ground and put together a proposal to develop programs for both women and men, on a properly constituted and funded basis, but their professional commitment and resistance to a feminist analysis of the issue made this a constant struggle.

During the remaining year or so of the task force's operation, there were several occasions on which women's groups' representatives challenged the relationship of the task force to the United Way. We expressed anger at the lack of emphasis on women's needs and the over-emphasis on professional education and on services to men. These acrimonious meetings led to more endorsement of the women's support groups and more active promotion of the need for funding. There was a constant covert struggle to include a feminist perspective in the highly successful regional workshops organized through the educational working group. The task force co-ordinator was under some pressure from United Way staff and board to tone down the overtly feminist presentations. She responded by rejecting as unsuitable the abrasive personality or 'narrow' (i.e., feminist) approach of the women involved.[14] Feminists themselves did not agree on how certain features of the issue should be understood and acted upon, and bitter rifts developed between some members and groups.

The task force reached the end of its term in 1979, but a 'holding' committee was formed by the co-ordinator, who continued, as an employee of the Social Policy and Research Committee of the United Way, to maintain the United Way's investment in the issue. This committee was designed to ensure a continuation of funding attempts and services for the support groups, and to co-ordinate various interested organizations. The committee was chaired by a supervisor from the Department of Social Services of the provincial government, who was responsible for both the now provincially funded Vancouver Transition House and the social-services child-abuse team for the Vancouver lower-mainland area. This choice of chair, presumably made by the co-ordinator, was a strategic one. It articulated the issue, the men's treatment groups, and the support program to the provincial-government department already responsible for general welfare, family benefits, and child welfare. A process of professionalization of the issue was already taking place through funding mechanisms and interagency linkages.

The conflict and contradictions experienced by the women's groups' representatives on the task force were intensified and magnified on this committee. We had developed a set of 'grounding assumptions' about violence and the family that had been published as part of my report in the task force's final document. In an attempt to find a common basis of understanding and co-operation, this document was tabled before the committee. It became apparent to the women's group representatives, after much time-consuming discussion and discord, that the difference between those who could accept these specific assumptions and those who found them contentious was one of principle and ultimately of political commitment. Therefore, this matter was not one for negotiation and compromise, but was a struggle between people taking up two fundamentally opposed positions. On the one side, the grounding assumptions named men as doing the beating, questioning the basis of women's oppression in the family and the part played by social institutions in maintaining that oppression. On the other, those who could not accept this analysis wanted to read wife-battering as an indictment of outdated sex roles, traditional attitudes, and inadequate institutional procedures, to be remedied by professional intervention at appropriate levels.

At this point, a series of incidents finally brought it home to the women's group members that there were also fundamental differences between what happened in the women's support groups and what was being done in the men's treatment groups, in terms of both talk and action. We found that the men's groups, by taking a clinical perspective, did not sufficiently emphasize the serious and dangerous implications of battering. Thus, the batterers were allowed to excuse their actions, since blame for the violence was placed on men's insecurity in the face of the challenge to traditional sex roles afforded by women's increasingly independent behaviour. We decided that the emotional energy being expended in attempts to co-operate and the time the male professionals took up in meetings were preventing us from doing our own work. The six women who represented women's organizations or their own concerns as feminists then withdrew from the committee in September 1979. Eventually, with a small grant from the Family Services Association, we set up our own program, a collective called Battered Women's Support Services. The committee foundered and disbanded within a few months.

THE WOMEN'S MOVEMENT STRUGGLE TO DEVELOP
A GENERAL POSITION

This experience took its place in the ongoing process of trying to understand and analyse for ourselves both the issue and the response of various aspects of the social-problem apparatus to the issue as raised. When we withdrew from the final United Way committee, it was in recognition of some profound differences in commitment to what was to be done to protect battered women and to change the circumstances that led to their situation. We had not, at that time, however, any very clear analysis of the conflict, and characterized it in terms of right or wrong ideas, negative personal relationships between members, lack of good will, or sometimes as radicals versus reactionaries, or women versus men.

Throughout the period prior to the involvement of the United Way and continuing after our withdrawal to form our own program, there were ongoing debates and discussions among women attempting to come to grips with the circumstances and experiences of women being beaten and to develop strategies for tackling the problem. One early event that sticks in my memory was a session in a graduate seminar in women's studies at the University of British Columbia. Seminar participants were women with experience in the women's movement as activists in union work, feminist counselling services, community organizing, politics, and women's studies. They brought to it a number of increasingly distinct, often contradictory and divisive, formulations and positions on the causes and manifestations of women's oppression. At the time, women were beginning to express anger over the nature and content of the upcoming Symposium on Family Violence, and Gene Errington, who was a participant in the seminar, was researching and preparing her challenging address. Using Pizzey's book,[15] and our experience with local women's initiatives such as Transition House, we attempted to develop a general context for women's experience within the family and the society at large.

Dorothy Smith, the seminar instructor, proposed a framework that examined women's economic dependence on men's wages to support the family, and the presence of an implied social contract in which, in return for such support, women would supply a range of domestic and sexual services. This implicit contract, she suggested, leads to a situation where men can demand that their needs be met and punish women to enforce their authority in the process. This framework, while making analytic sense, addressed the situation in broad terms, which seemed to some participants to be too remote from the pain and tragedy that made up women's everyday experience. As we looked at the historic dimensions and the indifference and hostility faced by women trying to get help to change their situation, the problem took on horrifying dimensions. I remember one woman saying over and over, 'Why do men hate us? Why? Why? They hate us and want to destroy us.' We experienced in the seminar the beginning of a division, and the emergence of different and sometimes conflicting positions within the feminist analysis.

These positions began to be differentiated as two types of analysis: one, of the organization of the structural dependence of women in the family, enforced by men's use of their authority in a range of ways, including violence; the other, of wife-battering as an example of the direct male domination of women throughout recorded history through various forms of violence, such as rape, incest, and sexual slavery. In taking up these positions, we drew on our experience and on scant material from a general discourse on wife-battering that was beginning to be circulated in books, articles, and papers written by feminists in Britain and the United States. These two positions amplified and differentiated the base from which feminists worked in their struggles within the United Way. They were cross-cut by a third position that connected some feminists to a professional framework and delineated the issue as one of inappropriate expression of the basic human emotion of anger. Within this third position, some analysed the problem as arising in dysfunctional masculine stereotypes that encourage rather than inhibit violence as an expression of anger. Thus, exponents of such a position could propose working with men and women alike to learn impulse control and to rechannel anger into an appropriate non-violent expression. This position presented no contradictions for its adherents when it came to developing modes of professional intervention to be offered by appropriate agencies and institutions and supported by the state. Adherents of the other emerging feminist analyses rejected this position as dangerously apolitical in its individualization of the issue into one of interpersonal relational dynamics, and saw institutionalization in this manner as a form of co-optation and control.

CONCLUSION

The events described in this chapter tell us something about the first stage in the process being studied, and lead us into the second. The experience of women working to make wife-beating a visible and action-able phenomenon took a particular form in Vancouver; the existence of Transition House, other subsequent shelters, and a number of women's groups and organizations made the women's movement a recognized part of the community. There was already a movement in place at the local level, one of whose aims was to present women's lives in ways that would be visible in the public arenas where action could be taken on what had heretofore been seen as private matters. Wife-beating, the stronger term 'wife-battering,'[16] and other such designations were adopted freely as marking and making visible a newly recognized issue. Even domestic and family violence at first appeared to be useful in as much as they named a problem and put violence in the previously private realm of domestic or family life forward as a matter of public concern. The involvement of the United Way of Greater Vancouver brought women's groups and others working in various institutions and agencies into a relationship of conflict and struggle, as professional agencies sought to depoliticize and appropriate the issue in their own terms. It was a process of seeking recognition and a struggle for control of 'the issue'; for control, that is, of how it should be defined, understood, and acted upon. This struggle took place not only between women's groups and institutional representatives, but also between women working as and with battered women themselves.

Both these aspects of the process were carried forward from the local to the national level, when the government-appointed Canadian Advisory Council on the Status of Women called together women from across the country to provide input into a 'consultation' on wife-battering. The consultation and subsequent federal initiatives provide the substance of chapter 3. It can be seen as providing a transition, and in some ways marking the development of the second stage, in which work continues on shaping up and generalizing the concepts being used and challenging the objectifying institutional terminology of family violence and domestic disturbances, the proliferations of which were such terms as 'spouse abuse,' 'marital abuse,' 'conjugal crime' and 'interspousal violent episodes that "break out" between couples.' This transitional phase of the process, and the beginning of coming to grips with the power of knowledge as embodied in conceptual forms, set up the protracted struggles of the third stage of the process of absorption and control.

3 Translating the Issue
to the Purview
of the State

The last chapter looked at some of the struggles involved in developing a
concerted analysis that would make the issue of wife-battering actionable in general terms. This chapter concentrates on developing the
second stage of the process of appropriation and absorption, that of
working on a conceptual framework, a way of understanding that
would co-ordinate the work of getting something done about the
problem of wife-battering. It was a practical matter; women working in
the area needed access to the resources essential for the continuation of
their work, while maintaining control over how services would be
provided. We also needed access to the policy-making forums where
changes could be made in the mandated reponse and jurisdiction of
institutions. We had to be able to produce our own research to validate a
general position and provide a knowledge base from which to respond
to the many task forces, committees, and hearings that were set up to
work on aspects of the issue as it was successfully raised in the public
domain.

My description has focused on these events as an entry point
provided by my own involvement in the developing issue, which was
increasingly being identified as wife-battering. The local nature of the
struggle, however, was also a feature of the organization of the women's
movement in Canada. Though the history of the movement's development is complex and diverse, its character, at this time, was essentially
regional. A number of national organizations existed, some rooted in
the women's rights movement that preceded the 'second wave' of
feminist political mobilization of the late 1960s; some established in the
wake of the report of the Royal Commission on the Status of Women,
published in 1970; and some arising from the development of national

positions on particular issues such as abortion. In the main, however, it was the work of organizing among women at the local level that identified new areas of oppression and introduced them into the broader political agenda of the movement. While we were aware that transition houses and support programs were being organized in other parts of Canada, our work on the issue and our involvement in the women's movement were centred in Vancouver and the surrounding area. British Columbia at that time had no coalition of transition houses. There was a federation of women, which provided links on a regional basis between women's groups organized around a number of concerns. Many towns had women's centres, which provided the focus for local organizing. Our knowledge of and connection to other regions and to a sense of a broader Canadian women's movement was largely based on individual contacts; informal networks; participation in particular actions such as the abortion caravan;[1] and the availability of a developing discourse in the form of newsletters, periodicals, and several books on women in Canada and the Canadian women's movement.[2]

The previous chapter was concerned with a local struggle for recognition of a thitherto private and even secret feature of the lives of women. Women worked to make women's experiences of beating, brutality, and neglect by the social-problem apparatus a matter of public and political concern. Soon, as the events described show, a battle developed over how these experiences should be defined, understood, and acted upon, initially in relation to the professional appropriation of the issue, and increasingly in terms of differing feminist analyses and strategies.

The involvement of the United Way focused both these aspects of the struggle and at the same time played a role in extending it to a wider area of the province. The series of workshops organized by the educational working group of the United Way task force actually performed several functions beyond their information mandate by bringing together professionals and women's groups in local areas and exposing them to the range of positions that divided the task force itself. These conflicting positions affected the suggestions for action to be taken in the different locations. Addressing the problem of family violence implied the need for co-ordinated social-service intervention. Identifying the issue as wife-battering and a women's issue implied something else; though those of us working on the issue tended to talk in terms of feminist services or support services, we saw 'self-help,' 'support,' and 'service' both as complementary and as part of a process of politicizing women to the broader features of their oppression, thus involving them in the women's movement. This view was based in the belief that women could help other women to help themselves, by virtue of their own life experiences and feminist analysis, not through authority derived from the professional discourse, and that this process was a crucial part of political organizing against women's oppression.

GOING FEDERAL

Events such as the United Way symposium and the subsequent publication of the task force's report on family violence were paralleled by similar occurrences in other regions, which while they differed according to location contributed to an increasing awareness at the national level of the problem of family violence.

Until the late 1970s, the federal government's involvement with the problem took the form of activities undertaken by different departments according to their jurisdictional responsibilities for policing, child welfare, and so on. The work of women involved in rape crisis centres and transition houses had identified violence against women as a phenomenon to be taken up by the women's movement.[3] Increasing pressure on behalf of women's concerns by a number of lobby groups inside and outside government resulted in a general plan of action, *Toward Equality for Women*, released by the office of the Status of Women Canada in March 1979. In it, the federal government included the identification of violence against women among its areas of concern. The document made a number of commitments, one of which was to undertake a major study of violence against spouses and women, violence in the family, and crisis assistance in communities. The study was to be done under the auspices of the departments of Justice, the Solicitor General, and National Health and Welfare, and the emphasis was to be on developing a co-ordinated and comprehensive approach.[4]

That same year the Canadian Advisory Council on the Status of Women decided to do its own research in the area, to focus specifically on wife-battering. The result was the publication, in January 1980, of *Wife Battering in Canada: The Vicious Circle*,[5] the first Canadian book on the subject. The advisory council, formed in 1973 by the federal government on the recommendation of the Royal Commission on the Status of Women, was made up of paid and volunteer government appointees. It was and is based in Ottawa, with regional offices in Manitoba and Quebec and representatives from the provinces and territories. The council employs a staff of researchers and information officers to carry out what it describes as a dual mandate of informing the public of women's issues and pressuring government to effect needed changes.[6] As part of the strategy of making wife-battering a public issue and recommending changes in legislation and administrative practices to the federal government, the council followed up the publication of the book with a 'consultation' on wife-battering. According to the council, the aim of the consultation was to give women who have been battered and women who provide support services to them a voice in the process of deciding on the action to be recommended to the federal government.[7] Actually, the consultation came about as a result of an internal strategy by feminists in the bureaucracy, spearheaded by a member of the advisory council, directed at allowing movement women to come together to do movement work while being funded by the state. The council was persuaded to endorse it as a viable part of the overall strategy of making wife-battering a public issue.

THE CONSULTATION PROCESS

The consultation brought together a number of women working with shelters and programs in Ontario, Quebec, and British Columbia, and a few from Alberta, Saskatchewan, and Nova Scotia. Of the thirty or so participants, ten were members of the advisory council and its staff, of the Office of the Status of Women, or of the Office of the Women's Program, Secretary of State. There were mixed feelings and suspicions among the representatives of women's movement groups about the function of the council and its intentions with regard to the consultation. These reflected the general ambivalence in the women's movement about the status of the council as a quasi-governmental body that spoke for women but had, at best, tenuous connections with the movement itself. These concerns were somewhat mollified, at least for those of us who had been involved in the Vancouver events, by the presence among the organizers of the consultation of Gene Errington, at that time working in an advisory capacity with the federal Office of the Status of Women. It was largely through her influence, and that of Sue Findlay, the original director of the Office of the Women's Program, Secretary of State, who, in that capacity, was intimately involved in attempting to shape federal government response to women's movement demands, that Jan Barnsley from the Vancouver Women's Research Centre (a founding member of the Battered Women's Support Services Collective) and I were invited to be among the 'consultants' in the first place. Findlay's position as vice-president of the advisory council and instigator of the consultation lent the occasion additional legitimacy, as she was a respected member of the women's movement.

The role of the government women was never clear to me as a participant. Some of them took no active part in the process, sitting impassively round a huge microphoned conference table. The setting and composition gave a strangely formal air to what participants understood was to be a chance for women working with the issue across the country to share what they knew. The aim of the consultation, as presented to participants, was to provide an opportunity to work together to analyse both the nature of the problems being faced and the solutions that should inform the recommendations of the advisory council to the federal government. This process of analysis was to be facilitated by summaries and suggestions provided by Dorothy Smith, who had previously been involved in working on the issue in Vancouver.

Some of the women who were invited to the federal consultation had some connections through previous communications or work on this issue and other women's concerns. Many did not know one another personally and the occasion itself became one of communication and exchange, which served to break down the regional isolation of the movement groups. Even the women from various parts of British Columbia did not know one another and took the opportunity to learn about one another's work. Information-sharing was organized to address the experience of battered women; the response of aspects of 'the system' at the local, provincial, and federal levels; and the work of the women's movement in different places. Women also pooled resources in the form of articles from popular and academic journals, talks they had prepared, and other written materials. These were photocopied by the consultation staff and made available on a 'hand-out' table. This distribution of materials performed a useful function, especially for women's groups who simply did not have the resources to copy and mail out articles and information to those who requested it. At this stage, this distribution of information was an important part of how a general discourse on wife-battering was developed and disseminated at the informal level, at the same time as it was being developed at the more formal or public level of published articles and books.

It was clear that there were a number of divisions and differences among participants at the consultation. These divisions were located in the contradictions between movement women's efforts to maintain a concerted position in relation to women's oppression and those who wanted to carry the struggle onto the terrain of the state and the professions, as a way to secure resources and to get things done. The struggle at the consultation was, at one level, a dialectical one between political definitions with strategies for mobilization and organization and definitions that provided for professional and governmental action. Even within these major positions there were divisions over how wife-battering was to be understood. Some took issue with the format and formalized milieu as too bureaucratic and male-derived; others wanted to co-operate fully in getting a response from the federal level that would legitimize their work provincially. A fairly vocal group saw the attempt at summary and analysis as a futile academic exercise. The analysis for them was a given: all women are battered to some degree and all men are potential batterers. The issue was one of direct male domination through violence under a patriarchal system, and the solution lay in the development of alternative structures and culture for women. Another woman spoke of the importance of integrating men into transition-house staffs to provide women, and especially children, with male role models who were not violent. Jan Barnsley and I tried to describe the tangle of professional and political struggles that had taken place over the focus on groups for male batterers by the United Way task force. We explained our decision to work outside the agencies and institutional structures that the United Way appeared to mediate and co-ordinate through its committees and task forces. These differences demonstrated not only emerging divisions within the women's movement, but also the varied ways in which the issue had been taken up in separate and insulated local settings.

Smith's concluding analysis of 'the system' provided a different dimension from the 'all women are potential victims of all men' approach. Acknowledging that, from the perspective of grass-roots work, it is hard to see how the system is organized, she said: 'It's not just men, it's that there are definite political and business interests in keeping women in the home and keeping them subordinate ... We can't change these things by looking just at sexism. Sexism is locked into these interests, this power structure.'[8]

A number of other contradictions were present in the consultation but were never really directly addressed. Perhaps the chief one was our relation to 'the state,' or at least to the federal government through the council and the representatives of women's programs within the government, and to the levels of government for which strategies for obtaining more adequate funding and other resources were being proposed. The complexity of these relations was exemplified by the ambiguous position of the participants: activists, paid staff in transition houses and other support programs, government appointees and employees, professionals, and a representative of academe. Some participants were actually members of more than one of these categories. All appeared to be united by a commitment to 'women's issues' and to doing something about this particular issue.

It is clear in retrospect that there were several agendas being played out at the consultation. The council, and particularly its then-president Doris Anderson, whose connections were to the media and the Liberal party in power, saw its role as mediating between women and the federal government. This was to be done by raising important 'new' issues to public awareness and using forums such as the consultation and media coverage to apply pressure on the government in those areas where changes were within its jurisdiction, for example, the Criminal Code. For Anderson, the consultation was only a minor part of a strategy to promote the council's research findings and the recently published book, by involving the women working in the area in endorsing recommendations for legislative change at the federal level. Above all it was to cement an understanding of the issue as one of wife-battering, in a way that would gain media attention and provide an avenue to pressure the government. A public forum at which a new National Film Board release, *Loved, Honoured and Bruised*, was presented, and a closing press conference were additional aspects of the strategy of creating a high-profile public issue in relation to the government.

Most participants, including the feminists working inside the government or with the council who had conceived of the consultation in the first place, saw it as a chance to use the government's funds to accomplish their own ends; to 'network,' exchange materials, continue the work of making the issue visible, and develop strategies for getting the various components of the system to take action that was consistent with the broader political goals of the movement.

The council staged the consultation as part of a strategy on wife-battering, thereby legitimizing its role in relation to women in general and the women's movement in particular. The event was followed by the distribution of a summary of proceedings written by Linda Mac-Leod, author of the council's book on wife-battering. These proceedings do a particular kind of work with what they present. They situate the consulation within the context of the advisory council's concern with violence against women as a major focus for action. The council's energies are reported to have been specifically directed towards wife-battering in response to requests from 'women across Canada.'[9] In realization of the council's philosophy, which recognized the importance of women themselves having a voice in the process, the proceedings explain that 'participants (or more correctly "consultants") were invited to attend on the basis of their long term experience with the issue and were asked to cover a range of experiences including direct service through transition houses and support groups, advocacy work with the legal system, and research. Dorothy Smith, professor of sociology at the Ontario Institute for Studies in Education in Toronto, was asked to facilitate the work of the consultation by summarizing discussions and identifying common themes that would provide directions for Council recommendations.'[10]

The title of the proceedings is a clear indication of the council's framework and agenda as far as defining wife-battering is concerned. It is called *Wife Battering Is Everywomen's Issue*, and opens with a quotation from one of the presentations, listing a number of circumstances that can be defined or perhaps redefined as 'battering.' These range from being put down by your boss; to being offended by a movie or newspaper article; to being slapped, shoved, kicked, or forced into sexual activity or inactivity. Experience of any of these indicates a battered women; 'wife battering affects every women, none of us is exempt.'[11] While this analysis would not have satisfied every participant, it did capture a particular position and is reflected in the proceedings' 'Themes of Dialogue.' The first of these states that wife-battering is only one manifestation of pervasive violence against women in a patriarchal society that keeps women 'dependent, subordinate, victimized and poor.'[12] The other themes deal with a part of the discussion that arose from some of the presentation material, particularly that describing the Vancouver United Way experience and federal government involvement. Government and social agencies' reliance on 'professionals' for expertise is seen to have led to ineffective solutions 'based on the assumption that wife battering is a private problem of abnormal family interaction.'[13] This assumption negates the seriousness of wife-battering and ignores input from women who have been battered or who work at the grass-roots level in the field. The inconsistencies of the system that purports to help women but further prevents them from escaping provide the final 'Catch 22' theme.[14]

The 'action goals' developed from the consultation show how the content of participants' presentations affected the way the council took up the issue and how, in turn, these were shaped to conform to the council's agenda. First and foremost was the aim of publicly redefining wife-battering as a crime against women and asserting the expertise and credibility of women's groups in this area. It had actually been strongly recommended by Shirley Small, from Support Services for Assaulted Women in Toronto, that we stop using the term 'wife-battering' at all and name the issue 'wife assault.'[15] Although this renaming was soon to become a major strategy among women's groups, it did not get picked up as such in the goals for action in the report. Publicly redefining wife-battering as a crime had been, in fact, only one of many issues raised and was emphasized in the discussion on legislative change, one of the organized working groups' topics. The second goal involved anlaysing the place of women's groups in the system and looking at how parts of the system perpetuate wife-battering though 'Catch 22' solutions. The final action goal was to maintain women's perspective in controlling directions for change and broadening the base of support in order to do so. This goal reinforced the position of the council as mediator between a grass-roots constituency of women and the federal government.

The body of the proceedings served to shape the issue of wife-battering, a public concern, and an addendum provided a variety of documents that represented aspects of women's work on the issue. The addendum carried forward the process of linking local efforts with a general position and collected together some pieces of material that women had brought with them from their organizations. At the same time, the proceedings document was part of putting in place a strange kind of amalgam definition of wife-battering designed to unite us all, as women, against an unnamed opponent, presumably 'patriarchal society.' Both document and definition served to link us, across Canada, in an unprecedented manner as representatives of grass-roots women's movement groups, battered women, concerned professionals, feminists of all stripes, in working on an issue now constituted on the terrain of the state and in terms of recommendations to the federal government for legislative and administrative changes.

INTEGRATION AND APPROPRIATION

Occasions such as the consultation perform a number of functions, not all of them overt or acknowledged. Even a brief examination of the circulated proceedings document indicates, in its selectivity and emphasis, how the conflicting positions present were shaped and amalgamated in the reporting. At the same time, the illusion of a safe working environment for women's movement women was shattered by the consequences of distributing detailed and somewhat distorted accounts of what went on to all and sundry involved in the area, a move that exacerbated the various local struggles. The benefits of making much-needed materials available to isolated and underfunded groups across the country were offset by the way in which this distribution assumed the effort was a concerted one and obscured the rifts that were developing. By this seemingly contradictory process, women's movement positions were absorbed into an overall definitional structure, but women were set against each other in their practice at the local level.[16]

When we look at the struggle over definition in the context of the work that was being done, we can see that there were different work practices in operation and that different terms embodied more than semantic differences. The definition worked to confuse the issue so that, to all intents and purposes, almost everyone concerned – women's groups, social agencies, and government bodies – wanted to get something done about the problem defined as wife-battering. Sometimes the means for achieving this end seemed to coincide and sometimes not, but the end appeared to be a common cause. This seeming commonality of purpose obscured the significant political implications of the different solutions proposed by consultation participants.

These contradictory positions were not just differences of ideas. They signalled the emergence of responses that began to be differentiated in relation to the possibility of getting particular institutions to take responsibility for dealing with particular aspects of 'the issue.' The issue itself, then, had to be shaped and put forward in a way that allowed for this possibility, and the position of women's groups was organized and conceptually co-ordinated as they worked to align and articulate it to institutional imperatives. Thus, the broader political aims of the women's movement, encapsulated in Dorothy Smith's closing injunction to participate in building political relations with allies working in other spheres, in order to develop a power base from which to act, were stripped away. 'As long as we work only in the institutional frame,' Smith said, 'we are working within a power structure and a communication system that is not on our side, that doesn't serve women.'[17] Here, then, we can see a linkage between two aspects of the process of appropriation and absorption: the struggle within the women's movement for a satisfactory understanding in terms of our political agenda, and the political process of ruling and control that organizes our work in relation to the state and other aspects of the ruling apparatus, such as the media.

The consultation brought together a dispersed and localized women's movement with disparate analyses of the issue. On the one hand, there were women who shared an understanding of the integral nature of women's oppression as fundamental to the social, political, and economic organization of society. Regardless of conficts over the determining relations of oppression, the goal of the liberation of women required the overthrow of such a system and a reconstruction of social, political, and economic relations. On the other hand, there were women whose analyses encompassed an understanding of the system as discriminatory by virtue of unfair and outmoded legislation and administrative practices. For them, the goal for women was equality under just laws and favourable, fair treatment by the institutions of government, the professions, and society in general. United as 'we women,' all battered to some degree by a sexist system, 'we' became one with the council as a force demanding government response.

In fact, the definition of wife-battering put forward in the consultation proceedings reflected an amendment of the council's position as presented in *Wife Battering in Canada* earlier in the year. The author of both documents initially presented wife-battering as an important aspect of family violence and set out some critical views of previous attempts to enforce criminal sanctions, citing such sanctions as ineffective, at best, and damaging, at worst.[18] The professionalized framework of family violence, so fiercely disputed by a number of consultation participants, became the object of criticism in the proceedings, which stressed the criminality of wife-battering and the need for women to eschew professional definitions and take control of the issue as one of violence against women. This was an important outcome of the work done at the consultation by women in and outside government, and it provided the women's movement with a voice in subsequent events in conjunction with the advisory council rather than its being subsumed and represented by the council and other professional bodies. At the same time, it stripped away the broader, more revolutionary goals of the movement and involved movement women as experts on wife-battering in taking the issue onto the terrain of the state in a particular way, as a particular line of development in relation to the legislative framework of criminal law. This line of development differed from and ran parallel to the directly professional line of development expressed by family violence and directed towards the provision of social services through the mandate of such institutions as the Department of Health and Welfare.

FOCUS ON ASSAULT

The process of struggling to find definitions that would act as conceptual co-ordinators for strategies to carry the work forward was not an isolated or merely theoretical one. It was part of the work, an important and urgent aspect of which continued to be the effort to ensure women's safety and protection. While transition houses provided this protection, it was obvious that all women in need could not be accommodated there, nor could they be kept there on a permanent basis. In the early 1980s, as part of various initiatives concerned with policing and the justice system, and in response to pressure from both activist and professional bodies, monies were being made available for research and consultation work from both the federal and some provincial departments of the Solicitor General. Women's groups, such as the Women's Research Centre in Vancouver, felt bound to compete for such funding, which was going almost exclusively to male researchers who had established expertise in the area.

'Wife assault' and 'wife abuse' were terms that tended initially to be used synonymously with 'wife-battering.' As the process of working on the concept developed, in areas such as the advisory council's consultation, the significance of the term 'assault' as placing the issue in a legal framework became increasingly evident. It provided for both research funding and changes in law-enforcement procedures as a response from the justice system. Feminists' anger and outrage were fuelled by the struggle to get the issue recognized on our own terms, as one of violence against women. That anger found an expression and vehicle for action in the Criminal Code. Defining men's violence as the crime of assault, for which they could and should be punished, offered a way to protect women by demanding that men be arrested, charged, and imprisoned when necessary. In the United States, women had had some success in bringing, or threatening to bring, class-action suits against police and local-government officials in several cities, charging them with failure to provide the protection from assault stipulated by law. Though such class actions were not possible under Canadian law, the effectiveness of the stategy used by the u.s. groups influenced the approach of Canadian activists.

The Toronto group Support Services for Assaulted Women had chosen its name with care to concentrate awareness on precisely this issue.[19] Its *Conceptual Framework for Wife-Beating*, introduced at the 1980 advisory council consultation and subsequently revised to contain a clearer legal focus, set out what became an increasingly acceptable framework for feminists working in or concerned with the area:

A Conceptual Framework for Wife-Beating

1 *Wife-beating is an assault, not interaction gone wrong.* When it's defined as an 'argument gotten out of hand,' the victim gets blamed for provoking the argument. The offender is tacitly given permission to use violence as a way of winning an argument.

2 *It's violence against women, not family violence.* If you view wife assault as one form of violence against women, then protection is your first focus. 'Family violence' leads to a focus on interaction which leads, in turn, to blaming the victim.

3 *It's not a sickness, it's a crime.* Women should not have to accept responsibility for 'nursing' a man through a so-called sickness. To call it sickness means saying that a man is not responsible for his behaviour, his violence.

4 *Freedom from assault is every person's basic right.* A woman should not have to earn the right to freedom from assault by being submissive, going to counselling or whatever.

5 *Men beat their wives because they're permitted to.* Wife-beating is best understood as an extension of the social permission given a husband to exercise authority over his wife. The lack of protection given to an assaulted woman is an important part of that social permission: violent husbands quickly learn that they can get away with assaulting their wives. Until that social permission is removed the search for psychological causes will be fruitless.

6 *Wife-beating should no longer be defined as a woman's private dilemma.* Wife assault should be seen as a public and community issue. A helpful analogy is the way in which neighbours rally to lower speed limits when a child is injured by a speeding car on a residential street. The injury is not seen as the child's private dilemma nor as the private problem of the parents, but the concern of the entire community.[20]

Naming the issue as one of violence against women and disputing the family-violence approach was central, the problem with 'family vio-lence' being seen as one of psychologizing and victim-blaming. This challenge to the term 'family violence' provided an unspoken critique of types of professional intervention that reinforce family relations of ownership and dependency, while maintaining the predominance of the 'assault' theme.

The shift involved in introducing the 'wife assault' framework can be seen by contrasting the Toronto document with 'Grounding Assump-tions: Groups for Women Who Are Beaten,' which was written in 1978–9 and published in my contribution to the United Way task force report. These had also been used as a guide-line by other groups and bodies. The assumptions named men as doing the beating, but were focused on a critique of the organization of the family, the part professionals play in keeping it in place, and the lack of real alternatives for most women with children. While some further 'assumptions' for running groups were based on concern for women's safety and acknowledged the inability of support groups to offer protection, there was little legal alignment and no reference to assault. The closest approach was the declaration that not only do women not deserve to be beaten, but 'nobody deserves beating, ever.'[21]

Adopting the term 'wife assault' provided an organizing focus for women's anger, linking it to the 'violence against women' conceptual frame, which mobilized broad support among women for rape crisis centres, 'Take Back the Night' marches, incest survivors' groups, and anti-harassment procedures. At the same time, it committed us to working on the terrain of the state in relation to the institutions responsible for justice and law-enforcement activities. The shift was not, of course, uniform or immediate. As women's group women were increasingly drawn into relationship to the state by such events as the consultation, and their work was entered into the liberal-democratic representational process, they had to break the issue into various components that would fit with state funding and administrative practices. In order to be heard, women served on committees and task forces; they shaped funding proposals to fit governmental imperatives; they scrambled to prepare briefs for official occasions such as the consultation and later for the various government hearings and confer-ences. Working in this way reorganized the women's movement concerned with the wife-battering issue into a more professional mode as pressure and lobbying groups or service providers. At the same time, wife-battering, though continually raised by women's groups and identified as a public issue under the aegis of the advisory council, was consistently absorbed or collapsed back into concepts such as 'spouse abuse' and 'family violence' in the work of professional bodies and associations.[22]

THE FEDERAL GOVERNMENT

Sufficient attention was generated by the strategies of the advisory council (such as declaring, in *Wife Battering in Canada*, that one woman in ten was a battered wife) and by the activities of women's groups and professional bodies to alert the federal government to the area of concern. When, in 1981, the Honourable Robert Howie presented a motion to the House of Commons that the subject of intrafamily violence be addressed, it was carried unanimously. The Standing Committee on Health, Welfare and Social Affairs, a working committee of the legislature, made up of members of Parliament for all three political parties, was directed to consider the issue. It did so by holding public hearings in 1981 and 1982. The order of reference for the committee reads as follows: 'That the Standing Committee ... be empowered to examine, inquire and report from time to time appropriate measures for the prevention, identification and treatment of abused persons involved in intra-family violence and in particular, without limiting the generality of the foregoing, to address the issue of battered wives and dependents and for such other measures in the same matter as the committee may consider desirable.'[23]

What appears to be a surprisingly concerted approach to the issue of wife-battering was evident in the presentations and briefs to the Standing Committee from a range of women's groups, professional agencies, and individuals. The kind of unified definition of battered women as victims of violence put forward in the advisory council's consultation proceedings seems to have provided a co-ordinated focus, which had shifted and sharpened so that opposing and competing analyses coincide in presenting a recognition of the criminal nature of violence and the appropriateness of the use of the legal terminology concerning assault to emphasize this as a public issue of public concern. A description and analysis of some of the briefs and presentations shows how this took place and what it made available to the federal committee members as a way to respond to the mandate they received from Parliament.

The brief prepared for the public hearings by the Canadian Advisory

Council on the Status of Women was written on contract by Debra Lewis, another founding member of the Battered Women's Support Services from Vancouver and a participant in the United Way task force. In the brief, Lewis spoke passionately about the realities of women's lives and the circumstances that trap them in situations in which they are treated with brutal cruelty by their husbands.

The brief challenged the language used to define violence in the family and cited as euphemisms many of the terms employed; an estimated 72 per cent of cases of so-called 'family violence' were, in fact, the brief suggested, wife-battering. Lewis went on to outline the institutional forces ranged against women's attempts to leave 'the battering situation.' She then detailed the problems of providing adequate responses: underfunded transition houses and other women's services; inadequate housing options; unresponsive welfare provisions; and the failure of the justice system to offer protection and remedy. These concerns were shaped into suggestions for action to be addressed at the federal level, recognizing that many of the changes required were not under direct federal jurisdiction. These suggestions were ones that, with the exception of those specifically related to the funding of transition houses, would affect a wide range of issues for women in general. They were grouped into three subject areas: funding, jursidictional and legislative questions, and policing. The brief and its reference list demonstrate a conceptual framework that can be traced to the experiences described thus far and the discourse prevalent in feminist circles. It lacked, however, any sense of the debates and differences in these experiences and not only reiterated the argument concerning the inadequacy of existing resources and responses, but also tied together definition, discourse, and practice.

Lewis did not, in fact, fully take up the amalgamated definition from the consultation proceedings. She referred throughout to battered women, and echoed the original grounding assumptions of our work in Vancouver by questioning the organization of family relations. Only once, in the section on policing and legal practices, was there a reference to the inequitable application of assault laws where husbands and wives are concerned.

Lewis appeared before the committee with the then-president of the advisory council, Lucie Pépin. Pépin placed the issue of wife-battering within the mandate and work of the council and named it as a women's issue, raised to awareness by women's groups. Thus, she formally aligned the council with the women's movement and placed it in the postition of a broker or mediator between women and the state. It was, Pépin noted, an issue of concern to everyone, a matter of the quality of society as a whole: 'When a woman does not receive just treatment, it is not simply and only her who is affected. We all suffer. Family violence – wife beating is, of course, a case in point.'[24] The principle of justice was evoked early in Pépin's testimony when she said: 'We accept that every citizen has a right to protection from physical and mental abuse, from assault. Yet, we know that a women beaten or abused in her own home is denied this fundamental right. And, as I said, the situation not only endangers women; it greatly endangers the family itself. A family wracked by violence and children who see their mothers beaten – these are not the ingredient of a healthy and productive society.'[25]

Pépin's verbal presentation located the issue from the start as family violence and introduced the principle of fundamental rights and justice under the law as a basis for providing protection for women. She folded wife-battering and assault together in a 'legal rights' framework and set this within an overall acknowledgment of the issue as one of family violence, bridging two lines of development to shape her presentation to both justice issues and the professional and social-service mandates of Health, Welfare and Social Affairs.

The beginning of a co-ordinated framework presenting wife-battering as assault can be seen in the presentations and briefs to the federal hearings from the transition-house representatives. Its significance is highlighted by the supportive questioning these witnesses received from some members of the committee, particuarly Margaret Mitchell (Vancouver East), Thérèse Killens (Saint-Michel), and Flora MacDonald (Kingston and the Islands). The presentation by Donald Dutton also contained clear and definitive statements about the criminal nature of the problem. Dutton, a University of British Columbia psychology professor, had been a protagonist in the struggles over the operation of the support groups for batterers in Vanvouver. He was also a recipient of major funding for research on 'domestic violence.' Dutton confirmed the fact that it is men who are assaultive and women they assault, and proposed a conjunction of clinical and criminal frameworks. Though he focused on various methods of handling men's behaviour through a combination of legal sanctions and treatment, he started from the position that wife assault is a crime against the state and should not be treated as a civil tort between individuals. It should be handled as a criminal offence that involves the state's obligation and power to protect the individual. This position was significantly different from the one that caused our withdrawal from the Vancouver committee, when our raising the issue of male violence and women's dependence was countered by the men's group leaders with arguments, literally, at the level of 'I knew a man once whose wife beat him' or 'I've got a friend who is unemployed and his wife works so he can't leave.' In fact here Dutton not only made strong statements supporting transition houses and the work of women's groups, but also repeatedly countered attempts by one member of Parliament on the standing committee, a family physician, to find ways of blaming women for their predicament, a process this member engaged in throughout the hearings.

The committee also heard testimony from Peter Jaffe, a psychologist from London Family Court Clinic. He was accompanied by a superintendent who was the officer commanding the uniformed divisions of the London police force. This officer described a family-consultant program that was developed in response to the concern of the local police chief about 'the major role the police were playing in the mental health field and family problems.'[26] This report again demonstrated the conflation of clinical concerns and police work. The presentation made by Jaffe showed how conflicts and overlaps of jurisdiction, and contradictions between philosophies such as whether to punish or help offenders, were actually practical issues in dealing with wife-battering. It further illustrated the need for a conceptual co-ordinator for institutional practices. Whereas the police testimony was entirely couched in terms of service to families, Jaffe reported on a focus on wife-battering. The research papers (produced for and funded by the Solicitor General's department) that he made available to the standing committee were titled The Criminal Justice System's Response to Abused Women and An Integrated Response to Wife Assault: A Community Model. Most of his testimony and questioning dealt with the response of the criminal-justice system and ways of making it more efficient and cost effective in proceeding with assault charges.

Though later in his appearance Jaffe very briefly mentioned that there was a 'community house' in the city where women could go if their situation was really dangerous, most of his testimony addressed the need to co-ordinate professional responses. This need he set within the context of London, which had a police chief who saw himself as 'an agent of social change and social consciousness for the community.' This fact, he suggested, may account for the relative sensitivity and progressiveness of the local police and the rates of change in practices for effective handling of the policing of wife-assault cases.

The final presentation I want to describe briefly is that given by Jan Barnsley from the Women's Research Centre in Vancouver. She was a founding member of the Battered Women's Support Services Collective, involved in the United Way task force, and a participant in the advisory council consultation. Her presentation came late in the proceedings and was acknowledged by committee members as having a strong impact on their deliberations. Speaking of the research report just produced by the centre, the study *Protection for Battered Women*, Barnsley detailed ways in which the criminal-justice system had failed women in dealing with the issue as assault. This study actually dealt with the medical and social-services systems in equal detail, but it was funded by the Justice department and the Legal Services Society of British Columbia, and it was the legal aspects that were emphasized in Barnsley's testimony. She used examples from women's experience with the obstacles that stand in the way of getting justice and that, she noted, illustrated what so-called 'sexist attitudes' actually look like in practice. Current practices in British Columbia involved the diversion of wife-battering cases to family court, and this gave the overall impression, the study suggested, that 'family court charges are seen as a way to provide a counselling service, not a legal end in themselves, and that keeping families together is seen as more important than making criminal charges to protect the woman.'[27] Barnsley pointed out that the Law Reform Commission in 1976 actually encouraged the screening out of domestic disputes from the criminal process, a move that seemed to have been sucessfully generalized to all other aspects of the legal system, making it hard for serious charges of assault, and even attempted murder, to be laid.

Concluding her comments and recommendations concerning the criminal-justice system, Barnsley noted that change in the system alone is not enough. She endorsed the recommendations in the briefs from the Canadian Advisory Council on the Status of Women and the Ontario Association of Interval and Transition Houses, and added recommendations for specific protocols for wife-assault cases, like those that exist for child abuse, in the health-care and social-service systems. Women's economic dependence in the family, and inadquate funding for transition houses and support services for battered women, must also be addressed. This, she insisted, was more than a matter of attitudes; it was a matter of policies and practices that must be changed. The priorities for such changes must be: first, to acknowledge and adequately fund transition houses so that the expertise gained by women working on the issue contributes to its solution; and second, to formulate directives towards and engage in work with the criminal-justice system. Diversion to family court should be stopped, and advocacy and victim-assistance services funded, to allow cases to be heard in the criminal courts, but with the advantage of the kind of supports necessary to help women through the process.

Members of the standing committee engaged in a long period of questions and answers, with Margaret Mitchell (MP for Vancouver East) drawing the session to a close by acknowledging the women's impact: 'I would like to pay tribute to women activists and to the women's movement that has really brought this to the fore. It seems to me that sexual politics really does have a very important part to play in this, both from an activist point of view and from the point of view of creating more public awareness and change in societal attitudes.'[28]

Very early in the standing committee's meetings there was an in-camera incident involving Margaret Mitchell, which she formally protested during the first public session. It appears that the chair of the committee had disallowed her line of questioning of one of the internal government witnesses because he felt that asking about the economic context of wife-battering was an attempt to score political points at the expense of the government. Mitchell was supported in her protest by a number of colleagues, and economic factors were established as a legitimate area of concern to the committee. Mitchell's struggle with the chair and other members of the committee, notably the physician mentioned earlier, against setting the issue in a traditional clinical framework, opened up the ground for definitions that attempted to include a questioning of the organization of family relations. This was superseded, however, by the increasing emphasis on the criminal nature of wife-battering as the favoured strategy for protecting women and forcing men to face imprisonment or treatment as a way to stop them from assaulting their wives. The approach provided a common basis for action, aligned previous opponents, and modified combative positions within a law-enforcement framework. It was by no means, at this point, a fully co-ordinated conceptual frame, but it signalled the development of the enterprise of locating an aspect of the issue within the criminal-justice system. This provided the federal committee with a position from which to respond in their report to the legislature in ways which will be examined in chapter 4.

CONCLUSION

In the processes and events detailed here I have shown something of the way in which members of the women's movement, who became spokeswomen on the issue, came together on a public position that named wife-beating as a public issue. One of the dimensions, that of defining it as an issue of assault, aligned feminists with others, particularly academics doing research on policy and policing issues, who were working in the area. This provided a co-ordinating basis for a variety of positions in an effort to get an acceptable response from the criminal-justice system. There was an insistence on claiming expertise on the issue of wife-battering, even when defined as assault, within the territory of the women who provide the services, and on pressing for adequate funding to do the necessary support work. The need to co-ordinate the existing social-service, medical, and legal systems was presented as an auxiliary to this work.

We can see the stages being identified as ones that may have overlapped and proceeded at different rates in different circumstances but delineated a process of gathering up a range of women's experience of harsh treatment at the hands of their menfolk to constitute a phenomenon of wife-battering in two major ways: as violence against women, to be addressed by separate and safe shelters, ideally protected by the external structures of policing and legal procedures; or as violence in the family, suffered by family members – including women and children – who must be protected by policies regulating any behaviour that infringed on the right to safety of individual family members. Once constituted in this manner, the enterprise of getting policy and procedures put in place was focused on getting various institutions to take responsibility for the phenomenon as defined and in relation to either a grass-roots alternative-service position or a professional-agency setting. The advisory council played a role in translating the local concerns of women's movement activists to the national level where women's movement experts spoke for battered women in public forums designed to influence the administrative and policy-making processes of the state.

4 Documents as Organizers

I have examined the way in which the advisory council's consultation and published proceedings and the ongoing work of the women's movement groups provided for a concerted definition that began to coalesce around renaming 'wife-battering' as 'wife assault.' This was only one of a number of forms of conceptual organization whereby the issue was entered into a general discourse of family violence, and was the subject of a struggle within the women's movement and against a process of professional appropriation. 'Wife assault' aligns the issue with a particular segment of the social-problem apparatus, that of the legal system, made up of departments of Justice, the Solicitor General, and the Attorney General. 'Family violence,' as initially conceptualized, provides for different alignment, one in which legal procedures are secondary to provincial social-service provisions and those of the Department of Health and Welfare. These provide for professional intervention in the relations of the family rather than the arrest and prosecution of men who assault their wives.

The process of appropriation and absorption, therefore, had two relatively distinct lines of development on the terrain of the state, which can be diagrammed as:

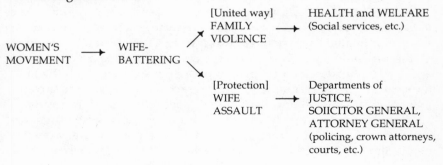

Throughout the process explored so far I have referred to a number of reports that were integral to how the work proceeded; they performed specific functions in the process I am analyzing. In this chapter I look at documents as work processes, which are moments in a social relation, in order to see how they carried forward the practices and activities of the people who were the players in this process of absorption. I want to draw attention in this analysis to two separate but related functions that can be seen in the way in which the documents operated. The first involved a writing out or reorganizing of the actual work, experience, and knowledge of women, whether they were women who spoke out of their own experience of being beaten or women who worked in transition houses and other women's movement programs. The second was concerned with putting in place particular understandings or conceptual co-ordinators that constructed the issue and articulated it to institutions and agencies as an ideological or 'ruling' concept. The previous chapter was mainly concerned with the development of wife assault as a direction for women's movement strategy. Here I focus on the way in which the concept of family violence operates, within a documentary process, to organize the professional approach.

I consider three reports, which did three different things in three different ways. Each successively organized and reorganized the relations of the women's movement to the issue and to the work of mobilizing to do something about it. The first report analysed is the initial United Way survey, done in 1976, which started in the social-science discourse, provided a framework for understanding wife-battering as family violence, and attempted to organize the relations of both professionals and the women's movement to the issue thus framed. In doing so, it in fact alerted activists to the potential for absorption of the issue. The fight thus engendered took place in the subsequent symposium and on the task force that the United Way set up to deal with the recommendation that emerged from the symposium. It continued in and around the task force's report of its activities. The initial draft of this second report, prepared by the social-work researcher who co-ordinated the task force, was framed as an acknowledgment of all the professional groups, women's organizations, and government agencies that had taken part in or supported the task force. It then put forward a series of recommendations directed at agencies and govern-ment departments, indicating how they could respond more appropri-ately to the issue of family violence. This draft was rejected by many members of the task force, particularly those from the women's movement, as too institutionally oriented. The report analysed here represents the result of the ensuing struggle over what it should contain. I will treat the conceptual framework of this second report in some detail in order to explicate the dimensions of the struggle and the integral problems with the ideological nature of the 'family violence' position.

The United Way task force report also had a key function in organizing how our work was to be seen in relation to ruling practices. By including representatives of women's groups in the planning and implementation of the Symposium on Family Violence within the structure of the United Way, the procedures allowed us to be construct-ed as 'members of the community' or a 'special interest group.' When the report then put forward its recommendations to government, institutions, and agencies, women's groups became one of a number of pressure groups credited with alerting the United Way to the deficien-cies in the system and then enlisted as 'lay' 'watch-dogs' to monitor the progress made by the social-problem apparatus, that is, the profession-als, in remedying these deficiencies. In this way, our work was, in fact, entered into a particular liberal-democratic framework for understand-ing social action and social change, and was constituted as that of merely one interest group among many concerned with the issue. We were then put in the position of having to take part in planning and appearing in these and other such events in order to represent feminist concerns and counteract this reorganization and obliteration of our work. The task force experience provided the basis for the position we took to the advisory council's consultation, which carried our voices on to the terrain of the state.

The third report considered resulted from the hearings before the federal government's Standing Committee on Health, Welfare and Social Affairs. I examine the impact of the testimony from women's movement groups, reviewed in chapter 3, and show how the develop-ing assault strategy was absorbed into a framework that took up the rights of the individual within the family. This framework produced a definition of family violence that accommodated some of the concerns advanced by feminists, but organized them alongside professional positions in an attempt to locate and co-ordinate the issue of family violence in appropriate administrative procedures.

THE UNITED WAY REPORTS

The textual analysis of documents provides a way to see aspects of the generalizing relation in operation. The two reports already mentioned as playing a part in the early stages in Vancouver will serve to show how the process was taken up and moved forward in documentary forms. The 1976 United Way survey was part of a larger research project that included concomitant studies concerned with child abuse and the social-service role of the police in managing domestic crises. The survey was funded jointly by the United Way and the Non-medical Use of Drugs Directorate (Health and Welfare) as being an alcohol- and drug-abuse–related issue.

The result was *Wife Battering: A Review and Preliminary Enquiry into Local Incidence, Needs and Resources.*[1] This report placed wife-battering very decisively within a framework most frequently delineated in the report as that of family violence, thought 'conjugal violence,' 'domestic violence,' and 'marital violence' are common terms in the authors' vocabulary. It did this by beginning with the discourse on violence, homicide, aggression, and the use of force, describing how these features of human behaviour are treated within the disciplines of ethology, sociology, social psychology, criminology, psychology, and psychoanalysis. The authors then examined violence as it is manifested in a particular setting, that of the family, where patterns of violent interaction are practised and passed on from generation to generation.

Having set up this framework for understanding wife-battering, alongside the abuse of children, the authors reported on their survey of local agencies. It was clear that, with the notable exception of the response from Vancouver Transition House, they had considerable difficulty in collecting any usable data because most of the agencies and organizations contacted either did not respond or simply did not collect statistics on or even record wife-battering as a distinct and recognizable problem. It was not, at this point, formulated as an issue for agencies and professionals.

Given the analytic framework and findings that indicated a dearth of interest or concern, the recommendations of the report formed a logical response. The authors noted that they had borrowed many of them from studies conducted in other communities and other countries. The major one was for a network of family crisis centres in large urban areas in British Columbia. These were to be under the auspices of existing agencies but designed both to act as an emergency service to wives, husbands, and children and to co-ordinate the access of those in need to lawyers, doctors, health visitors, housing and financial services, clergymen, probation officers, marriage guidance counsellors, child-care workers, and so on. The centres were also to be responsible for developing specialist advisory education and publicity programs; for data collection on incidence, treatment, and outcomes; and for providing group support for women with similar problems. In this way, they would potentially remedy the then fragmented and inadequate nature of existing services, which were 'not oriented to the violent family.'[2]

Several recommendations dealt with the need for more support for transition houses as the best form of temporary relief and shelter for women in danger. The needs of children, especially in a refuge setting, were detailed in the context of the disruption of their everyday lives. It was recognized that they would be 'living in crowded conditions in a totally female environment and an atmosphere of hostility towards their fathers and men generally.'[3] The rest of the suggestions and recommendations took up the lack of available information on causes and incidence, proposing studies of violent husbands and family dynamics, and the means to identify children who are themselves vulnerable to the possibility of becoming perpetrators of violence in their own families. The violent husbands were to be encouraged to seek help and be 'treated considerately.'[4]

Health-and-welfare agency personnel were seen as needing proper training to identify family violence. The role of the police was also deemed 'crucial in the identification of domestic assault cases, in the enforcement of the law, in the protection of the battered wife, and as a referral link to the helping system.'[5] Consistent policy in intervention, and use of family-crisis techniques and human-relations education in the dynamics of family life, were recommended for the police. The whole issue of the processing of wife-abuse cases through the courts and the functions of the criminal-justice and Unified Family Court systems were seen to need study. Communication mechanisms and education were urged for the public, agencies, and government, along with information on legal and social services, plus steps towards getting help. The work of women in transition houses, while acknowledged, was presented as offering a last resort in crisis and as potentially harmful to children exposed to an environment hostile to men. The solution of choice for the problem of wife-battering was a crisis resource for counselling treatment of the family unit. Women with direct experience of being beaten were not consulted in the survey.

We can see how the issue was shaped up and formulated according to the existing social-science discourse on violent and aggressive behaviour, at the same time being linked with the abuse of children as a matter for professional intervention. This intervention was to take the form of social services to which legal proceedings served an ancillary function. The same vocabulary was applied to both problems and the connections made were ones that were later used to initiate and justify the link made in organizing the United Way symposium, not on wife-battering, as recommended, but on family violence. This link then carries over to the work of the task force set up to implement the symposium's recommendations, and the resulting task-force report.

The United Way task force report, *Family Violence*, actually started with an introductory section that detailed the connectedness of the issues of wife-battering and child abuse and the reasons for taking them up together. This task-force report was widely distributed[6] and felt by its author/editor to have been instrumental in making wife-battering an acceptable subject for United Way funding across Canada.[7] Its distribution was a conscious strategy on her part to raise awareness of the issue of family violence, and co-ordinate a more adequate response from agencies and relevant departments.

The report provides an avenue for exploring in greater detail the actual workings and consequences of the process of making ideology. Such an exploration develops the analysis of the function of absorption of issues into institutional forms. An analysis of the way in which the report operates shows us that the author provided directions for how to understand and work together on the issue of family violence, as professionals and as activists. These directions did not acknowledge the contradictions between professional ideology and the position taken by women's groups, which were the basis of the conflicts that took place within the task force.

Starting with the rationale for treating child and wife abuse together as family violence, the report's introduction set the frame not only for reading the document but also for understanding and acting on the issue in the terms set by the introduction. 'Family Violence' becomes something to be discovered in the work and opinions of field workers, professionals, and knowledgeable lay people, and acted on as such by their organizations. Professional services are to be monitored and evaluated by 'the community,' that is, by the knowledgeable lay people who, with the professionals, make up the board of the United Way, and presumably also by women's groups and other private agencies and organizations.

The problem with this method of producing knowledge is that it refers us back, not to the lived world where people experience their diverse and particular situations, but to a world that is already constituted in the activities of those whose work it is to make such situations comprehensible and actionable in certain and specific ways. It refers us back, not to what actually goes on, but to a theory or view of the world that is constituted by ideological practices. This process of referencing its own theoretical framework forms an ideological circle, providing an interpretive schema cut off from the experienced world. The ideological circle keeps out any possible explanations or ways of knowing that do not conform to the framework.[8] This kind of process might be represented as:

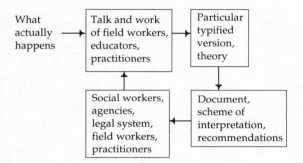

Critics and reformers within this ideological framework can see that institutions in society progress at different rates or become moribund. The state may not always live up to its task of establishing and maintaining equilibrium and moderating the self-interest of particular groups or individuals. Therefore inequalities and lapses in the democratic process are constantly being revealed. The community, the press, opposition party members in the government, and special interest groups or concerned individuals are seen to have a function within the system. This function demands eternal vigilance to ensure that anomalies, injustices, or new problems are brought to the attention of those who are in the position to amend or remedy them. This function is seen as being particularly important in times of rapid social change. For example, the law with respect to the family may be seen to be archaic and inadequate, or may not be properly administered, through ignorance, apathy, or the maintenance of traditional attitudes and values, perhaps even those of misogyny or sexism. The same may be true of the social services or the education system. There may be a need to adjust or even reform existing institutions in line with liberal-democratic notions, but the basic structures are regarded as both sound and inevitable.

Organizations such as the United Way, as representative of the community (defined as people from all walks of life), appear to be taking a bold stand when they take up an issue such as family violence and make recommendations as to how the system should upgrade its practices. They are going well beyond their generally perceived role as conscience of and to the community, a role that consists of encouraging and co-ordinating philanthropy and determining the legitimacy of worthy causes or those deserving of community support.

When concepts such as family violence operate in this ideological manner, they obscure all the diverse, different, and various situations and ways in which women have experienced forms of ill treatment from the men with whom they have intimate relationships, and all the diverse, different, and various ways in which children are mistreated by those who have charge of them, under the headings of 'wife-battering' and 'child abuse and neglect.' A detailing of the common features of the two justifies their inclusion together in the concept of family violence. When we try to use family violence as a way to understand what is happening in the lives of women and children, however, we can see only theories about or instances of family violence or, at best, of wife-battering and child abuse. It is impossible to tell what is really going on when the idea of 'family' is a given within the frame, unless we understand, as the first common theme in the report's introduction suggests, that 'the family is a violent place.' This statement, attributed to symposium keynote speaker Murray Straus as the academic expert, confirms the family as 'the most violent group or setting that a typical citizen is likely to encounter.'[9] This statement is seen to apply to all families, of all 'cultural and social backgrounds, ages or income levels.'[10] Similar terms often used in other bureaucratic settings are: domestic violence, domestic disputes (the police term), interspousal violence, or even 'interspousal episodes.' If we can even gather who does what to whom in these 'instances of family violence,' they can be explained only in terms of the deviance, breakdown, or pathology of the family or the individuals concerned, or, in some recent theories, as a 'maladaptive interactional pattern.'

We cannot recover from 'family violence,' as a concept, what is going on for women and children who are harmed. Nor can we account for reports that in more than 70 per cent of all known cases of so-called family violence, it is women who have been harmed by their husbands or mates. In 20 per cent of cases, children are harmed by parents, other related adults, or those who have charge of them, and the remaining 5 per cent covers every other possible combination, from 'granny bashing' to fights between uncles and cousins – almost any dispute where the assailants are related by blood or marriage, including presumably the ubiquitous battered husband.

With regards to child abuse and neglect, it is even clearer that there is no way to tell what is going on that is different when mothers harm their children, father harm them, both parents are involved, step-parents are involved, or whatever. Every instance of family violence comes to be seen as equivalent to every other, part of a universal theory of family violence as being the same for all races and classes, dropping from sight both the local and the particular features of the situation and any other ways in which there might be factors in common. Most particularly, 'family violence' glosses over the experience of women – a classic example in this report is the situation of women who are punched or kicked during pregnancy, particularly in the stomach. They become, through the 'work of researchers,' instances of 'intrauterine child abuse.'[11]

Using the overarching concept of 'the family' in this manner puts forward violence as an interaction between two or more people within the family unit rather than as a matter of how men treat women. This forms one of the major dimensions of an ideological circle that cuts off any linkage to violence against women outside the family or, indeed, any other way that the organization of the relations of men and women into family forms might be conceptualized.

I am not in any way suggesting that this ideological method of proceeding is intentionally oppressive. It is a way of proceeding that those of us who have been educated and trained as professionals and social scientists have learned to see as the only appropriate way. We have learned to see it as neutral, objective, scientific, and producing untainted 'knowledge' upon which to build theories that provide a base for both understanding and action. In the face of this 'objective' stance, however, the anger and outrage expressed by feminists, in relation to what they know and experience, appears as biased, subjective, inappropriate, strident, and divisive. It falls outside the ideological circle provided by the concept of family violence.

This frame, then, is what is given us in the introductory section of the United Way report. It instructs us to read the document from the standpoint of the ideology I have identified, which takes the family as a natural and universal form; takes the statements of the professionals as expert, objective knowledge; and gives the women's groups their allotted place as identifiers of wife-battering. They are also presumably, knowledgeable lay people and monitors and evaluators of the system's response to victims of family violence, but they are outside the system's ideological circle, which appropriates knowledge and power.

This frame in the introduction is not what is to be found in the body of the report itself. The struggle over its production resulted in the voices of the women's movement's groups being included. In the accounts of the working groups on wife-battering and education, for example, and in the reports from those groups, there is reference to a different under-standing of the situation, one that comes from starting from the stand-point of women. When we start here, it is clear that there are other ways of accounting for some of the questions and issues constantly raised (such as the perennial 'Why does she stay?' or 'What did she do to deserve it?'), in the commonality of women's experience, in the common sources of their oppression, and in the bases of their inequality, not in their membership in the category of battered wives or as instances of family violence. However, as Smith points out: 'The standpoint of women discloses the distinctive power relations of professionalism – hierarchy preserving the authority of theory where theory is ideology, in preference to the working knowledge of an actual everyday world; in rationality having as its secret form opposition to those who take up the side of the oppressed; neutrality having as its secret form taking sides against those who take the side of the oppressed.'[12]

There is no easy way to see this division in the frame set up in the introduction to the United Way's task-force report. The frame is clearly addressed to professionals and governmental and other agencies, but since it includes reference to women's contribution and takes the institutions strongly to task, it appears to strike a balance and represent all viewpoints.[13]

DEVELOPING A FEMINIST FRAMEWORK

What the women involved in the struggle at the time learned from analyzing our experience on the United Way task force was that the family-violence approach made wife-battering a subset of an overall problem of violence in the family, and in so doing 'professionalised' the issue.[14] Professional courses of action and the solutions they implied were not, in fact, the same as those we were working for in any long-term sense; they rendered our own work and women themselves invisible, and our insistence on disputing these courses of action and solutions disorganized the work the professional task-force members were trying to do.

'Fixing up the family' and helping 'it' take responsibility for 'its' violence[15] involved a variety of treatment strategies aimed at certain behaviours and interactions but did not provide for any long-term change in the family forms maintaining women's dependency and subordination. Nor, at this particular juncture, did it seem to offer women any protection from men who beat them. Indeed, it potentially encouraged women to remain in dangerous, even life-threatening situations. This had been one of the major concerns in relation to the support groups set up under the auspices of the task force, and particularly in relation to the handling of the issue of women's safety by those involved in providing treatment groups for men.

It seemed clear that these clinical strategies did not work. Even in the small proportion of cases where men actually agreed to treatment, women, in a variety of ways, were still being made responsible for being part of an interactive pattern of communication. In some programs in the United States, women were expected to act as quasi probation officers in diversion projects where men were allowed to return home rather than face charges or jail sentences, on condition that their wives reported on their behaviour. Systems-theory approaches to treatment tended towards ever-more sophisticated versions of the professional ideology of blaming the victim.[16] In the United States, agencies used information gained from professional intervention into 'violent families' to check into welfare frauds and other governmental concerns.

Feminist activists on the task force came to share the view that the only safety for women was to get them out of the situation and into a transition house of some kind. The need to provide proper and long-term protection for women began to be a priority increasingly emphasized in Vancouver and across the country, along with issues of funding and control. It was entirely congruent with the initiatives being put forward by those feminists within the rape crisis movement who favoured changes in the Criminal Code to redefine rape as sexual assault (rather than as some particularly unique crime related only to women as sexual objects) that the women concerned with wife-battering should begin to highlight the issue as assault. While women's movement activists still embraced the goal of connecting individual women's experience to the larger struggle against oppression through self-help support groups, self-defence classes, 'Take Back the Night' marches, and so on, this signalled the beginning of a strategy that came to override the putting forward of a critique of the organization of 'the family' and family relations, and focused on co-ordinating a conceptual framework that would move forward the action in relation to the definition of male violence as assault.

FEDERAL INVOLVEMENT AT THE GOVERNMENTAL LEVEL

A further step in this process can be seen in the deliberations of the federal legislature's Standing Committee on Health, Welfare and Social Affairs, published in May 1982 as the *Report on Violence in the Family: Wife Battering*. The previous chapter contained an account of some of the testimony put before this all-party working committee. Here I review the impact on its findings of the women's movement's wife-assault formulations and the family-violence framework already recognized in the federal approach to the issue.

The committee's report to the House of Commons focused on wife-battering. It opened with an account of the experience of a woman subjected to horrendous physical and sexual assault during the process of legal separation and custody proceedings. Her husband won custody of his terrified children, beat his new girl-friend, and was apparently committing incest on his eleven-year-old daughter. This experience was presented in the professionalised format of a 'case study.' There followed a clear rejection of the aspect of the family-violence framework that denotes battering as rather vigorous arguments that get out of hand: 'We have found that wife battering is not a matter of slaps and flying crockery. Battered women are choked, kicked, bitten, punched, subjected to sexual assault, threatened and assailed with weapons. Their assailants are not simply men who have had a bad day, or who drink and become temporarily belligerent: they are men who, for whatever reason, behave violently towards the women they live with.'[17] In its conclusions the committee acknowledged the complexity of 'the problem' and the corresponding jurisdictional difficulties. It identified the assumptions from which its recommendations arose, including the implications for areas outside its jurisdiction. While upholding the privacy of the family, the report stated: 'In the case of wife battering society is justified in intervening to assist the family. To ignore the problem is to ignore society's fundamental obligation to preserve the life and health of its members. Our institutions must occupy themselves with the problem more actively than they have done in the past.'[18]

In its self-appointed task of helping the family, the report first took up the needs of the battered wife, concluding, on the basis of 'the evidence which was so eloquently and forcefully put before us by every group who [sic] appeared'[19] that the first priority was protection as well as the opportunity to gain financial and emotional independence from her partner. Protection was defined as having two elements: the enforcement of assault legislation and legislation for keeping the peace, and the provision of a place to live away from her assailant, ideally in her own home or alternatively in a nearby shelter. There followed a plea for means to ensure both the economic and the emotional independence for women in terms of freedom from assault, a steady income, and the understanding and support of the professionals and others with whom they come in contact.

With regard to the battering husband, the committee went on to insist that he be treated as a criminal and processed through the criminal-justice system. Measures must be taken to lay charges on the woman's behalf and to encourage her to co-operate in the prosecution. As a longer-term solution, the committee pointed to the need to research ways of treating wife-batterers that might prove more effective than a system of fines and imprisonment. It favoured criminal sentences that referred the batterer to treatment programs, where they were available.

The final assumption picked up on the learned and interactive aspects of violence within the family unit:

We have been given reason to believe that wife battering is learned behaviour, on the part of both men and women. Many batterers as children see their fathers beat their mothers and their mothers unable to respond. Society teaches women to be passive in the face of violence; many battered women are encouraged to continue their relationship even when there is no reason to believe that the situation will change. These lessons must be unlearned. It should be a commonplace in our society, as it is not, that no women ever deserves to be threatened, punched, maimed, sexually assaulted. More generally, it should be a commonplace in our society, as it is not, that no action short of violence justifies a violent response. We must educate ourselves, our children, those who enforce and administer the law, and those who are involved in preventing and curing our physical and emotional ills, to identify violence and to control its consequences, for the sake of battered women, for the sake of us all.[20]

The report then made a number of recommendations. First, RCMP training must acquaint them with problems, needs, and services, as identified by 'people in the community who are responsible for providing services to battered women.'[21] Affirmative-action hiring must increase the number of female officers, and a system of rewards should acknowledge the importance of competent or outstanding performance 'of duties associated with family violence calls'[22] commensurate with other duties. A number of recommendations then addressed federal impact on funding for shelters and other housing needs. Treatment for wife-batterers should be researched and funded by programs within the department of National Health and Welfare and Justice; Health and Welfare should also encourage and help fund research into the causes of wife-battering and the development of educational programs to change attitudes towards violence and acquiescence to violence. The rest of the recommendations dealt with ways of publicizing the problem, the jurisdiction of federally appointed judges over family matters, and the agenda for a recommended federal-provincial conference. It is stated that the agenda should include: the issue of civil orders regarding the matrimonial home and restraint against harassment; the centralization of various forms of protection orders on province- and country-wide computers; arrest for breach of such orders; regular laying of charges by the police; the victim as a compellable witness against her husband at the option of the Crown; the development of uniform sentencing practices; the development of treatment facilities as a sentencing alternative; and a program of training for provincial and municipal police officers on the lines of the prior recommendations for the RCMP.

CONCLUSION

The reports examined here indicate some of the documentary processes involved in 'getting something done' about wife-battering. It is possible to see how family violence worked as an ideological concept set within a dominant view of society and laid out a course of action that attempted to organize and co-ordinate the response of the existing social-problem apparatus. The difficulty of differing jurisdictional imperatives and responsibilities was addressed by bringing together the clinical and the criminal in the form of proposals for mandatory treatment for men who are violent. This was itself a concession to the increasing pressure from women challenging the family violence ideology to make its gendered component visible as assault.

In the various forums described here, it is apparent that women struggled on the terrain of the state for a voice in how the issue was shaped and dealt with. The increasing insistence on definitions that named wife-battering 'assault' reflected women's anger, and the need to find ways to make the system offer women protection from physical danger. The strategy was itself dictated, however, by the terms available upon the state's terrain – that is, the institutional forms available for redress. The collapse of wife assault into the family-violence framework, which, in fact, keeps it within the domain of Health, Welfare and Social Services (at the federal and provincial levels, respectively), displays the reorganization of a ruling concept[23] and consequently of the relations through which governing is accomplished. The federal report acknowledged the jurisdictional difficulties, upholding the privacy of the family, but emphasizing the rights of individuals to safety and protection. Not unexpectedly, the federal report presented the same liberal-democratic ideological position identified in the discussion of the task-force report. It proposed the shaping of existing institutions, the co-ordination of existing policies, and the creation, where necessary, of new ones that would alleviate the situation of individual women and deal with the violence of individual men within the family unit. Attitudes and sex-role expectations were seen as needing to be examined and brought up to date via better educational methods, and it was determined that equality needed to be instituted as a basic value in the family, as elsewhere. The problem was formulated as uncontrolled and unmitigated violence, not as structural issues of power and dependence, which render all women and children vulnerable to abuse, not only from individual men but from a society not organized with their interests at heart. Instead, the report offered solutions that addressed the internal practices of state agencies and departments and suggestions for ameliorating the legal framework to allow for clinical responses to criminal charges.

It becomes evident here that both the family violence and the battered wife/wife assault lines of development onto the terrain of the state were present in the deliberations of the federal standing committee. The violence-against-women position taken consistently by the women's groups had a significant impact and was represented in the text and, to perhaps a lesser degree, in the recommendations. The overall framework of family violence, however, prevailed in the report, in the statement of commitment to the privacy of the family, and in the linking of wife-battering to other forms of family violence not focused on by the committee in these particular hearings.

The federal hearings and report examined here link us directly to what occurred in Ontario later in the same year, both in its form and in the content. Some of the same witnesses appeared, namely Trudy Don from OAITH and Peter Jaffe from London. The same brief from OAITH and research reports from Jaffe were made available to both committees. Peter Lang (MP for Kitchener) represented the federal committee before the provincial hearings, and the federal report was available and frequently referred to in the sessions at Queen's Park. This cross-fertilization provided for a correlation of information on policies and practices and at the same time contributed to the negotiation and shaping of the dimensions of the issue to be considered. It is a useful illustration of the way in which documents contain and carry the discursive organization of ruling practices, linking institutions and individuals in the larger structures of the political process.

What we can see at this point is a struggle that increasingly takes place on the terrain of the state, but with the input of women both inside and outside the state's institutional forms. Women speaking from their practice as well as those women and men who speak as politicians, academics, researchers, and experts of other stripes, some of whom also show the influence of feminist arguments, have an impact on how the issue is understood and taken up. The result is a far from clear and vigorously contested concept of family violence in which the ideological circle set up by professional practices of thinking about and dealing with the issue is constantly challenged to admit the information women bring. Women insist that the issue to be considered is gendered, is concerned with male violence towards women, and must be treated as wife assault. The various experts concede that this is so, but subsume and thus contain the issue by insisting that it is none the less a subset of family violence, both a product and a reflection of a violent society. This is the framework that goes forward into the Ontario hearings through the direct links of individuals whose actions embody their organizations in each of the settings examined, through specific documentary material available to each constituency, and in the academic discourse that is discussed in chapter 5.

5 Discourse as Dilemma

The events and activities described so far had as their correlate the development of an elaborate discourse, made up of books, articles, papers, films, videos, radio programs, and so on, that became part of a general and public knowledge about the issues of wife-battering and family violence. The organization of such a discourse has come about through some of the kinds of processes we have been examining. I have touched on various aspects of this development in discussing the stages in the process but have not focused on one particular feature that is an important part of how the discourse both developed and gained legitimacy. This feature is the academic work that produces theory-building, accounts, and formulations that influence and feed into policy and practice, at the level of political organizing and as a feature of ruling. These discursive practices are a crucial aspect of how such activities are linked and co-ordinated. It is important to theorize about the way in which the professional academic discourse was reworked to accommodate the critique and knowledge of the women's movement and, in turn, incorporated this knowledge in particular contained and limited ways.

ENTERING THE DISCOURSE

In the initial stages, movement women in Vancouver and elsewhere chose a range of tactics for bringing the issue of battered women to the fore. Most were designed to reach women, break down their isolation, and tell them about the existence of such support programs as shelter and transition houses. Other tactics addressed our own isolation as women working to do something about the problem. Increasingly women were faced with demands for 'facts,' for documentation of the existence of the problem, explanations, recommendations, justifications, in order to legitimize requests for even the most basic supports for women; it was beyond the limited resources of the movement to provide women with income, employment, housing, or protection. Already, then, the approach and the work in the movement were being organized by the need to provide some kind of 'account' of the situation. Women spoke out of their experience; for some of us, it was our own experience. Others of us spoke of our work and what women told us of their lives. Women identified other experiences of subordination and fear from which to develop a variety of possible analyses.

Though women turned to each other for information first, we also used what some of us knew from our common status as educated, middle-class, and predominantly white women; we entered our work into the existing discourse. We documented and analysed our work but we also turned to texts, to media productions, to anything that provided information that was sympathetic towards women's plight, to anything that provided a general feminist position on which to build. This process was part of a feminist networking of the kind described as a crucial feature of the growth of a women's movement.[1] Most of us did not initially analyse these materials in terms of their origins either of place or of discipline, only on the pragmatic grounds of their usefulness in understanding and working with the problem.[2] It was only certain aspects of professional and academic practices that appeared problematic, those that were overtly non-feminist and anti-women in nature.[3] Almost anything else was eagerly embraced.

The exchange of ideas and information was, as we have seen, an integral part of the process of making women's plight visible and actionable. Both sharing relevant information and putting forward our own knowledge to dispute harmful or distracting approaches to theory and practice were ongoing activities. These we recognized as a part of the political struggle to claim and define the issue in terms that would allow our work to go forward and battered women's plight to be recognized and addressed as a women's issue.

It is also important to reiterate that what I am addressing here is a set of institutional relations, not just a case of differing or competing ideas that act to influence people's understanding. The frameworks to be considered arise out of and contribute to the particular material situations and the work practices of particular people and groups of people. The books, papers, reports, protocols, studies, articles, and films that were available to bodies such as the Ontario Standing Committee on Social Development, whose public hearings are the subject of analysis later in this book, are the conceptual coinage that brings into being the phenomenon as we learn to understand it. This conceptual process also provides us with ways to develop a range of practices with which to address, ameliorate, or provide solutions to the problem as we have come to formulate it. The theories identified here have a specific history and particular areas of overlap and diversion that relate directly to the institutional and organizational settings in which they arose and into which they are inserted by actors such as those described in this study. The work of the Ontario committee represents yet another moment in the history of the development of a discourse. Therefore I propose to explore, in the main, material that was available in 1982 when the public hearings took place, supplemented by some more recent sources to support my critique and subsequent analysis of the relation between the discourse and the proceedings of the committee.

REWRITING THE DISCOURSE

The larger feminist project of rewriting the discourse to incorporate the women's movement's critique took two main forms. The first and most immediate was concerned with identifying and disputing what already existed in the professional and academic discourse. These discourses either absorbed the experience of women beaten by their husbands into terms existing within psychological and psychiatric formulations or failed to recognize the problem as existing at all. The second and somewhat later critique took up emerging psychosociological formulations that recognized wife-battering as a phenomenon but subsumed it under the definition of family violence. In the process, the discourse was reworked to accommodate both the knowledge and the critique presented by feminists, but the accommodation was also an appropriation of the issue.

The material examined here shows the work that women have done to define the issue within the discourse so as to reconstruct the way violence is taken up. The second part of the chapter looks at how feminists themselves took up and incorporated aspects of the discourse to develop a modified definition. This definition obscures some of the political aspects of the process of struggle, and results in compromise concepts that have the potential to co-ordinate administrative practices within the social-problem apparatus.

In her 1984 study 'Abused Wives: Their Perceptions of the Help Offered by Mental Health Professionals,' Pamela Johnston developed a schema for identifying a variety of material.[4] I am going to adopt the three models she identified, but use them rather differently. Instead of presenting three theoretical frameworks that sometimes cut across one another, I will show the relationship between the frameworks, the generalizing process that informs my analysis, and the institutional locations and jurisdictions that organize the terms of the struggle to reconstruct how violence is conceptualized. I will extend Johnston's discussion of her third model, the feminist position, into a critique of my own concerning the major approches to the issue, and locate models in the work processes involved, including those of the feminists considered.

When Johnston's models are set in the context and practices of those who adhere to them, we can see that there are, in fact, political divisions rooted in locations within or outside the discourse. Some feminist writers and researchers have taken up pieces of two of the frameworks to be examined or used methods and information offered by the social sciences. This taking up is, itself, a feature of the work they do in order to make visible, comprehensible, and legitimate both their own work and the difficulties faced by women who are beaten and abused. Those whose work as professionals is located entirely within institutions that use specific approaches or theoretical frameworks may be in search of ways to deal with the problem, but their definitions of it and their explanations, responses, and solutions are set within a particular set of institutional relations. Within these relations the actual features of women's lives are the resources and raw materials from which data are worked up, as instances of wife-battering or family violence, into conceptual forms. These, in turn, provide for courses of action related to the imperatives and relevancies of the existing or available institutions rather than to the needs of the women themselves. Since, in most cases, counselling is the only method of intervention available to the organizations, these definitions provide access to their own solutions. Thus the institutional locations organize the work of professionals within them, regardless of whether or not such professionals have a commitment to feminist principles and analysis.

PSYCHODYNAMIC FORMULATIONS

In her review of the literature, Johnston identifies three theoretical schools that offer competing explanations of why men beat their wives. She starts by delineating a clinically oriented psychodynamic framework that reduces the abuse, when it is acknowledged at all, to a symptom or manifestation of pathological intrapsychic processes. Adherents of this approach are divided. Some hold the woman responsible for her abuse because her innate masochism leads her to provoke and enjoy it. Others see the problem as residing in male pathology, such as paranoia or alcohol addiction. A third variant in this school identifies a relationship in which abuse occurs as itself in some way pathological, providing rewards for each partner.[5] The problem, then, is explained as one of intrapsychic dynamics to be treated either as an entirely individual matter or as a result of a dysfunctional, that is, 'sick,' relationship. Johnston sets this model in place first as the one that has been the dominant one in the field of mental health since the early years of this century. It still informs the approach to (or avoidance of) the issue by many professionals, particularly in medicine and mental health. Most important, much of what is significant in the succeeding models arises, she notes, from a variety of dissatisfactions with and critiques of this approach.

THE FEMINIST CRITIQUE OF PSYCHODYNAMIC FORMULATIONS

Johnston identifies in this model the psychodynamic discourse as it existed prior to the formulation of wife-battering as an issue. Women were dealt with in relation to existing formulations; their experience of being beaten was pathologized, treated as shameful or insignificant, or seen as elicited and thus deserved.[6]

The first target for feminist criticism was, of coure, the psychodynamic framework in place when the issue was constructed in the early 1970s. Feminists took up the inadequacies and harmfulness of pathological models, linking much of their criticism to existing feminist arguments against Freudian formulations of femininity as passive and masochistic. Also under fire were theories of innate and uncontrollable male aggression, a socio-biological variant of the male-pathology model that justifies male behaviour as a residual survival trait and, like models of mental illness and alcoholism, implies that men cannot be held responsible for their outbreaks. As a number of critics, feminists included, point out, most men beat their wives in private, some only on selected parts of their bodies, showing considerable 'control.'

The need to dispute existing psychodynamic precepts was not only a reaction to the offensiveness of the notions when compared to the experience of women speaking out about the brutality and abuse to which they had been subjected. It was rooted in the fact that practitioners working from these formulations in settings where such analyses were part of the policy and practices of the agency or institution provided services based on the understanding of sick individuals or relationships, minimized both women's pain and the danger they faced, or failed to provide services at all. Service, where seen as necessry, took the form of 'treatment' through counselling or psychotherapy focused on intrapsychic and behavioural patterns. These patterns were seen as located and maintained within the individual, and caused by childhood experiences within the family.

This is a universalist and a historical view of the interaction of individual and culture as mediated by parents in the earliest years and virtually unamenable to influence from other or later environmental factors. It was, and is still, the orientation of a number of psychiatrists and counsellors, who operate in clinical settings, using clinical frameworks to inform clinical solutions. They are recognized as the official experts on personal problems, often have medical affiliations and hence status, and are the only source of treatment covered by medical insurance. Since this means they are available free of additional charge, they are often the most evident and affordable source of 'help.'[7] If such 'help' holds women responsible for their plight, it offers neither safety nor protection; the accounts that women give of the treatment they have received have led to a recognition by critics from various other positions that it constitutes a second victimization, at the hands of the 'helpers.'[8]

When feminists took issue with prior formulations, therefore, it was because such formulations provided for intervention that shamed, immobilized, and endangered women and militated against the recognition of a women's issue to be organized and worked on in political terms.

PSYCHOSOCIAL FORMULATIONS

The second model Johnston labels as psychosocial. It derives partly from social psychology but more generally from sociology and seeks to establish an understanding of wife-beating that covers the use of violence and the inflicting of physical or psychic harm as an interactive pattern between intimates and family members. This approach then is seen as part of a larger system or context of family dynamics, cultural norms, and societal values that condones violence in a variety of forms. The mode is a departure from psychoanalytic formulations that fail to address violence as a feature of family relations.[9] There is a range of explanations for the problem, variously described as spouse abuse, domestic violence, conjugal violence, marital violence, and family violence.

Johnston identifies three major components or views within the psychosocial frame as to why men are violent towards their wives.[10] She labels these as explanations that advance socio-economic and personal stress as causation, social learning theory, and theories of how the sexist organization and traditions of society encourage wife abuse. The socio-economic factors put forward in this framework as having most impact on the occurrence of wife abuse are: 'lower class; low income; unemployment, family size; low occupational status, and social isolation.' The 'personal' causes offered in this literature have, Johnston suggests, limited empirical support. These include frustration; poor communication; lack of impulse control; poor problem-solving skills; stress caused by unemployment, financial, and medical problems, unequal power balance in the marital relationship; the man's inferior achieved status; the extreme need for men to demonstrate their masculine power; and perception of violence as the only method of solving problems.

The most influential precepts of this model originate in the work produced by Straus, his colleagues, and his students at the University of New Hampshire Family Violence Research Program. Initial frameworks did not identify gender as an issue, but focused on violence. Straus himself acknowledges the significance of the work of the women's movement in making wife-battering visible and forcing researchers to consider it as an aspect of violence in the family. Family-violence theorists are highly critical of psychodynamic formulations as being misleading and inadequate when it comes to understanding and dealing with the problem. They show some awareness of women's disadvantaged position in 'western society.'[11] Johnston notes Straus's statement:

The existence of wife abuse reflects the cultural norms which implicity make the marriage licence a hitting licence in the sexist organization of both society and the family system. Cultural norms legitimizing marital violence are found in the legal system, in literary works, and everyday discourse ... Sexism contributes to the frequency of wife beating because: one – the need of men who lack superiority in personal resources [to] use violence to maintain a superior power position in the family; two – the antagonism between the sexes engendered by sex-role differentiation and inequality; and three – the male-oriented organization of the criminal justice system which makes it difficult or impossible for women to secure legal protection from assault by their husbands.[12]

One of the most critical features of the family-violence framework, since it initially tied together child abuse and spouse abuse, is the aspect of social learning theory that argues that violent behaviour is learned within the family and passed on from one generation to the next. Strauss, Gelles, and Steinmetz, in separate and collective studies,[13] present evidence that children who are battered or who witness battering will grow up to be victims or batterers. This theory has come to be referred to as the 'cycle of violence.'

The concept of violence organizes this approach. Straus, Gelles, and Steinmetz,[14] in particular, make a case for the importance of focusing on conceptualizing violence as' the problem.' For these researchers, child abuse and wife-beating are 'different manifestations of the general problem of family violence. Their work underscores the similarities in patterns, causes and remedies of child abuse and other kinds of family violence.[15] In fact, Gelles, in a defence of their major study, states categorically that 'the study was primarily concerned with violence.'[16]

As the basis of their initial, and indeed subsequent, survey research, they constructed a behavioural scale, a number of items of which were categorized as degrees of physical violence. These include such acts as: throwing things; pushing, shoving, and grabbing; slapping and biting; hitting with fists or with an object; and threatening with or using a knife or gun. The survey provided figures that indicated that women were as violent as or more violent than men, and that there were as many battered husbands as wives or more. Since the items measured neither circumstances nor consequences, it did not, as Gelles himself points out in his retraction of these implications, account for actions taken in self-defence or for the severity of the injuries caused.[17]

This framework in its various forms provides a dominant model in the social sciences where violence has been primarily conceptualized, as Dobash and Dobash point out, 'as a breakdown in the family relationship or in the social order, in which either individuals or social structures are thought to be deviant or aberrant.'[18]

Although initially focused on violence as a matter of family dynamics, this framework has been amended to incorporate a definition of spouse-battering as assault, which should be treated as a criminal act. When it comes to dealing with the issue, however, counselling with couples is the method preferred. Based on the belief that abusive behaviour is learned, intervention is concerned with 'unlearning' and relearning. 'Men can learn to control their violent behaviour and couples can be taught ways to reduce and control dysfunctional anger and violence in their relationships by learning new ways to communicate, to "fight" and to solve problems. The focus of intervention, therefore, is on restructuring relationships through modeling and teaching changes in behaviour.'[19]

Strauss, Gelles, and Steinmetz also advocate structural as well as personal change, which will attack the broader social system in order to 'alter some of our most fundamental values and attitudes.' The structural changes envisaged would:

1 eliminate the norms which legitimate and glorify violence in society and the family, such as physical discipline of children, the death penalty, corporal punishment, domestic firearms, media violence;
2 reduce violence provoking stress which causes some men to abuse their wives, such as underemployment, unemployment, and poverty;
3 integrate families into a network of kin and community; this requires more community resources and better living conditions for all people;
4 change the sexist character of society and the family by eliminating sex patterned allotment of roles and tasks in the home and in the workplace.[20]

THE FEMINIST CRITIQUE OF PSYCHOSOCIAL FORMULATIONS

Through the work of this group and their various systems-oriented associates the concept of family violence has been circumscribed so that wife-beating (more so than child abuse, which as a different institutional location) has come to be understood in a general, cultural, and common-sense way as something that can be separated from but always refers back to family violence. The major rationale for this view appears to be the cycle-of-violence concern with the transmitting of socialized behaviours generation by generation. The result, however, is often an emphasis on the influence on children rather than on the safety and suffering of women. The degendered, depersonalized, and abstracted use of such concepts as 'rigid unilaterial control,' 'method of resolution,' and 'relationship violence' allows the reality of women's experience of being beaten, injured, and killed to be denied or obscured, despite the apparent attention paid to feminist concerns. Institutional factors such as the prior existence of child-welfare agencies and departments within the social-problem apparatus with responsibility for family services provide the operational context for this framework and account for the way that family violence as an issue has been taken up by the state.

Criticism of the psychosocial approach, and of concepts of family violence, domestic violence, spouse abuse, and so on, developed more slowly and has been less evident than the critique of psychodynamic models. The sociological focus and the incorporation of a number of the contextual issues that affect women's lives gave the psychosocial approach a more benign and even useful appearance, thus allowing it to be adopted or tolerated by some feminists who saw the need for properly co-ordinated professional services as the primary solution to the problem.[21] The most cogent critique of this approach developed out of the practical concerns of grass-roots feminist groups and activists in working alongside proponents of this position in professional agencies, on task forces and community liaison bodies, much as in Vancouver and elsewhere.[22]

Breines and Gordon, however, raise the problems and the dimensions of the critique in their 1983 review, 'The New Scholarship on Family Violence',[23] expressing their reservations about the function of the family-violence framework itself and pointing out its limitations and drawbacks. They recognized that, as de Lauretis points out, a concept of a form of violence institutionally inherent – if not quite institutionalized – in the family could not exist without the terminology of family violence. Theirs is one of the few papers that draws attention to the fact that most researchers fail to analyse the terms of their own enquiry, such as 'family,' 'power,' 'gender,' and even 'violence.' They maintain that 'violence between intimates must be seen in the wider context of social power relations, and gender is absolutely central to the construction of and is constructed by, the "family". Violence should therefore be conceptualized, not as a breakdown of social order, but rather as the reflection of a power struggle for the maintenance of a certain kind of social order.'[24]

They propose several overlapping categories into which studies of wife-beating break down.

There is a feminist school of thought which views the problem as a microcosm of the social relations between the sexes; in contrast non-feminist (but not necessarily anti-feminsit) analysts tend to view the problem (often called, not wife beating, but spouse abuse or marital violence) as gender-neutral or at least as a mutual poblem of both sexes. In addition there is a division between those who approach the problem primarily psychologically – and these may include feminist and anti-feminists; those who look primarily to social stress factors for explanations – and these too include people with a range of attitudes towards feminism; and those who rely on systems theory approaches. Most non-feminist sociologists emphasize similarities between child abuse and wife-beating both in their patterns and causes and in their remedies. Indeed, these scholars argue that treating the problems separately may obscure their commonalities.[25]

The concerns expressed by these authors are an indication of the confusion caused by the amalgamation of diverse and contradictory elements into compromise and seemingly comprehensive definitions such as family violence, which can then be treated as a subject for academic research. Discursive practices work to render equivalent various 'viewpoints' and models by treating them at a theoretical level rather than grounding them in institutional locations and political positions as features of ruling relations.

FEMINIST FORMULATIONS

Alongside and in some ways cutting across these theoretical models is a third framework, or model, which Johnston identifies as a feminist position. The 'cross-cutting,' as Breines and Gordon suggest, arises from attempts by feminists to discover, in the various models available, some useful causal, explanatory, and accountable theory to inform and extend the work of finding solutions to women's dangerous circumstances. It also arises from attempts to insert into these models women's knowledge and political commitment. The existing models are, however, the very forms through which appropriation occurs.

A feminist position starts with a validation of women's experience, expresses anger at the range of victim-blaming stances put forward in many varieties of the other models, and is determined to locate the abuse of women in its historical and political context as part of the systematic subjugation of women. Within these parameters some feminists assume positions that could be included in the previous models. Pizzey,[26] influential founder of the first of the current wave of women's shelters, believes, for example, that a small but significant proportion of women do indeed display characteristics and behaviour well described by the

Freudian formulation of masochism; Walker[27] makes sensitive and persuasive use of social learning theory. An even larger number of women working from a feminist perspective would find themselves in some agreeement with family-violence researchers such as Gelles and Straus when it comes to recognizing the systemic, socio-economic, traditional sex roles and stress/frustration related theories they offer as being useful explanatory tools. In the main, however, feminist theorists refute such explanations and seek to build knowledge from women's experience of subordination by the use of coercion and force.

Johnston's third model elaborates on what she has identified previously as 'the feminist literature.'[28] This she describes as representing 'only a small percentage of the total literature in the area,'[29] but as providing a more valuable explanation and analysis of violence against wives. Although I shall include my adaptation of her review and other feminist summaries to give the reader an appreciation of the content, I intend to use the review itself to draw attention to a problem with this method of approaching the material. Treating feminist scholarship in this way introduces it into the discourse as merely another perspective to be championed or dismissed. Thus, the discourse can be seen to operate at the level of ideology as if it were simply an interplay of ideas, relative and viable views of a reality to be adopted where relevant or discarded as useless.

Johnston notes that a feminst analysis provides for a broad view of the context of individual behaviour in the structural and institutional organization of a patriarchal and capitalist society. It usually sets wife-battering, or as she prefers to call it, 'violence against wives,' in its historical context: 'What stands out most clearly when discussing wife abuse from a feminist perspective is the historical-legal precedent of male supremacy and the subordination of women in marriage and in society. The reasons men have historically beaten their wives originates from the belief that man has property rights over his partner. In return for economic dependence, women are expected to obey their husbands' demands. Wife abuse then is an extension of the social permission to control women.'[30]

A second significant feature of the feminist 'approach' stems from the critique that has been developed with regard to the other models considered here. A number of women and some men writing from the standpoint of women's experience have taken issue with theoretical underpinnings; victim-blaming; inadequate, positivistic, quantitiative, and idealistic scientific methodological procedures; sexist, patriarchal, and biased formulations; and misleading assumptions.[31]

Summarizing the two models from a feminist position, Johnston identifies the larger political issue, suggesting that 'All the theoretical work within the psychodynamic and psychosocial literature addresses the question of why men may hit their partners at a particular moment. While analyzing this question is important, it is not the same as designing a theory of why men as a group direct their violence at women ... Theorists have failed to make this distinction. While individual characteristics, relationship or familial problems, stress levels, low socio-economic status or being brought up in a violent family, in individual cases may contribute to abuse or heighten the likelihood of its occurrence, they do not explain the consistent target – women as wives.'[32]

The feminist position, though divided, does concern itself with this larger question of male violence against women. It sees such violence as a reflection of unequal and oppressive power relations between the sexes, and this as not just a matter of tradition or cultural values but as integral to the unequal social structure of society as a whole. Writers such as Barnsley, Dobash and Dobash, Martin, Pleck et al., Small, and Schechter[33] see power as the root issue in wife-battering. Power is the overriding issue to be addressed, within the specific historical context in which battering occurs. Oppressive power relations must be recognized if the situation is to be properly understood.

As Schechter points out in her study of the shelter movement in the United States: 'Feminists were the first to analyse violence against women as part of the power dynamics operating between men and women in a sexist society ... Professionals then moved in to claim violence as a mental health or criminal justice problem. The political analysis disappeared, was changed or was considered beyond the scope of professional concern.'[34]

THE RELATIONS OF DISCOURSE

Schechter's observation returns us to the problem of the political relations of the struggle to get women's needs addressed. The kind of 'review of the literature' that Johnston provides, and on which I based the previous section, is, I suggest, itself one of the many ways in which 'the political analysis disappears.' Incorporating a range of feminist work into the discourse as representative of particular 'perspective' obscures a number of contraditions. The different locations, activities, and implications are lost. Lost too are the distinctive properties of research that attempts to start outside existing theoretical formulations and the relations of discourse. Efforts to create knowledge for women's use rather than for the imperatives and relevances of those who order, administer, and rule, are obscured by being incorporated into the discourse as a particular 'perspective.'[35]

The work processes by which academic discourse is accomplished and the discursive procedures through which it is disseminated create a depoliticized and homogenized knowledge that can be put forward as a range of views and perspectives. Feminist researchers, scholars, and writers have an impact on how violence is taken up but are also incorporated through such processes; they produce their work within particular existing disciplines, or they enter the discourse by presenting their work at conferences and in publications, or they draw on, review, and apply work done in different locations. Some texts that have been influential and some that are merely significant in terms of their actual organization, which in itself creates certain discursive relations, serve to illustrate my point.

Much of the work done by feminists has been located outside the mainstream discourse on family violence and maintains a critical postion towards it. Pizzey's early and influential book, for example, was not written as an academic text, though it provided a corner-stone for much of the succeeding work. It was largely made up of Pizzey's first-person description of how the original Chiswick centre was set up and became the model for the Women's Aid Movement in Britain.[36]

Dobash and Dobash[37] and Schechter[38] took explicitly critical, though differing, positions in their analyses of the history of wife-battering and of the battered women's movement, respectively. Others, such as the Vancouver Women's Research Centre, deliberately worked to produce knowledge by methods that start outside discourse. They researched the experience of battered women and transition-house workers and examined the policies and procedures of the social-problem apparatus as they affect women.[39] The work of Del Martin[40] and Lenore Walker,[41] by contrast, illustrates the different ways in which feminists entered into and used existing discourse. Martin raised women's plight to public awareness as wife-battering, displaying the inadequacy of the response of various social services and institutions. She named a phenomenon, claimed it as a women's issue, and attributed responsibility both to men as perpetuators and to society as failing to provide adequate sanctions and supports. In doing so, she disputed prior psychodynamic formulations but called upon existing theoretical material from the social sciences to develop explanations and accounts of the situation.

The author's actual relation to the subject is not clear in her influential book, *Battered Wives*, published in 1976. The timing of her book, her analysis of the oppressive nature of a patriarchal society, and her activist affiliations locate her as a radical voice in the newly emerging movement, but within that context her aims incorporate professional objectives. She states her purpose in writing the book as being to investigate the problems of battered wives and suggest solutions. But, she goes on, 'any lasting solution to this complex problem should come from the collective thinking of researchers in government and private social agencies, the institutional religions, and political action groups. Such cooperative and constructive thinking will continue to be impossible, however, unless men as well as women come to realize that violence in the home is not a private affair but a grave social problem.'[42]

The text is then organized in a manner than brings together: a review of violence in the home; the hidden nature of wife abuse; the structure of marriage in a patriarchal society; the social-science discourse on violence and aggression as it relates to understanding the behaviour of the batterer; the victimization of women in relation to the societal structure of the family; and the failure of the legal and social-service systems to address the problem and women's needs for protection and assistance. Part of the book deals with individual survival tactics, remedial legislation, the availability of refuges for battered women, and strategies for gaining various forms of government and private funding for their establishment.

Though Martin insists that male violence towards women cannot be eradicated without changing the poor relationships between men and women, which would involve a complete restructuring of the traditional family and a transformation of the division of domestic labour, she locates the problem in 'historical attitudes toward women, the institution of marriage, the economy, the intricacies of criminal and civil law, and the delivery system of social service agencies.'[43] Having done so, she proceeds to acknowledge the contribution and influence of a variety of people: feminist activists and academics such as Pizzey; Straus, Gelles, and Steinmetz, whose work forms, as we have seen, the core of the social-science framework on family violence; and various legal experts, psychologists, and police consultants such as James Bannon. Bannon's analysis, she states, 'shows a high degree of feminist consciousness and a keen awareness of the victim's predicament that is generally lacking in police attitudes.'[44] The various locations and positions of the people and institutions that are acknowledged appear as equally valid grist to the mill of Martin's analysis.

Here we begin to see women's experience taken up (the book begins with a long and detailed letter written to a friend of Martin's by a woman identified as a battered wife) and is inserted into the social relations of the broader determinants of social organization. At the same time, however, this is accomplished, at least in part, by calling on the social-science discourse on family violence for ways to account for and explain men's behaviour. Thus, we are presented with the beginnings of an organization of conceptual co-ordination by amalgamation or even merely by approximation of often dissenting, and sometimes contradictory, frameworks melded to form a seemingly homogenous whole in relation to understanding 'battered wives' as 'a grave social problem.'[45] A similar format was later used by MacLeod to organize the advisory council's book *Wife Battering in Canada: The Vicious Circle.*[46]

In Lenore Walker's 1979 book *The Battered Woman*, the author deliberately set out to bring a feminist analysis to bear on the pyschology of battered women: to make women's experience of battering part of the framework of the pyschological discipline and at the same time to make a psychological perspective on battered women part of the discourse on family violence. In the introduction to her book, she writes:

When I became interested in studying battered women's problems in early 1975, no other psychologists were doing similar research. Several sociologists, such as Murray Straus, Richard Gelles, and Susan Steinmetz, were documenting some of the social causes of violence in the family. Feminists like Susan Brownmiller were studying the history of rape as a means for men to control women. Feminist pyschologists like Phyllis Chesler were re-evaluating the usefulness of traditional pyschoanalystic therapy for women because of its strong anti-woman theoretical basis. No one, however, was studying the psychology of battered women as victims. I decided to begin at the original source, the battered women themselves.[47]

This she does, using extensive interviews from which she selects and orders women's words to dispute myths; reveal patterns and commonalities; expose the nature, severity, and bizarreness of what she calls the 'coercive techniques' men use to control women; and draw attention to the previously little-discussed sexual aspects of the abuse, including the sexual abuse of the daughters of batterers. From this material she develops theoretical constructs by setting it within existing social learning theory, particularly that of 'learned helplessness,'[48] accounted for by a cycle of violence within the abusive relationships she studies.

The aspects of physical, sexual, and 'social' battering combine with 'economic abuse' to become the features of a 'battered women's syndrome,' to which Walker alludes but which she does not emphasize in this book. Walker became something of a celebrity in the course of this work, giving speeches and appearing on radio shows and television specials. As a result she became a recognized expert in the area, and her ideas have been widely disseminated. In her own words:

My feminist analysis of all violence is that sexism is the real underbelly of human suffering. Men fight other men to prove they are not 'sissies' like women. Women show passive faces to the world while struggling to keep their lives together without letting men know how strong they really are for fear of hurting their men's masculine image. And men beat up women in order to keep themselves on the top of this whole messy heap. Little girls and little boys learn these sex-role expectations through early socialization. Unless we strive for equal power relationships between men and women, women will continue to be victims of the kind of assaults I share with you in this book.[49]

ABSORPTION BY ASSOCIATION

The second process, that of producing coherence by juxtaposing a range of different frameworks and adding women's experience to the discourse in the form of professional knowledge, is even more evident in another early and influential book, Maria Roy's 1977 *Battred Women: A Psychosocial Study of Domestic Violence*.[50] This text is a collection that addresses the issue by bringing together the author's own social-work study (a survey of 150 'cases') and papers by experts in the area of neurology, psychiatry, psychology, sociology, law and law enforcement, history, and child abuse. Roy proposes a model for services and appends documents that attest to the work done by the service she founded and directs in New York, including conference proceedings and legal actions.

Roy's direct experience of the situations faced by the women with whom she worked as a social worker in New York, concern about which led her to found a refuge and engage in an energetic campaign of public education and legislative change, is subsumed under the various theoretical positions presented by other authors of papers in the book. The text itself is organized into sections presenting each position, framed by historical quotations, and introduced by a historical overview article that, together, function to demonstrate the transhistorical and universal nature of wife-beating and abuse. It is, as the title suggests, a psychosocial problem. The positions put forward by various experts appear as representative of different ways of accounting for aspects of the phenomenon as defined, each offering a seemingly complementary or cumulative analysis. Starting, as Roy does, within the professional and bureaucratic practices in which her work is located puts her avowedly feminist concerns and insights directly into the discourse, the coherence of which she herself contributes to in the production of the book. Unlike Martin, Roy fails to embed women's experience in the social organization of the family in relation to the economy and the legal structures that maintain that relation. Women's experiences do not appear at all in any primary narrative sense except as cases, but are replaced by the terms and concepts of the various disciplines that are drawn upon for expertise and are thus entered into the developing discourse.

The final text I want to consider brings together aspects of the academic discourse in a way that demonstrates fully the process of coherence by proximity and absorption by appropriation that has taken place. Called *The Dark Side of Families*,[51] it contains twenty-three papers from the 1981 National Conference for Family Violence Researchers, held in New Hampshire. The editors describe it as a collection of writing by some of the best-known authorities on family violence and abuse, containing 'not only some of the newest research and theoretical perspectives but also articles from a wide range of disciplines.'[52] Contributors include 'sociologists, psychologists, psychiatrists, physicians, human developmental theorists, social work researchers, social policy researchers and others.'[53]

Even a cursory perusal of the table of contents is enough to clue the reader into the problem I have been identifying. Among the range of 'family violence researchers' and 'others' contributing to the apparent emergence of a coherent position are not only representatives of all the diverse, divergent, and often contradictory approaches identified in Johnston's first two models (and more), but also representatives of a range of feminist positions. These positions are represented, first, in Lenore Walker's paper, 'The Battered Woman Syndrome Study,' which directly follows an introductory section identifying the 'common features of "family abuse."' Among the other papers are at least two that are specifically critical of the paramount family-violence frame, one by Dobash and Dobash, whose analysis is specifically designed to set the problem of wife-battery in the context of patriarchal family structures,[54] and one by Stark and Flitcraft, which questions the social construction of knowledge about the abuse of women and does so from an overtly socialist-feminist position.[55]

The conference and resulting book demonstrate two particular ways in which feminist input has impact and is at the same time absorbed into an overall framework that appropriates it, contradictions and all, as just one of many perspectives on family violence. The process of absorption consists of, first, a somewhat cursory acknowledgment of the serious consequences of wife-battering and its structural determinants by naming it criminal assault. At the same time, practitioners continue to advance the professional ideology of treatment for individuals and families. Second, the organization of the conference and its proceedings incorporate feminist tenets and positions, alongside other, often irreconcilable, formulations. The conference itself may well have been the site of conflicts between participants but the document that presents it to public view, like the United Way task force report and the proceedings of the federal advisory council reviewed in chapter 4, organizes the relation of participants and their positions into a discourse that has the character of co-ordinated and authoritative knowledge production. Political issues, dissent, and conflict, if they arose, are homogenized in the text and presented as complimentary perspectives.

INCORPORATING FEMINIST AND MAINSTREAM DISCOURSE

The process of discursive development parallels the process of struggle and contradiction that has been identified in the stages delineated in chapter 1. My argument can be illustrated by a final consideration of a piece of work that relates back to the Del Martin text, which I noted as being an early example of this discursive procedure. The second printing of her book, *Battered Wives*, contains a concluding section entitled 'Update, 1976–1981 – Five Years Later.' The structure of this section is, in itself, significant. It starts with an account of the acquittal of a woman charged with the attempted murder of her batterer-husband, pointing out that five years earlier such an acquittal would probably not have taken place. The change is attributed to legislative rulings that instituted three important procedures: the definition of a different standard for women for what could be considered justifiable self-defence; the admissibility of evidence of previous incidence of battering; and the allowing of testimony from an expert witness on 'the battered woman syndrome,' Lenore Walker, 'enabling jurors who may have little knowledge of the phenomenon to consider the evidence in perspective.'[56] The next section, 'Domestic Violence Is a Crime,' reviews the success of the Battered Women's Movement in changing police and court procedures, removing the onus of prosecution from the victim, and, in some cases, transferring responsibility to the district attorney to file charges as a crime against the state. Martin then includes a section noting a shift of treatment focus from the wife to the couple and then to the 'offender' and programs designed to deal with violence as 'his problem' and a learned behaviour to be unlearned.

We can see here a description that has much in common with the stages identified in the local processes we have been following: a phenomenon has been constructed, identified as wife-battering, a syndrome with a clinical organization of sufficient persuasiveness to be considered as a defence under the law, and responsibility has been designated as belonging causally to the pathological aspects of masculinity and remedially to the state through the law-enforcement apparatus and therapeutic treatment programs.

Missing from the process, however, are the battles between professionals and activists and the struggles within the movement over which definitions and strategies would serve which ends. What we get, instead, is a review of recent research that has inserted the 'specificity of wife-beating' into the framework of 'family violence' and contributed to 'our understanding of the battered wife syndrome ... [as] the *result* of the beatings, not the *cause* of them.'[54] Walker, Dobash and Dobash, and Pagelow are here lumped together, and their very different analyses presented cumulatively to support Martin's formulations on the negative effects of sex-role sterotyping.[58]

Next, Martin details the progress of the Battered Women's Movement in terms of its expansions, the struggles against co-optation through funding processes, and the take-over of some refuges by professionals. The failure of legislative strategies is counterbalanced in her account by the success of initiatives to get the government to respond to the problems of military wives by instituting extensive social services for battered women on a number of military bases. After a section dealing with the politics of funding and the need for state coalitions against domestic violence to ensure the continuation and expansion of refuges and other actions, Martin addresses what she calls 'psycholinguistics and domestic violence.'[59] Here she struggles to come to grips with some of the definitional issues that have been my concern so far. 'Domestic violence,' she says, 'is the euphemism we first employed to attract public attention at a time when there was so much resistance to dealing with wife abuse per se.'[60] The problem, as far as she is concerned, is that news stories and police reports still use misleading terms such as 'disputes' or 'quarrels' that 'deny wife-beating as a crime and diminish the impact of the violence, and preventing people from coming to grips with reality.'[61]

The kind of connection Martin makes between terminology, professional practices, and the politics of social action does not question the grounds of our construction of the issue, only the effectiveness of certain linguistic strategies. These, she suggests, should be intensified to 'say what we really mean,' that is, we should abandon the 'diplomatic language we used in the past to get people to listen or to keep them from alienating those whose help we needed,'[62] and start to address 'conjugal terrorism.' Battered women must be seen as political prisoners. 'Male domination and protection of the patriarchal system that breeds sexism and homophobia are the political issues at stake.'[63] The section ends with a reference to the letter from a battered wife that begins the book, noting that the woman took action that threatened publicity for her physician-husband if he continued to beat her. He stopped. Martin closes by suggesting that when a man has something to lose, he can quickly learn to change violent behaviour.

I have described Martin's postscript in detail because I think it displays some features of both the process of action and change towards increasingly institutionalized solutions which are being traced in the events I describe in this book. It also draws attention to the conceptual processes, an aspect that has received less attention except in accounts by Schechter and Morgan.[64] These conceptual processes are the focus of chapter 6.

CONCLUSION

In this chapter I have identified the dilemma I see in the relationship between the grass-roots and academic aspects of the women's movement: how to construct our own knowledge for our own use and how to have an impact on other institutionalized knowledge-making processes in society in order to bring about our political ends. I sketched briefly the content of the various academic frameworks that take their place in the discourse that has developed around the issues of wife-battering and family violence and showed how these have had an impact on each other. The success of feminist input into the discursive frameworks during the period being analysed here resided in the recognition of wife-battering and the fact that much of so-called family violence is violence by males against females as features requiring acknowledgment. This feminist input was being absorbed and reorganized so that wife-battery took its place as a subset of family violence and was given a specific clinical and criminal classification as 'the battered-woman (or wife) syndrome.' This classification was accomplished, in part at least, by the work of feminist researchers such as Roy and Walker.[65]

This discussion of discursive relations raises questions about the practices of knowledge production and the relation of feminist ways of knowing to the political process. It returns us to the consideration of ideology as it has been defined and discussed in previous chapters. It is here, I suggest, that we will find the underpinnings of the dilemmas raised in the book so far.

6 The Concept of Violence

I have been tracing a crucial progression whereby the anger and mobilization of feminist activists concerned with wife-beating have been transformed and absorbed into existing institutional structures. The result of this process is that, although we may still be working, struggling, and angry, the sites of our struggles are dispersed, disconnected, and depoliticized. It is not a magical or mysterious process. Because, however, it has many complex features and, largely, I would suggest, because it involves ways of thinking and of using language that obscure important aspects of what it is we need to understand, this process is not an easy one to uncover. Now I want to emphasize some of the ways in which the dilemmas we face as feminists in our various locations are embedded in the conceptual practices that we necessarily adopt when we take up our struggle in relation to the state.

In the early years of recognizing and organizing around the plight of women beaten and brutalized by husbands and intimates, women did not have a term that would particularize or define their situation. The process of making the experience of oppression in our own homes visible to ourselves and then getting it accepted as a matter of public concern was one that involved defining it as an issue or problem in our own terms. The language we have available to us to do this kind of work presents us with a contradiction: it is the 'oppressor's language,'[1] controlled by those who have the power to define its content and meaning. We have, however, to use it to express our cases.

The chapter pulls together the conceptual processes underlying the developments described so far. In it I consolidate my thinking on the key concept of 'violence' and put in place the conceptual elements that are the focus of the second part of the study. The use of language presents me with a problem here. It is important that language used descriptively in relation to activities and experiences be distinguished from the conceptual forms produced by ideological practices that identify the generalizing relations of ruling. I am in no way denying the fact that men treat women in a variety of oppressive ways, some of which are brutal and coercive, in order to enforce their demand and desires. What I am addressing here is something different: I am mapping a discursive process embedded in the work of intellectuals, professionals, and administrators. This process selects and names certain activities as categories identifying particular problems and leading to particular solutions. To mark and clarify this distinction, I have placed certain terms in quotation marks when I address the technical nature of their ideological functioning as ruling concepts.

First, I want to look at the way particular aspects of women's experience have been isolated and described so as to become accepted as a discrete phenomenon, that of wife-beating, – battering, or abuse, a 'women's issue.' Then I shall review the struggle over terms and definitions – 'male violence,' 'domestic violence,' and 'family violence' – that took place both within the women's movement and in relation to institutional structures and professional practices. Finally, I will argue that the common ground provided by the concept of 'violence' has allowed for combined strategies among activists and professionals that have led to the acceptance of wife-battering as primarily a problem of assault under criminal law. While this definition of assault has important short-term implications for the protection of individual women and the possibility of public sanctioning of men's violent behaviour, I argue that it is part of the process of institutionalization that we need to understand if we are to analyse our struggles and develop strategies to avoid fragmentation and the appropriation of our concerns in the future.

THE BATTERED WIFE

When women first spoke out about being hit and beaten by husbands or common-law partners, the terms 'battered wife' and 'wife abuse' were not available as ways to think about the experience. As women strove to make the situation public, these terms were extrapolated from the existing discourse on child abuse, already 'discovered' and designated as a 'syndrome' by medical practitioners in the 1960s.[2] 'Battered babies' had made media headlines, especially in Britain, and the use of 'battering' in this conjunction refers to legal terminology of assault and battery, which is one of the categorizations of degrees of severity of assault under the British Criminal Code. Though the terms may have arisen in the professional discourse in Europe and the United States, they were elaborated in the media and their use in reference to wife-beating was sufficiently widespread to have become common parlance by the early 1970s. Women identify themselves as battered wives in some of the letters that Erin Pizzey published in her 1974 book. She herself uses 'battering' occasionally as an adjective to describe continued and severe beatings and refers to 'battered wives' only once, qualifying the reference by the use of quotation marks, which imply some scepticism about the professional implications of the term: 'As far as I can see the reason why "battered wives" are getting a hearing is that for the first time a middle-class woman has said, "It's happened to me." That makes it respectable and all the more shocking. Now – just as "battered babies" were once called "manslaughter" – wife beating has become the "battered wife syndrome." But it is not enough to call it a new name and then carry on as before.'[3]

My memory of working with the women who ran Transition House and other related projects in those days is that we initially used the terms 'wife-beating,' 'battering,' and 'abuse' in a loose and relatively inter-changeable way. Any concern we may have had at the time about the implications of the terms related more to considering whether using 'wife' would act to prevent women who were not legally married to their abusers from seeing themselves as welcome at the house or to allow professional agencies to refuse them welfare and other services.

Del Martin's book *Battered Wives*, published in 1976, contains an introduction by Diane Russel, an activist and academic doing research in the area of rape. Russel defines battering as a recognized term denoting a more severe and extreme form of the phenomenon of wife-beating, which she links with rape as a means of coercion and control of women. Martin takes up the term 'wife-battering,' in the same way we did in Vancouver, as problematic only in relation to the marital status of the victim and explains her use of 'wife' as conveying the intimate nature of the relationship involved.[4] For Martin, too, 'battering' seems to have taken its place as a specific descriptive term. Her book was a significant factor in promoting the adoption of the term 'battered wife' as one around which women mobilized their efforts to define the issue on their own terms and to counter neutralizing and degendering alternatives such as 'spouse abuse' and 'interspousal violent episodes.' These terms were employed by professionals faced with responding to the issue, which was increasingly linked with child abuse under the rubric of family or domestic violence.

Activists in other places shared similar experiences to ours while working with the United Way in Vancouver. We found that linking wife-battering and child abuse focused the issue in such a way that women's experience came to be subsumed under 'family violence' and marginalized by the professional emphasis on child abuse and services to men who battered their wives. We had to be vigilant, vigorous, and persistent in putting forward the situation of battered women in order to counteract the way that the framework of 'family violence' allowed for an obscuring of the actual actions of men, and the suffering of women, in an objectified professional language.

The designation of violence as occurring in the family or in the domestic realm also maintained it as a private matter concerned with the dynamics of interpersonal relations between individuals. This framework arose out of and fed back into the work of professional agencies and institutions whose mandate and objective it was to maintain the organization and existing power relations of the family. The political objective around which many of us focused our work at this point thus became one of forcing the professionals in the field to recognize wifebattering and abuse as an issue to be addressed in its own right, and as representing the overwhelming preponderance of instances of 'family violence.' We also became involved in a critique of 'the family' as such; the feminist analysis of the family as an institution that embodies the political oppression of women at its most personal was not readily accepted by the professionals with whom we struggled. We fought against the removal of the issue from its context in a political movement, and for the maintenance of women's control of their definition of the issue.

For some feminists, however, the use of the terms 'family' and 'domestic' violence served as conscious change strategy. Martin, in her 1981 update to the second edition of her book *Battered Wives*, notes, as we have seen, that in the early stages of raising the issue to pubic attention as 'domestic violence' it was sometimes necessary to cloak 'the realities' in 'diplomatic language ... to get people to listen or to keep from alienating those whose help we needed.'[5] The co-ordinator of the Vancouver United Way task force reacted with anger to the suggestion that 'family violence' as a term worked against women's interests. She insisted that, on the contrary, it allowed her to 'slip women in' in circumstances where wife-battering itself would have been 'too contentious an issue.'[6]

MALE VIOLENCE AGAINST WOMEN

The division over the uses of such terms as 'family' and 'domestic' violence was not the only one among feminists working on the issue. Increasingly we insisted on attributing responsibility for the problem to the men who do the beating and the society that condones it. This position involved us in recognizing similarities between wife-beating and other forms of coercion and control, especially rape, incest, and sexual harassment. Many activists united to struggle in an arena of male violence against women, to which all women are vulnerable and of which all men are capable.

The account of the rifts between women who met at the Canadian Advisory Council on the Status of Women consultation, which I described in chapter 3, reveals attempts made by the council to find a common position. Such a position had to address professional concerns for the proper management of the problem, and activists' analyses that put forward differing and divisive accounts of the roots of the issue. Some of us, including Dorothy Smith, whose function at the consultation was to pull together an overview and unifying analytic framework, concentrated on the structural features of women's dependence in relation to the family and the work-force, emphasizing the trap that this creates for women, particularly women with children. At the same time, we had no difficulty in agreeing that men's violence towards women must be addressed in the short term in any strategy for change designed to alter the overall relations of dependence and control. Others of us saw the organization of the family as only a manifestation of the overriding issue, that of the ultimate control of women by force or the threat of force in a patriarchal system. Male dominance and male violence thus became the primary target for action.

The proceedings published by the council after the consultation show how the work of the women there was drawn together to emphasize this latter position. By taking up the theme of one presentation (that battering is something we all share), which extended the definition of wife-battering to include almost every form of women's experience of oppression, the document packages the various positions into one that can be adopted to stand for all. 'We women' stand opposed to male violence, which must be countered; we women must maintain control of the issue. This position attempts to marry definitions that operate at a bureaucratic and a professional level, such as family and domestic violence, to those with a political mobilizing intent, such as wife-battering, violence against women, and male violence. Language such as 'Wife Battering Is Everywoman's Issue' (the title of the document) organizes an undertaking that brings us together as women and dissolves differences between professionals, service providers, activists, and women who are beaten, all of whom become women vulnerable to male violence. The document takes up the term 'wife-battering,' which is already mobilizing women, in a way that links movement organization and impetus to bureaucratic and professional forms.

ASSAULT UNDER THE LAW

At this stage of the process the beginnings of a marriage of the male-violence framework with that of family violence was accomplished by focusing on violence itself as the problem that unites them. Thus, women who occupied a range of positions were given a way to organize their work in opposition to violence as behaviour beyond the rule of law. The issue of wife-battering has thus been reformulated in terms of the laws on assault, which ostensibly protect everyone from violent attack by other members of society. The struggle is joined around pressure to extend the application of the law to those women whose status as wives or intimates is seen having left them unprotected within the private realm of the family, traditionally beyond legal intervention in most situations short of murder. In the process, the analysis of women's oppression in the broader structures of society becomes secondary to the strategy of invoking women's rights as individuals under the law. The coalescence of this strategy and its consequences for lodging wife-battering, formulated as wife assault, within particular institutional sites of the social-problem apparatus is the focus of my analysis of the events that took place before the Ontario legislature's Standing Committee on Social Development. Some of the conceptual underpinnings to those events are detailed here.

CONCEPTUAL PRACTICES

I have described the struggle over definition and control of the issue sequentially to demonstrate the process as one taking place over time and within activities and events, not as merely an abstract or linguistic concern. It could equally be presented schematically as:

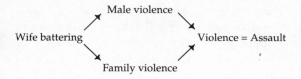

Male violence

Wife battering   Violence = Assault

Family violence

Such terms require an analysis that takes into account the way language operates at the conceptual level, to demonstrate how the process functions and why it is consequential for the absorption of the political mobilization of the women's movement around the issue of wife-battering.

Concepts, when they operate in this 'technical' way, are not simply descriptive linguistic conventions; they organize the social construction of knowledge: ways of thinking about, defining, and giving abstract and generalized meaning to our particular experience. Knowledge, thus produced, provides for particular ways of taking action. Thus concepts can be seen to do more than name a phenomenon. They are part of a social relation (used here to signify an ongoing, concerted course of action, involving more than one person) that brings into being and organizes particular phenomena in specific ways, providing for responses to what has thus been identified.

'Family violence' as a concept organizes both a phenomenon and a course of action. How it is constructed, however, is in some way invisible. It appears as the natural conjunction of two recognizable features of our society: 'the family' and 'violence.' This conjunction is not a straightforward naming of related entities; it has developed out of the work of professionals, researchers, theorists, and information disseminators, to become a discourse with distinctive properties. Putting together 'family' and 'violence' both treats as naturalistic and conflates two concepts that have already been developed for our understanding by sociological procedures or as administrative products. These procedures construct as social facts the 'ordinary forms in which the features of our society become observable to us as its features – mental illness, neighbours, crime, riots, leisure, work satisfaction, etc.'[7] The process by which these features are constructed is the making of ideology. Ideology, understood in this way, is a method of thinking and working that severs our ideas from the practical, everyday world of lived experience in which they arise and uses them as the building-blocks for theories that serve the purposes of those whose job it is to order and rule.

Feminists have struggled against the concept of 'family violence' per se, but I want to suggest that there is a prior conceptual stage with regard to wife-battering itself, as a category, that has seldom been addressed in our definitional debates. Pizzey acknowledged some ambivalence towards the naming of women who were beaten as 'battered wives' but it was Smith who challenged the category itself.[8] Her quarrel with the category, though based in the same recognition of the professional organization of a syndrome that Pizzey noted, takes it up from a different angle of concern. Smith points out that taking a particular aspect of women's experience of oppression out of its context and putting it through the process of abstraction that constructs such a category as the 'battered wife' is an ideological process. It produces the conceptual forms through which professional intervention operates and is justified. Such a process is, she suggests, one of the ways that women's protest is absorbed into institutional structures: 'The issue of men's violence against women in the family setting is being transformed into a professional psychiatric or counselling problem. The "battered wife" concept is substituted for the political analysis of violence by men against women. There are conferences, a literature, the elaboration of a professional practice (often focusing more on men than on women).'[9] The significance of Smith's challenge was not fully appreciated at the time it was issued. The struggle over 'family violence' and the efforts made by women to combat the subsuming of wife-battering as an issue obscured some of the implications of the term itself. Wife-beating or -battering might perhaps have some claim to the status of mere description, but 'the battered wife' is clearly a social construction. Its ideological properties as a category removed from the social relations of women's lives allows 'the battered wife' to be treated as an instance of 'family violence,' or any other larger theoretical framework implicated in the ideological process of separating out features of people's lives into manageable administrative portions.

A subsequent development adds a dimension to the problem that was not evident in 1979 when Smith wrote the passage quoted above. The political analysis of violence by men against women has itself been elaborated into a framework that had become a major organizing focus for feminists by the early 1980s and absorbed 'the battered wife' as an instance of the victimization of women by male violence. I would argue that this framework is also an ideological feature of a discourse equally cut off from the social relations in which women's lives are embedded. It allows for the abandoning (or marginalizing) of the women's movement's initial mobilizing focus around the analysis of the oppression within the broad social structures of the division of labour in the work-place and in the family. Thus, the acceptance of men's domination of each other and of women through the use of 'violence' as the overreaching determinant of women's oppression throughout all time is provided for. This shift in focus from the earlier analysis for the structural determinants of women's oppression in the family and the labour force represents a major rift in the contemporary women's movement.[10] It has provided the basis for the conceptual co-ordination of the issue of wife-beating in terms of 'violence' defined as assault under the law.

THE CONCEPT OF 'VIOLENCE'

Feminists on many fronts have taken up the ideological construction of 'the family' as both normative and problematic for women.[11] 'Violence,' in contrast, appears to have been used extensively as if it was a purely descriptive term for behaviours or activities in which physical force is used to inflict injury, either randomly or to gain some specific end, such as control. Its definition has been extended in the case of male violence against women to include verbal threats and abuse, economic deprivation, sexual coercion or deprivation, and the creation of a general climate of fear that limits the full participation of women in society. If, instead of seeking to extend its definitional adequacies, we were to examine 'violence' as a term to be investigated by methods that reveal its construction as a concept, we would find that like 'the family' it, too, holds properties beyond the descriptive. It is not my purpose here to attempt a full-scale analysis of 'violence' as a concept, but simply to sketch in what I see as some of the dimensions and implications of its current usage.

When a concept such as 'violence' is constructed by the process of 'making ideology' identified by Smith,[12] it is detached from its grounding in the social relations in which events and activities take place. It is then put through an abstract reorganization that conforms to the relevances of a particular discourse or a number of them. It takes on, in this process, a reified form to which causal efficacy, as well as explanatory powers, can be ascribed. In the process, there is a shift in the concept. It ceases to describe what someone does – hitting, punching, kicking, stabbing, shooting someone else – replacing the idea of a person doing things by that of action in a general form, but without the actor. Violence 'breaks out' in families, in the streets, on the picket line; outbreaks of violence 'occur.' 'Violence' can then be treated as a causal factor and motivator in a range of discourses that intersect and correlate several disciplines. Within the broad discourses of the social sciences, 'violence' appears as integral in the psychosocial and socio-biological discourses concerning aggression, dominance, instinctual behaviour, and sex roles. In sociology and criminology, it operates as a feature of the discourses of law and order and victimology. In legal discourse, 'violence' is of particular significance in relation to the rule of law. 'Violence' knits together these discourses and is given both a clinical and criminal organization, each of which is salient in the analysis I am making here.

Already made available to us by the ideological practices of mainstream social scientists, building upon 'the primary administrative work which constitutes murders, suicides, etc.,'[13] 'violence' has taken its place as the unquestioned focus of two relatively new and developing discourses, the professional discourse of 'family violence' and now a feminist discourse of 'male violence.' It provides a link between both discourses and the socio-legal discourse on 'violence' in relation to the state.

'VIOLENCE' AND THE STATE

The sanctioned use of force in contemporary society is monopolized by the state as a feature of the practices of ruling. The state has developed myriad bureaucratic procedures to license and control its use by the police, the military, and other functionaries such as coast guards, prison guards, and mental-hospital attendants. It is in relation to the state's claim to the legitimate use of force in certain circumstances that 'violence' as a concept can be seen to designate uncontrolled, unregulated, and illegitimate use of force. 'Violence,' within this framework, has been worked up ideologically. It is no longer merely a term in common usage to describe a wide range of activities used to enforce one's way and desires, inflict injury, or express one's discontent. It is also a technical category for the designation of non-sanctioned acts beyond the bounds of the law. Its status as such a category developed as part of a historical process in which the use of physical force to gain power and maintain order and control has been increasingly superseded by ideological procedures that regulate society through bureaucratic and professional operations.[14]

Use of brutal physical practices such as hanging, flogging, maiming, and torture as a regularized feature of the rule of law is no longer officially accepted in democratic societies. Even corporal punishment in schools is increasingly prohibited and in some countries, such as Sweden, it is illegal to smack one's own children. The outlawing of such acts represents both a change in methods of law enforcement and a shift in the designation of the realm to which the rule of law applies, extending it into the hitherto 'private' relations of the family. The internal governance of family matters was, until relatively recently, regarded as the domain of the male head of the household, though it is only in later forms of capitalist organization that the family has taken on the restricted nuclear grouping that we take as normative today. The patriarchal organization of earlier family forms resulted from a hierarchical social structure whereby the chain of authority of the state was extended to the 'paterfamilias,' whose responsibility it was to ensure the law-abiding behaviour of the family members, servants, apprentices, and employees within his household.

The juxtaposition of the concept of 'family' with that of 'violence' within the professional discourse is a historical process that has taken place over the past decade and a half, along with the medicalization and legalization of child abuse.[15] Indeed, as I noted in chapter 5, a concept of a form of violence institutionally inherent in the family did not in fact exist as such without the terminology of 'family violence.' Previous campaigns in Britain and the United States, at least, were fought in terms of 'crimes against women': cruelty, wife torture, men's brutishness and brutality, issues of temperance and social purity. These were designed to draw attention to men's abuse of a husband's legal rights over wife and children as property and to create legal conditions under which such rights could be challenged and revoked.[16]

Pressure from the current women's movement forced contemporary researchers to acknowledge the fact that women, like children, have historically been subjected to harsh discipline and cruel treatment in the household. As late as 1969, however, wife-beating had not yet been fully included in what prominent sociologist James Q. Wilson designated at the time as 'domestic violence': 'There are two kinds of domestic violence for which we would like to estimate future rates and thus two kind of problems which make such estimates very difficult, if not impossible. The first kind is individual violence – murders, suicides, assaults, child-beatings – and the second is collective violence – riots, civil insurrections, internal wars and the like.'[17] Conceptualizing 'violence' as spanning a range from individual pathology to large-scale social pathology opens the way for a set of relevancies that are capable of designating protest, dissent, or resistance to the dominant class as riots, insurrections, terrorism, or mob rule. That such definitions are operating unseen when 'family violence' is considered can be seen in both the definitions of 'domestic violence' offered by Wilson.

The kind of theory that this conflated framework of individual and collective behaviour allows for can be seen in a study by Dutton et al. They pull together a number of seemingly contradictory possibilities, theoretically reconciled into a causal hypothesis that suggests a form of personalized, 'deindividuated violence' engaged in by men towards their mates. 'Deindividuated violence' is a construct that refers to theories of mass, uncontrolled, uninhibited, and pleasurable rage expressed in vandalism, mob rampages, and riots. 'Violence' as a conceptual organizer enables the actions of individuals (here acknowledged as men) to be treated as if the acts are governed by a force independent of the will of the actors. Women are thought to remain with 'violent' men because they in turn develop inappropriate but intense 'trauma bonding' as a result of the erratic nature of their partners' behaviour. This theory is based on studies of the hostage, or 'Stockholm' syndrome. Triggers of male rage are stress and 'interpersonal aspects of the battering relationship.'[18] A feature of the theory of individual yet 'deindividuated violence' is that men, once past the rage threshold, have no control over and no memory of their actions and thus presumably no responsibility for them; women are helplessly unable to escape because of their own trauma.

THE DILEMMA OF 'VIOLENCE'

The positive aspect of the 'male violence' discourse lies in making visible the gender and power relations involved in 'family' or 'domestic' 'violence.' It has been crucial in advancing the struggle for definitional control and the action that comes out of it, and in making the professional discourse accommodate women's awareness. It does, however, produce a number of anomalies that challenge its ultimate usefulness as a strategic base. At the simplest level, it presents an explanation that suggests that the use of force to control women is either an inevitable outcome of pathological concepts of masculinity or a problem in which society is at fault for the way it socializes the genders. This explanation obscures any understanding of society as being structured and built on fundamental inequalities that render it disastrously out of tune with human need. At the other extreme are theories of innate, inherent, and socio-biological characteristics that doom all men to dominate each other and all women by aggression and force for all time.

These two positions seem to offer us the option of a massive and immediate resocialization of the entire society or the setting up of a separatist society divided on gender lines. At the very least, neither of these positions accounts for the anomalous situation of 'violent' women or of men who do not beat, rape, harass, and abuse women, in spite of growing up in so-called 'cradles of violence,' or for those who did not experience or witness physical abuse and do not perpetuate it. Such positions also open the way for clinical and legal initiatives that tie the most seemingly radical aspects of feminist mobilization into a conservative law-and-order framework for social control. In doing so, men's actions towards their wives become instances of assault. The actors are again subsumed under the legal terms 'perpetrator' and 'victim' and both the gender and the relational aspects are dissolved.

DISSECTING THE DILEMMA

The process I have examined can now be assembled schematically in a more complex and elaborate fashion:

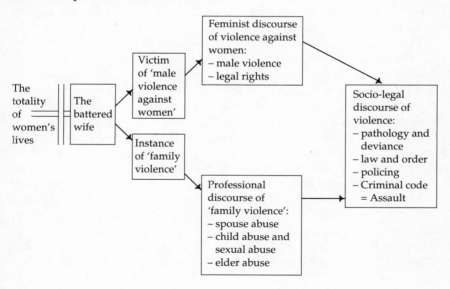

The dilemma of 'violence' as a conceptual practice points to the larger dilemma for the women's movement that has been discussed in this chapter. In order to act in ways that will make changes in the conditions of oppression that women experience in differing ways in the totality of their lives, experiences that have been designated as belonging to the private realm and to personal relationships have to be made public. The terms available in the public discourses, however, are more than a mere language of description. They are the conceptual features of methods of governing contemporary society. When we take up such terms as the 'battered wife' or 'violence,' we are participating in the bringing into being of the very phenomenon we seek to name and make visible. The language of abstraction is part of the making of ideology that transforms our understanding of our daily experience and implicates us in our own regulation. It does this by shaping our concern into 'issues' organized on the grounds and with the relevancies and imperatives of the institutions and practices of ruling. We have taken up the issue of wife-beating, but the 'battered wife' has proved problematic. She has become the 'victim' of 'violence' perpetuated by a batterer who must be prosecuted and treated for his violent behaviour. In the process she is turned into an abstraction by procedures that remove from the general context of women's lives the experience being named, constituting it as a category. The category can then be assembled, with others, as an issue or social problem from which professional intervention extracts all political focus. Social-service or legal solutions can be provided to the individuals concerned.

The dilemma faced by feminists is contained in the practices through which ruling is accomplished. Naming the experience is a double-edged weapon. It co-ordinates our mobilization and identifies our difficulties to ourselves and each other. Many women have spoken of the power that being able to identify themselves as battered wives gave them. It was a first step in recognizing the commonality of shared experience and the legitimacy of taking action. At the same time, it shapes the action to be taken in particular channels: 'help' in the form of social services or legal redress. Neither of these channels mobilize women without a feminist context nor do they address the totality of women's needs.

An example of the strange contradictions that these positions pose can be seen in Martin's 1981 update of *Battered Wives*. Opening with the experience of a wife acquitted of murdering her batterer, Martin notes the progress made in the previous five years. She attributes the acquittal to changes in court procedures and to the testimony of psychologist Lenore Walker as an expert witness on the characteristics of the 'Battered Woman Syndrome.' This marriage of the clinical and criminal does not perturb Martin; she is concerned, however, that progress on the legislative front has foundered and that the diplomatic terminology of earlier days is no longer sufficient to promote political change. Her strategy for repoliticization of the issue in the face of right-wing opposition and trivialization is to recast it in stronger language that will be indisputable in their terms. Battered wives, she suggests, should be seen as 'hostages' of their husbands' 'terrorism' and the ultimate form of 'political prisoner.' Thus the mobilization of women concerned with intervening to change this aspect of women's oppression is translated, in Martin's strategy, into the language of the state at its most bellicose and reactionary.[19]

CONCLUSION

'Violence' is no longer a straightforward term describing a natural or pre-existing phenomenon. It is worked up by ideological practices to become one of the concepts forming discourses that are the knowledge base for the exercise of power in contemporary society; it is a ruling concept, a building-block in the practice of ruling. As feminists we have taken the term into our own language to counter the ideology of 'family violence' and to attempt to reattribute the activities it names to the men who commit the acts of cruelty and coercion that it purports to describe. In the process, however, 'violence' comes to be accepted as an independent force directing the activities of all men for all time.

This, I suggest, has got us involved in some strange alliances. Within the women's movement the position of 'we women,' battered or oppressed in other ways, mobilizing to change the actual conditions of our lives and the structures that enforce them, has been fragmented by strategies that align us with different aspects of the state's practices. Our organization becomes its organization. We take up 'violence' within the family and use the linkages with the legal discourse to support the equation of 'violence' with assault. Thus feminists with differing political commitments can ally themselves with professional and civil-rights positions in seeking legal sanctions and protection for women under the law. We become actors in a process that reflects shifts and tensions in the jurisdictional boundaries of state practices.

As the organization of 'the family' around the assumption of a single wage deteriorates, men's authority in the family is challenged. At the same time, as the individual-rights model of participation and democracy permeates the ideology of the state, the right of women to be considered as persons, only relatively recently won and not by any means fully implemented, makes arguments against their right to freedom from assault harder to defend. 'Family violence' seems to present a way of deflecting part of the focus from the criminal-justice model and maintaining it in the hands of those professionals more directly concerned with maintaining or implementing 'the family' as represented in the ideology of the state. 'Violence' as assault allows for the treatment of men to 'cure' the individual of his violence or for the removal of men who 'abuse their authority in the family' and the supporting of a newer family form made up of women and children dependent upon the state.

When we look more closely at this strategy it is clear that what is being modified is not men's authority in the family but their abuse of it. 'Family violence' deflects the focus from the legal system towards health, welfare, and social-services institutions; 'male violence' is reformulated in professional discourses in terms of another recent entry into the conceptual stakes, 'spouse assault,' and paves the way for the entry of legal discourse. Patriarchal family relations are thus reduced to actions that support or defy the law and the hidden 'law-and-order' frame that 'violence' references.[20]

What is being examined here can thus be seen as part of a struggle in two areas, visible, in some part, through the issue of definitional control. One is concerned with women's relation to 'the family' as a form, and through this their relation to children and to men. The other relates to the oppositional force represented by the women's movement whose work in organizing against the various manifestations of women's oppression has been shaped, disorganized, reorganized and generally affected by its relation to and understanding of the state. To ally ourselves with aspects of the ruling apparatus by accepting the 'family violence' conceptual frame is to risk substituting what Brown has called 'public patriarchy' for private patriarchy.[21] It is an irony of significant proportion that the appropriation of 'male violence' provides for short-term solutions that invoke the rule of law integral to the very system that is seen as most implicated in the maintenance of male domination. Control of the issue is delivered to those in the social-problem apparatus who are charged with maintaining 'the family' and who now have the means to enforce legal sanctions against individuals within the family unit.

7 Particularizing the General

The next five chapters look in detail at a piece of the process I have been calling 'the enterprise' in action. They chronicle the insertion of a women's movement issue, that of wife-battering, into the administrative processes of the Ontario government. The federal hearings examined in chapters 3 and 4 provided an example of the generalizing relation through which discourse, policy, practices, and the work of the women's movement were brought together and organized into a general position on the issue. Only seven of the seventeen recommendations contained in the federal committee's report were actually actionable at the federal level; the rest related to concerns that were mainly under provincial jurisdiction.

At this point I want to trace an extension of the enterprise of getting the issue lodged in administrative locations that have the mandate to act on social problems. This shift of location is part of the larger and generalized process providing linkages between the everyday and local world in which people, in this case women, experience difficulties, disruptions, and oppression and the policy frameworks through which broad social issues are addressed. The generalizing process thus transforms issues from the local level into social problems for which policy solutions can be reapplied in local sites, in this case as a crime of violence in the context of the family. The final chapters of the sequence provide an analysis of the way in which these elements are ordered and weighted when the committee produces its report and what this provides for in the way of government action to advance the now incorporated issue.

The process considered in this section can be represented schematically:

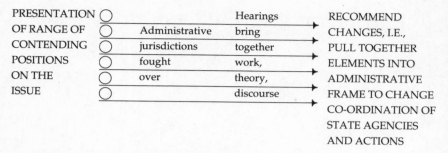

This examination is not designed to be a comprehensive review of the totality of the Ontario hearings, but is an exploration of how an overriding framework for co-ordination is negotiated and put in place, and the way in which this framework then organizes how the committee advances the issue for government action.

Though a certain schematic coherence is implied by the diagram, the process is not a smooth developmental one. It is a political struggle engaged in by members and supporters of the Battered Women's Movement outside and inside government circles. It can be described as operating on two levels. There is the actual orchestration of the struggle to get the issue put forward while controlling in some measure how it is to be handled; this results in it being entered into the parliamentary process but in very specific and determined ways. Then there is the need to address the issue in terms that relate to the parameters of the institutions available.

The parliamentary system provides for particular mechanisms through which such social issues are channelled. These most commonly take the form of task forces, inquiries, public hearings, and royal commissions, which operate to develop and co-ordinate government response to problems raised at the grass-roots level or otherwise outside the circle of government authority. Three moments in the process and the crucial linkages between them can be represented as:

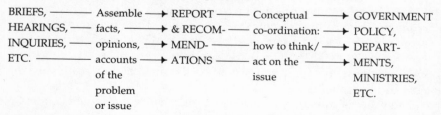

Rather than attempt to develop an adequate theory of the state and state functions and then search out examples of these in operation, I want to make an empirical examination of particular practices and the relations whereby ruling occurs.

The part of the enterprise that is of particular concern to my argument took place in Ontario in the spring and summer of 1982 when the Standing Committee on Social Development of the Ontario Legislature held public hearings on the issue of family violence. First I look at how the issue was raised, then taken up by the government through the committee process, and at how the committee set about developing the conceptual tools that would allow for the co-ordination of approaches and mandates. Next I examine the public hearings themselves and identify the process of negotiating the elements that make up a compromise co-ordinating conceptual framework with a clinical and criminal organization. Asking the government to take action requires that the issue be packaged and presented in ways that will align appropriate features with existing institutional mandates and imperatives. In this chapter we can see what this involves, where the issue has already been lodged, and what problems existing arrangements present for the state, for women's organizations, and for battered women themselves.

ONTARIO AND 'THE ISSUE OF ABUSE'

More than thirty interval and transition houses were in operation in Ontario by 1982, when the events being examined here took place. A number of service agencies provided programs of various kinds for women, and some for battering men. Funding had been obtained from federal, provincial, and municipal levels of government, as well as from private and community sources such as United Way agencies. In spring 1982, a variety of different pressures were applied to the government of Ontario in relation to the issue. The Ontario Association of Interval and Transition Houses (OAITH), at its business meeting in November 1981, passed a motion requesting that the provincial legislature 'form an all-party committee to look into all aspects of wife abuse, including specific legislation affecting the funding of the Transition Houses and improved General Welfare Assistance affecting its residents, with an added view of developing preventative education programmes.'[1] The association, through its co-ordinator, sent letters to all provincial parties, drawing to their attention the work of the Federal Standing Committee on Health, Welfare and Social Affairs in examining wife-battering and asking that a similar committee be established at the provincial level. Replies were sought by February 1982. A press release was timed for distribution at the same time as the arrival of the letters. Twenty-seven replies were received, all pledging strong support.

Meanwhile, members of the caucus of the New Democratic Party (NDP) signed a request that the Annual Report of the Ministry of Community and Social Services (COMSOC) be referred to the Standing Committee on Social Development. 'Referring out' requires that twenty members 'stand up' in the legislature – that is, sign a request – 'pursuant to Standing Order 33(b),' asking that the legislative assembly send a ministry's annual report to one of its working committees for consideration. This was done under the leadership of Richard Johnston (NDP MP for Scarborough West) on 30 March.[2] The tactic of 'referring out' was decided upon by the NDP caucus at the urging of Marion Bryden (NDP MP for Beaches Woodbine). Bryden, a feminist, was committed to supporting OAITH's strategy for bringing wife-battering to the attention of the provincial government.[3]

The committee in question is one of a number of working committees that serve the provincial parliament by reviewing budgets and annual reports for certain designated ministries, studying existing and proposed legislation, or considering specific topics of concern to the government. Its power to review legislation is strictly limited but it has more latitude in considering reports and special issues. The mandate of this standing committee is related to the jurisdictions of the ministries of Health, Community and Social Services, and Education. The committee is made up of elected members of provincial Parliament from all parties in proportion to the number of seats each party holds in the legislature. At the period under consideration here, there were twelve members: seven, including the chairman and vice-chairman, from the ruling Progressive Conservative (Tory) party, three Liberals, and two from the New Democratic Party, one of whom was Richard Johnston.[4] Johnston submitted the request to refer out the COMSOC report because, he later stated, he believed it 'of urgent public importance that the issue of abuse should be the subject of public hearings at an all party committee.'[5]

Johnston then sent letters in early April to OAITH and other people involved in the field, telling them that the report was to come before the committee and asking them to respond by pressuring the chairman to see that the committee gave it some consideration. A number of responses were received.[6] Members of OAITH kept up a campaign of lobbying MPPS and many sent letters of support for an all-party hearing to the chairman of the Standing Committee on Social Development.

REFERRING OUT

Having considered the events that led up to and provide a context for the Ontario government's consideration of the issue of family violence, I want to examine the actual process that took place at Queen's Park in spring and summer 1982. The rest of the chapter deals with the early meetings of the Standing Committee on Social Development that occurred after the New Democratic Party had successfully executed the manoeuvre of referring out the report from the Ministry of Community and Social Services.

When the committee met to deal with the report set before it as the result of the NDP tactic, Johnston had the task of convincing members that they should take up what he describes in his opening statement to them as 'the issue of abuse.' The content of the COMSOC report itself was irrelevant to the NDP strategy, except for locating the issue within COMSOC's jurisdiction over areas of family relations and its existing role in funding transition houses. The committee at this point could choose whether or not to proceed with considering the issue put before it. Johnston credits his success in persuading the committee to go farther in its initial meeting to a number of factors. One of them was the performance of the chair of the committee in trying to block the referral in the legislature. Johnston was able to make political capital out of the general embarrassment suffered by politicians over the laughter that greeted questions in the federal House of Commons when the Federal Report on Wife Battering was presented. He used this embarrassment to undercut the chairman's obstruction, and create a climate in which the committee felt obliged to take the issue seriously.[7]

TAKING UP THE ISSUE OF ABUSE

On 4, 10, 11, and 12 May the Standing Committee on Social Development met to decide how to deal with the problem that had been set before it. These meetings were recorded for Hansard, and the transcripts provide the basis for this analysis. Having been convinced by Johnston at the first meeting to take up the issue, the committee members called in two senior bureaucrats from the Ministry of Community and Social Services, two from the Ministry of the Attorney General, and the director of the School of Addiction Studies of the Addiction Research Foundation, to address the issue in terms of their own departments' involvement. In the process of setting parameters and priorities for the committee's consideration of the subject, the decision was made to focus on 'spouse abuse' at special public hearings to take place in the last two weeks in July. Remaining topics to be covered, such as child abuse and abuse of the elderly, would be tackled at future hearings in 1983. The committee also decided that it wanted to hear not only from 'academics' but also from victims of abuse and those involved with direct services in the field. The researcher attached to the committee was directed to prepare a list of witnesses to appear and places to be visited. The researcher also assembled reference material, articles, books, and bibliographies as background reading to provide information to committee members.[8] Thus the preliminary work necessary for the committee to take up its deliberations was put in place prior to the hearings in July.

By the end of these preliminary meetings, the committee and its advisers from the various provincial government departments had 'shaped up' the issue. They had assembled, or instituted procedures for assembling, materials and witnesses for a process of public hearings to be held later in the summer. Beyond this they had developed an understanding that the issue was not clearly or satisfactorily lodged in any one dimension of the social-problem apparatus. Thus the task of the committee had become one of finding a way to work together as a committee, that is, of developing the conceptual tools that would allow their approaches and the mandates of various ministries to be co-ordinated. The committee, in fact, had taken hold of the issue.

Already, in the process described so far, a certain shaping and forming had occurred in relation to what was to be taken up by the committee and how the matter was to be dealt with. For instance, although the parliamentary device of referring out the Community and Social Services report to the standing committee may have presented an opportunity to bring up for consideration the 'issue of abuse,' it also had a number of other results. First, the NDP caucus decision to use the tactic of referring out resulted in the issue being formulated in terms of the relevancies of the Ministry of Community and Social Services. Since the ministry is responsible for services to children and families the issue was seen as being family violence (although actually neither the term nor the topic occurs in the COMSOC annual report). An all-party task force as proposed by OAITH could have been mandated to consider wife-battering as its major focus. Consideration of 'the issue of abuse' thus became part of the purview of the standing committee rather than of any other body that might have been seen as appropriate, or a specific body mandated to deal with the concerns raised by OAITH. Second, it extended the work of the committee in this instance, as Johnston explained in the speech in which he made his case for taking up the issue during the first meeting of the committee:

The technique of referring out a report ... was used by myself and my colleagues in order that this committee, outside of our normal discussions in terms of the various estimates that we go through – Community and Social Services, Citizenship and Culture or whatever the field we might be looking at – might spend some time as a group looking at an area of concern, and a fairly large area of concern, which in this case is violence in the family.

It is our feeling that it is time that a legislative committee spent some time looking at this area of concern as a group in terms of our legislative responsibilities at a provincial level for the kinds of concerns that come out of the very unhappy level of violence in the family that is taking place in our society today, and how we might want to address ourselves to that, not in an ad hoc way of debating once in a while whether or not the child abuse registry is working or the Children's Aid Society is properly funded at another given time, or looking at the problems of distress centres individually, but rather looking at it as a grouping of concerns.[9]

While extending the work of the committee, however, the referring-out tactic restricted the scope of inquiry, and amount of time that could be spent, to the exigencies of the committee's work schedule and responsibility and its members' time commitments. This fact was recognized by the chairman during the extended deliberations concerning the timetabling and specific focus of the hearings when he pointed out that 'this whole topic is so vast that ideally it would require a special task force to spend almost a year on ... You are looking almost at a select committee focusing on this problem.'[10] The decision to focus the hearings on 'spouse abuse' came in the end to be based on scheduling priorities and the need to make the topic manageable.[11] Other reasons, such as urgency, lack of information, or the uniqueness and seriousness of the issue, were put forward at various junctures in the deliberations, but did not eventually determine the decision.[12]

The relevancies and imperatives of the groups applying external pressure may not have been the only ones in operation. One of my informants suggested that there may have been other interests than those overtly presented. MPPs of all parties, but particularly those in long-time opposition, may have seen this as an opportunity for input into the policy and legislation-making procedures of government and a chance to involve the committees in directions beyond the pro forma work of considering estimates and so on.[13] There was a momentary coincidence of interest between the women's groups pressuring the government and certain members of the government, who saw the issue as one that could further their own purposes. In the opinion of Richard Johnston there were several factors involved: the interest in the committee process, the climate of concern created by coverage of the federal committee's hearings, and the public consternation caused when MP Margaret Mitchell's question in the House of Commons concerning the incidence of wife-battering was greeted with laughter by members of Parliament. These circumstances were equally important if not more important than pressure from women in getting the issue accepted for consideration, both in the NDP caucus and in the provincial legislature.[14]

A process of political give-and-take can be seen to have been operating in other aspects of the shaping and formation with regard to both the hearings and the issue itself in these preliminary sessions. An important part of what was negotiated, discussed, and set up was the actual working plan and rationale for the committee, in terms of how it would proceed. Once the committee took hold of the issue, the work took on the particular character and mandate of a public inquiry. Procedures were set up to gather information, report to the legislature, and recommend changes designed to address the problem set before the committee. The committee had to be seen to listen to a range of representative 'witnesses' – rural and urban interests, service providers, and victims of violence – as well as to bureaucrats, in order to legitimate the committee's findings in terms of its accountability both to 'the public' and to the government.[15]

The initial choice of witnesses from among the ranks of the senior bureaucracy already began a process of lining up and apportioning aspects of the work and responsibilities for the problem among at least some of the various ministries designated to do something about it. The COMSOC representative who appeared before the committee in its preliminary meetings named these as the criminal-justice system, the medical system, the social-service system, the public housing system, and Employment and Immigration Canada. All were necessary, in her view, to serve the 'victim considered as part of a total family system.'[16] The witnesses from the two ministries and the Addiction Research Foundation gave accounts of how their institutions conceptualize and handle the problem. They brought forward what was already being done and how they saw this as relating to the work of the committee. At the same time, they provided facts and background information for the committee to use in formulating its own position.

EXISTING INSTITUTIONAL RESPONSE

The initial work of alignment of problem and resources involved consultation with individuals who, in Smith's words, 'perform' the organization or institution as part of the daily tasks and responsibilities that make up their work.[17] The committee called on representatives of various government departments who might be expected to have jurisdiction over or an interest in the issue. These bureaucrats brought forward, in their statements, the administrative and ideological features of the operation of each institution and of the discourse that informed and organized their work, linking institutions horizontally. Much of this linking took place through documents and documentary processes, involving reference to existing or incomplete reports, articles, books, items of legislation, and interministerial working papers. The witnesses made some of these available to the committee; others were promised at a future date or in time for the public hearings.

Identifiable in the preliminary sessions were a number of ways in which the issue of abuse could be seen to be problematic for the government and its agencies. These were reiterated throughout the hearings. The departmental representatives who appeared before the committee alerted it to issues such as the funding problems of interval and transition houses and of victims themselves inherent in the General Welfare Act, the Canada Assistance Act, and the Immigration Act.[18] These witnesses provided information that raised questions about the adequacy and effectiveness of police responses and record-keeping, the lack of proper statistics, and the nature of general court procedures.[19] Dilemmas arising out of conflicts and contradictions between the federal and provincial levels of government, especially in relation to the justice system and the enforcement of family law orders, were identified.[20] The committee's attention was drawn to issues surrounding appropriate services to victims, to children, and to men who batter,[21] and to the prevalence of unenlightened attitudes on the part of professionals and public in regarding family violence as a lower-class, alcohol-related, and culture-specific problem.[22]

From the point of view of this study the most crucial aspect of what happened during these four sessions was the delineation of the 'issue of abuse' as it was to be taken up and understood in the work of the committee. The final agreement was that the committee would concentrate first on 'spouse abuse.' The abuse of children would be considered at this time only in relation to spouse abuse. The July public hearings, however, were to be the beginning of ongoing concern with 'family violence in general.'[23] While it was clear that, for some members of the committee, the spouses in question were women,[24] the chairman twice made the point that 'the element of battered spouses is different from battered wives, children, or seniors,'[25] suggesting on one occasion that members should focus their questions 'not only ... on child abuse and battered women but on spouse abuse, meaning husbands may be victims as well.'[26] Despite this intervention from the chair, the committee decided to focus on wives as the main victims of spouse abuse. This, in fact, represents a considerable shift from the opening discussions in which Johnston, in his capacity as sponsor of the referring-out motion, put forward a strong plea for the consideration of all aspects of family violence and recommended that the committee review a whole series of reports on spouse, child, and elder abuse.[27]

Much of what was being done during the deliberations and planning that took place in these meetings was therefore not merely administrative involving details of time, place, and format. The conceptual practices to be made use of and the appropriate institutional designations to be made were also being worked out. How the committee should begin to understand and think about 'the issue of abuse' was being negotiated between the members of the committee in relation to each other, to the existing discourse, and to the expert witnesses called 'to help us determine our focus'[28] and 'to develop an approach, a concerted effort toward the problem.'[29] A suggestion was made by Johnston that 'some civil servants involved within the ministry [presumably COMSOC] could provide information on current ministry activities and that members of the Federal Task Force and one or two other key people who have been major resources to the task force be asked to talk to the Committee.'[30] A subcommittee made up of a member from each political party, including Johnston as NDP member, took on the final planning, and with the help of the clerk of the committee, organized the appearance of the representatives from COMSOC, the Ministry of the Attorney General, and the Addiction Research Foundation. Thus the government committee of elected representatives turned first to its own senior bureaucrats for information on how the situation was already being considered and acted upon by government at the provincial level, and also planned to hear from the federal task force, which had already considered the issue. The sphere of activity was established first and foremost within the internal institutional relations of the state.

THE MINISTRY OF COMMUNITY AND SOCIAL SERVICES

The representatives from the Ministry of Community and Social Services, who were the first witnesses to appear before the committee, stated that family violence was an area of concern that indicated the need to provide 'help' to families, both in the form of financial assistance and through support and counselling services. In the case of child abuse, the legal aspects of the Child Welfare Act, which carries penalties of 'a fine of up to $2,000 and up to two years' imprisonment or both,'[31] adds a further dimension. The committee could see how COMSOC was aligned with the issue, how it related to the institutional imperatives and structures. For COMSOC, battered women were a welfare problem in need of various services under the General Welfare Act and this, in itself, made for problems of co-ordination with other levels of government, notably the municipal. One of the problems was the perception and designation of such women as part of a family unit dependent on a male wage or family welfare allowance. If a women left her husband, she was not automatically seen as destitute since the money going to the unit was expected to support her, regardless of the circumstances. The legal aspects of dealing with child abuse were already in place, but the same was not true for wife abuse, although the concept of abuse had been extended through the term 'family violence' to include wife abuse, which was not formerly recognized as a problem within COMSOC's jurisdiction.

THE ATTORNEY GENERAL

The presentation by representatives of the Attorney General's office confirmed what the committee had learned from the previous witnesses: both 'spouse abuse' and 'family violence,' as concepts, failed to adequately articulate departments and discourses. It was also noted that the law did not address family violence in any direct way; if violence was recognized as assault, women could be responded to as victims of crime but treating them as such did not address the relational aspects of the situation. The relationship between victim and perpetrator could only be addressed, the witnesses suggested, by involving the civil remedies of family law, the provisions for support under the General Welfare Act, and clinical treatment for individuals and family units. If abuse was to be accepted as assault in a domestic setting, then the concept would have to be determined and defined in such a way as to shape and co-ordinate the work of both the jurisdictions of Justice and General Welfare. The Justice department had already handed part of its legal jurisdiction over child abuse to COMSOC, but was now being asked to consider spouse abuse as a different feature of family violence in relation to the law.

In general, what the Attorney General's representatives made clear to the committee was a rising awareness of the definition of assault of a spouse as a crime that should be adequately remediable under the laws on assault. The familial relationship, however, complicated the use of law to provide a solution for battered wives because they were often economically dependent on and living with their assailants.[32] The witnesses reported that the Attorney General issued directives in January 1981[33] to Crown prosecutors to prosecute vigorously in wife-assault cases and that other avenues were being pursued through committees and task forces. Proposals relating to the extension of an experiment with a unified family court containing both civil and criminal procedures, undertaken in Hamilton, were being considered.

The witnesses also detailed the ministry's current activities seen to touch on the two major components of 'family violence,' wife and child abuse. These were: an interprovincial liaison committee on the enforcement of family-law orders, representations concerning the federal Bill C-53 (amending provisions of the Criminal Code dealing with sexual offences to, among other things, remove indemnity from charges of rape hitherto enjoyed by husbands), and participation in a federal-provincial task force then looking into needs and services for victims of crime.

THE ADDICTION RESEARCH FOUNDATION

A represenative from the Addiction Research Foundation was, it transpires, invited to address the committee 'in part because of the presumption that alcohol does play a role in this.'[34] He provided a great deal of rather inconclusive evidence that disputed any causal notion of the relationships between family violence and alcohol, but indicated that alcohol was 'involved' in many cases where it acted on 'the personalities of the offender and victim of violence and the quality of their interaction.'[35]

According to this witness the myth of alcohol as the core of the problem had been replaced by clinical dispositions of personal and interactive dimensions. The agency was not involved in the issue in any way beyond some awareness of family violence in their approach to research over the past four or five years.[36]

DEVELOPING THE TERMS OF A CONCEPTUAL FRAMEWORK

If we look at the preliminary sessions in the light of the various frameworks identified in the previous chapters, we begin to see how these relate to the relevancies and work practices of the witnesses who appeared before the committee. In their presentations witnesses put forward, implicitly or explicitly, the ways in which the 'issue of abuse' related to their institutional affiliations and how it was conceptualized in that context. The process of assembling the issue to be considered and delineating its parameters tells us something about how the participants conceptualized the issue in terms of the various ways it was already being approached. This process was integral to the work being done by both the committee in its political capacity and the various bureaucrats in theirs.

The whole process of how the committee came to take up the issue of abuse bears further examination. The initiative from OAITH in its original appeal was couched as a demand for the government to address the issue of wife abuse. This was extended, in a private member's bill put forward at the same time by MPP Marion Bryden, to a consideration of violence in the family, victims of family violence, and the need for protection of battered spouses. Although this bill was not successful, serving as an alternative strategy to back up the caucus tactic of referring out, and does not relate directly to the proceedings of the Standing Committee on Social Development, it was presumably couched in terms seen as shaping the issue for relevance to the concerns of the legislature.[37] The Conservative government had at this point been in power in Ontario for forty years. It had taken a number of recent initiatives designed to reinforce the role of the family as a key focus for social-welfare policies in the areas of deinstitutionalization and community care of the elderly, the developmentally retarded, the mentally ill, delinquent youth, and abused children.

In the context of the government's family focus, Johnston's statements in the initial meeting about looking at the whole 'issue of abuse' and 'a grouping of concerns' were part of a recognizable strategy to get the subject of wife-battering raised and inserted into existing parliamentary structures. This expedient was effective in that it meant that the issue was taken up as part of the regular and ongoing work processes of parliamentary rule, but at the same time, by taking it up in relation to concern for the family, the tactic put spouse abuse into the framework of family violence and ensured that it would be examined only within such a framework since it must remain linked with child abuse to maintain the committee's original mandate. Though this committee, unlike its federal counterpart, did not have specific terms of reference in this case, the referral of the COMSOC report contains the issue within the family and sets the terms of the committee's mandate. Recognizing this process helps to make sense of the chairman's consistent reluctance to focus on wife-battering. He even regarded spouse abuse as 'too narrow a focus.'[38] In addition, moreover, according to Johnston the chairman had been instructed by the government to 'block the issue.'[39] His insistence on dealing with the broader issue of family violence would then be a significant way to at least diffuse the subject and avoid the recent federal focus on 'battered wives,' since he had failed to block the referring-out manoeuvre.

The first COMSOC representative to appear before the committee, Doris Guyatt, actively separated the component parts of the issue, focusing her presentation on the needs of battered women. She was a senior policy adviser for the Department of Adult's Policy development; her colleague's area of responsibility was child abuse and she left this subject to him. She did, however, insist that the needs of victims must be 'considered as part of the total family system.'[40] She then detailed the needs of battered women as she saw them from her reading of 'the literature' and from the contact she had with organizations who served battered women. This contact, it transpired, came about because she was in charge of her department's current policy review of hostels and half-way houses, which she had been visiting to determine 'what their problems are, how they view our legislation, and what ministry policy should be in the future in this area.'[41] She credited the feminist movement and its focus on the needs of women with the increase in public awareness and the numbers of interval and transitions houses in existence, and gave a cogent list of services that should be provided by various government departments to serve the needs of battered women and to support the shelters in their work. She also provided the committee with the name and telephone number of the co-ordinator of OAITH. Guyatt noted the problems with current funding provisions for hostels and set her report to the committee in the context of her work by concluding the formal presentation thus: 'We will be taking a special look at this particular area and doing some policy work on this target-group of abused wives specifically. We expect to have some kind of resolution by the end of this year of what the ministry's role is and how we see ourselves going in the future.'[42]

Responding to questions, Dr Guyatt gave a comprehensive description of services available through other social agencies – such as programs for men who batter 'to help them face up to their problem and to look at ultimate ways of dealing with their frustrations.'[43] When asked by Johnston about where the committee should be looking for causal information, she called on the discourse, detailing both prior and professionalized positions as well as that of the women's movement to respond:

DR GUYATT: *There is a lot of information in the literature about that. There tend to be two major areas that people blame. First, they blame the woman victim. They say it is her fault; she is obviously a masochist if she stays; she enjoys it somehow or other.*

I think the studies that have been done would refute that. They find the woman is really in a trap. She has nowhere to go. She does not see any other alternatives for herself and that is why she stays. She stays because he promises he will not do it again and she thinks it is going to improve, but it generally does not. Of course, all the psycho-analytic literature is more in that line; the woman has a masochistic relationship and so on.

The other area blamed is society. There is the general acceptance in society of wife-beating, that it is okay to beat your wife. That goes away back in our history. Our legal system is based on English common law. If you recall the expression rule of thumb, the rule of thumb was that a man could beat his wife with a stick that was no bigger than his thumb. That is the rule of thumb. So this whole business that it is all right for a man goes away back in our culture. A woman is a chattel and it is his duty to make sure she behaves herself. He has the right to chastise her and to use force. There is a lot of that in the literature.

Then if you get into the alcohol part of it, not all wife abuse is associated with drinking. I thought that was the case until I got into the literature. You find it is not the case. Some is clearly not associated with drinking at all.

There is also the economic aspect that has already been mentioned. When times are hard and men are unemployed and under a great deal of stress, there tends to be an escalation in family problems of all kinds. There is a fair amount of literature on that.

MR WATSON: *Could I have a supplementary on the culture? Do you have any*

information on various cultures now? Are there some cultures that believe in
wife-beating more than other cultures? Is that a fair way to put it, or do you
understand what I am trying to ask?
DR GUYATT: *I think it is true that some find it more acceptable. It is more com-*
mon among some groups, but it is still common among all. You have to be very
careful. The transition houses in Toronto do tend, in some cases, to get women
with certain cultural backgrounds more than others, Mediterranean back-
grounds for example. I was just reading a study I got from Hiatus House in
Windsor. Their most common cases were women with a French background and,
next to it, British. I think you have to be very careful. It depends very much on the
cultures represented where the study is being done.

Johnston then asked her to provide the committee with further basic
material and names of people doing Canadian studies and Guyatt
agreed to do so.

She, in fact, provided a complete list of all member organizations of
OAITH[44] and other possible witnesses, noting that 'there certainly are
many people who could speak to you from the women's groups, the
ones that are running transition houses, but not just those. There are
other women's groups, professional associations, feminist-oriented
groups that would probably want to be heard in this whole area.'[45]
While making sure that the committee included women's groups and
the information available from a feminist perspective, she clearly did not
see this as in any way anomalous with the understanding of family
violence that she and other professionals held. It was this definition that
allowed her to put in place the various funding mechanisms and
services to which she alluded. The victim's material needs must be met,
and also her emotional needs: 'These include counselling, with the
victim considered as part of the total family system. The children also
have emotional needs because they have been part of this whole family
violence system.'[46]

In the testimony and deliberations that took place in these preliminary
sessions, there was a tension between the rights of individuals and the
designation of 'the family' as the fundamental social unit at the level of
government policy. This ambivalence led to a slippage back and forth
between different frameworks, most apparent in the testimony of the
representatives of the Attorney General's department. The law with
regard to criminal assault could be administered to cover assault
between spouses, but familial relationships caused contradictions in its
operation. It was designed to cover the relation of individuals seen as

the 'victim' and the 'perpetrator,' presumed to be strangers, since, in fact, statistics and records were seldom kept of the relationship and even the sex of either. The interests of family members were presumed to be covered under civil law, which relates to property arrangements, support payments, and so on. Family violence was thus characterized as a social problem with legal dimensions, a jurisdictional difficulty that the conception of wife-battering as 'conjugal crime' exacerbates. Even the committee on victim services did not 'specifically deal with domestic violence in any way,'[47] only with what services could be provided to victims who must appear as witnesses, in order to make their time in court more comfortable and effective.

The testimony of the two representatives from the Ministry of the Attorney General, and Guyatt's recital of the lack of response to battered women's complaints from the police, the courts, medical and professional institutions, combined to present the committee with the picture of the whole system as 'really not helping a great deal. It is a sad state.'[48] This impression was reinforced by Guyatt's personal story of an attempt to intervene in a situation where a man was publicly beating a woman. In this case the police, though called, never came. The committee was being given a picture that clearly showed the shortcomings of the social-problem apparatus at the local level, where it was failing to respond appropriately to the situation as described. Committee members were also told of the discrepancies and inadequacies that exist between the central and extra-local structures that determine local practices, such as the justice system with its criminal and civil codes and the social-welfare system as represented in the General and Child Welfare acts. By the end of the meeting at which the COMSOC representatives made their presentations, McGuigan (Kent-Elgin, L) was moved to point out that there was an act of Parliament and a system in place for addressing child abuse, but very little, 'other than a pretty poor police system, for looking after battered wives.'[49] In the final session on 12 May, his was one of the voices that prevailed in the decision to focus on spouse abuse as the issue most deserving of the committee's attention.

By the time the committee reached that point, they had heard particular frameworks and aspects of frameworks advanced, defended, or defeated. A particular interaction that appeared as a skirmish fought on grounds of sexism alone provides an instance of this process. Here knowledge of the discourse on wife-battering and family violence provided Guyatt with a way to respond to questions that showed some committee members' commitment to particular understandings that were in the process of being superseded. Certain traditional views of the causes of wife-battering were raised by one member and rather firmly refuted by both Dr Guyatt and the one woman who was a permanent member of the committee, Sheila Copps (Hamilton Centre, L). Alan Robinson (Scarborough-Ellesmere, PC), first asked: 'Is the individual who batters, whether male or female, psychologically prone to acts of violence in a public way, or is this generally the only type of outburst?' Guyatt responded: 'I do not think you can generalize too much, but certainly in some of the studies the women say that their husbands have outbursts of temper. But there are some men who would never show it outside their own home and there are others who do.'[50] A little later Robinson returned to the topic:

MR ROBINSON: *Just carrying along with the same thing I was on, Mr Chairman, does the victim in these situations as a rule, perpetrate the incident, or is it simply an innocent bystander who happens to be in the wrong place?*

DR GUYATT: *You cannot generalize. There is some of both. There are certainly some cases where the women have been drinking with their husbands and they get into fights, and so on. But there are other cases, certainly recorded, where the woman has done nothing, where she has tried very hard to say and do nothing that would precipitate an attack. Her husband comes home and attacks her. It is sort of an individual situation.*

MR ROBINSON: *You talked earlier about the attitude of the law for battered wives and you mentioned wives specifically. I can only presume, and I am sure you will correct me if I am wrong, that the incidence of battered husbands is a very small percentage of that of battered wives.*

DR GUYATT: *Yes.*

MR ROBINSON: *Does the law have the same attitude toward a battered husband, or is he considered better able to fend for himself?*

DR GUYATT: *I have heard that a husband who takes his case to court is more likely to get a positive resolution to the problem rather than the other way around.*[51]

Then Robinson asked, 'Can you give us any sort of profile of a husband-beating situation?' and the following exchange took place:

DR GUYATT: *Any of the profiles I have seen are based on fairly small samples of studies which have been done on particular women in particular transition houses. It is really not fair to try to – it cuts right across society, all economic levels and all cultures.*

MS COPPS: *You are talking about husband-beating, are you not?*
MR ROBINSON: *Yes.*
MS COPPS: *Are you answering to husband-beating?*
MR CHAIRMAN: *This is battered husbands.*
DR GUYATT: *Oh, husband-beating. You are talking about the other way around.*
MR CHAIRMAN: *Is your question about battered husbands, Mr Robinson?*
MR ROBINSON: *I am sorry if I did not ask you more clearly.*
DR GUYATT: *I do not think there have been many studies on husband beaters. It certainly is a relatively small proportion as compared to the other way around. Some of the things you read indicate that a wife is more likely to verbally abuse her husband. What do you call the –*
MR ROBINSON: *The nagging wife syndrome.*
DR GUYATT: *The nagging wife syndrome.*
MR WATSON: *Sheila wants to react. I can just see it.*
MR ROBINSON: *Do not ask me why I know that.*[52]

Copps disputed with Robinson over the implications of his statement. He insisted that he was merely trying to ascertain whether the issue was one of mutual fights that end in violence or whether it was a matter of unprovoked attacks. Copps argued animatedly against the inference that women perpetrate the attacks to which they are subject.[53] This interchange was more than an exchange of information; it was a negotiation concerning how the 'issue of abuse' was to be understood – in terms of the individual psychological aberrations of the 'perpetrators' or the provocation and thus 'perpetrating' behaviour of the wife – and who could or could not be considered a victim of what kind of abuse. Guyatt and Copps refuted both the psychodynamic formulation of masochism and incitement and the contentious aspects of the initial family-violence framework concerning battered husbands.

With the exception of a final intervention from the chair of the committee, this skirmish was the last concerning whether women are violent towards men to a degree that warrants inclusion in the definition. The issue was taking shape here, in the activities and interactions of committee members, as one of spouse abuse, focusing on wives as victims and including dimensions of the discourse already introduced by Guyatt.

I have dealt with Guyatt's testimony in some detail because she played a key role in the preliminary meetings and in the orchestration of the subsequent hearings. Her input focused the task of the committee and 'the issue of abuse' on wife-battering. She acted as a kind of 'broker' between the women's movement and the state, inserting and legitimizing the feminist discourse and promoting OAITH and its members as vital witnesses and experts to whom the committee should attend. Guyatt put forward the elements that were eventually assembled into the framework that predominated when the committee made its report. These elements could be seen at this point to be: that wife-battering is a criminal act of assault that takes place in the context of the family as one of a range of violent activities; that victims and perpetrators of wife-battering, and their children, need counselling, support, and other services from a number of government departments, not all of which currently respond in an adequate manner; that properly funded transition houses are a vital aspect of these necessary services; and that police and court procedures are not sufficiently attuned to women's need for protection and safety.

Though Guyatt used her knowledge of the feminist position to refuse prior formulations and myths concerning wife-battering, she had no difficulty with the family-violence framework, once it is modified to encompass the feminist position on assault. 'There are other kinds of abuse, family violence and intersibling violence,' she noted. 'There is abuse by children of their parents, what we now call "granny-bashing." In Ontario and Canada we have almost no reports on that.'[54]

It is clear that the degendered language and clinical organizations of the conceptual framework of family violence provided for a course of action, policy, and practices that either treated all forms of abuse as being of equal severity and concern or focused on child abuse as the most pressing and most amenable to action under the Child Welfare Act and the child-protection mandate of the provincial government. Indeed, family violence as a bureaucratic category appeared to be used for exactly this reason. The category was unproblematic for Guyatt; when questioned at a forum on wife-battering in Vancouver about a year after the hearings, she denied that family violence as a concept concealed the true nature and extent of women's experience and insisted that the term allowed her to provide services to women, to adolescents, to the abused elderly,[55] and so on, as part of her bureaucratic mandate. It is this feature of Guyatt's testimony, the linking of professional positions and discourse while aligning institutional options and practices, that reveals the extent to which 'family violence' is in fact an administrative category and as such is implicated in the relations of ruling.

CONCLUSION

What began to be put in place during these sessions, then, was an understanding, a framework in which to assemble the information sought and given, with regard to family violence in general and 'spouse abuse' in particular. In this framework, family violence was described as a serious problem, one that cut across race, class, and culture (and gender, too, in the invisible degendered language of spouse abuse, victims, and perpetrators) and affected all family members to some extent, though husband-battering was felt to be relatively rare.[56] It was characterized as a difficult, if not intractable, problem that had been with us since time immemorial but had recently been recognized as a social phenomenon. The problem required intervention from a number of departments and levels of government, including, where necessary, the criminal-justice system. Statistical evidence was sought and causes and methods of intervention inquired into, as the committee began the work of developing a way to carry out the task it had taken up.

All this appeared as a statement or collection of the facts, or need for facts, about family violence. What can be read initially as a 'mere' factual account, however, can also be seen as the construction of 'facticity.' As such, it is part of a process of producing the particular understanding necessary to allow the committee, and eventually the government, to proceed with the work of responding to and managing problems brought before it. The initial conceptual frame of family violence, identified here, organized a course of action, albeit an imperfect one, for COMSOC in the way its representatives showed when they described their activities of funding, support, and intervention. It extended and co-ordinated the state's mandate to intervene in the hitherto 'private' sphere of behaviour within families.

What the Attorney General's representatives revealed was something rather different. Family violence, as it stood, even with the inclusion of a definition of assault, did not provide them with a direct course of action, or link the individual neatly to the justice system. They had to show the committee, in their presentations, which parts of their work touched on, were tangential to, or were relevant to, the issues being raised. In relation to the law, in particular, this presented some problems. The responsibility for children's programs and services had been transferred to COMSOC; women could be related to only as victims of assault and men could be charged as perpetrators of assault under the Criminal Code,[57] but in the context of family law the disposition of the problem presented a difficulty. Men had to be held accountable not only for the crime of assault, but also for the financial support of the victim and the matrimonial home. Difficulties in managing both aspects satisfactorily could be seen to be a focus of the working groups on both the enforcement of family-law orders and the provision of services to victims. Other aspects of family violence had to be compartmentalized and dealt with as assault, problems of property relations, problems of support payments in the event of marriage breakdown, services to victims of violent crime, and so on.

It was clear from the discussion in the final session, 12 May, that the committee no longer saw itself as deciding whether or not to review a report but as having taken on the whole problem of family violence and the 'issue of abuse.' It never made a formal resolution to this effect, but with Johnston's orchestration, Guyatt's testimony, and the generally sympathetic climate created by the support of other committee members, the issue moved forward. From a possible agenda item for review in time appropriated from the budget-estimates debate (the committee's next allotted task), it became a full-scale two-week public hearing to be held later in the summer.

In this process we can observe both the conceptual and the institutional or administrative 'facts' about the issue being assembled into an account of the problem. What we see here is not a dispute about whether or not there is a problem – at least in any overt way. We see, instead, a process of negotiation, dispute, questioning, and information-gathering designed to identify the characteristics, nature, and causes of the problem. The aim of assembling an account in this form was to provide directions for remedy of the problem. The 'issue of abuse' was on the Ontario government's agenda, at least as far as one of its working committees was concerned; public hearings would be held and would focus on spouse abuse. The enterprise had been successful thus far, but its very success had set both terms and the terrain for the next phase as those that align and co-ordinate the issue with existing institutional responses. The current situation had been identified in this early stage as being, at best, problematic and, at worst, inadequate or even damaging. The public hearings went forward, based on the parameters and priorities set in place, at least in part, during the four sessions examined here. In them we can already see the crucial lineaments of the issue and the courses of action in which the government was currently engaged.

8 Hearing the Issue

The Standing Committee on Social Development of the Ontario legislature held its public hearings on 'spouse abuse' in July 1982. I have used the Hansard-recorded transcripts of the hearings and briefs, memos, and background documents to identify the main elements of the conceptual frameworks that were put before the committee. My description of events is in no way an attempt to present a comprehensive review of the proceedings or the presentations of many groups who either appeared before the committee or submitted written briefs and letters. Rather, I have selected for analysis some of the testimony that can be seen to have put in place the positions that eventually become the crucial lineaments of the organizing and co-ordinating conceptual frame apparent in the committee's final report.

In the initiatives already taken by the women's movement and by concerned professionals within the social-problem apparatus, two predominant lines of development or frameworks have already been advanced, struggled over, and modified in attempts to confront the contradictions between mandates within different government departments and jurisdictions. This process of negotiation took place in some of the ways explicated in my examination of the events that culminated in the enterprise of getting the issue lodged within the administrative processes of the state. The impact of modification, amalgamation, and compromise can be seen in the presentations on which this chapter focuses. These occurred on the first day of the public hearings, when representatives from women's movement groups and from a professional treatment program for battering men appeared before the committee. Though other witnesses have a cumulative impact on the committee's understanding of how the two lines of development are to be characterized, the initial testimony was, I suggest, particularly significant. It confronted the committee with the issue as experienced and understood by those most involved in dealing with its conse- quences and indeed with men who themselves had battered their wives. At the same time, it revealed the aspects of modification and compro- mise that had taken place in the frameworks under discussion.

Concentrating on the early sessions in which representatives from the Ontario Association of Interval and Transition Houses and the London Alternatives to Violence Project appear also emphasizes the linkages with previous events. Some of the same individuals appeared before both this committee and the federal one that had held its hearings earlier in the year. Similar presentations were made and backed up with the same briefs and research reports. The OAITH brief even contained the same stories of the experience of battered women that were presented by Trudy Don at the federal consultation organized by the Advisory Council on the Status of Women in 1980. Initially, in this chapter, some of these discursive and administrative links are described; the testimony is reviewed and its impact suggested. Finally, the kind of factual account and co-ordination of conceptual practices provided for in the hearings is identified; it provides a link with what is found to be excluded or minimized by the framework that dominates in the committee's final report, which is considered in chapter 10.

PREPARING FOR THE HEARINGS

By the time we get to the hearings themselves, there is no mention whatsoever of the original report of the Ministry of Community and Social Services, which was instrumental in their institution. The preliminary meetings in May had provided an initial framework and set in action a particular approach that was apparent from the outset as the committee reconvened to consider the problem. It is impossible to gauge exactly what each member of the committee had read or heard in the time between sessions, but it is possible to note what was made available to them, what this provided for, and how it links into the presentation made by witnesses in the main hearings.

We do know that members of the committee were shown the National Film Board documentary *Loved, Honoured and Bruised* and had a package of background material made available which included Linda Mac- Leod's book written for the Canadian Advisory Council on the Status of Women, *Wife Battering in Canada: The Vicious Circle*. In addition, they received both bibliographies and suggestions for possible witnesses from the government officials who appeared at the preliminary meetings. The bibliographies reflected the interests and relevancies of the departments involved and contained a number of articles and books that represent work done within the framework of child abuse, alcoholism, legislative issues in relation to child abuse and wife-battering, and police practices in dealing with family violence and domestic disturbance.[1] Dr Guyatt made mention of a current Ontario study contained in Patricia Kincaid's doctoral dissertation and made a copy of this available to the committee.[2] Copies of the report of the federal standing committee hearings were provided to each member.

In a memorandum to the committee dated 17 June (1982), the research officer sent the members a list of suggested witnesses contributed by 'the School for Addiction Studies, the Policy Development Division of the Ministry of the Attorney General, and the Adult Policy Branch of the Ministry of Community and Social Services.'[3] She also included copies of appendices I, II, and III from the federal report.[4] These appendices list the witnesses who appeared before that committee, the written submissions received, and the departments and agencies of the federal government that provided information and offered expert advice to the federal committee in background sessions held in camera.

What we can see here is the assembling of materials and information from a range of academic and administrative discourses. These placed the work of the comittee in relation to what was already known and activities already undertaken. In this way its work could be properly linked to that of others dealing with the subject. Also evident is an aspect of the martialling of witnesses to appear at the main hearings. Here the list submitted by Guyatt provided a dozen or so of the seventy-three groups or individuals who eventually appeared before the committee, including some of the most prominent and influential.[5] Others were recruited by a process of invitation, response to previous initiatives by Richard Johnston, and requests from groups that wished to appear before the committee (some of which were upset at not having been asked).[6]

Many of the groups and individuals who appeared before the committee brought with them written submissions in the form of briefs, statements, and recommendations. Other written submissions were received from groups and individuals who did not appear in person. This material and the material referenced in the transcripts of the hearings will be discussed briefly when the antecedents of the final report are considered in later chapters. Here the focus is on the actual hearings and the conceptual frameworks that can be seen to operate in relation to the witnesses' testimony and in the questioning and concerns of committee members.

THE HEARINGS THEMSELVES

The committee held fifteen formal Hansard-recorded sessions between 19 July and 30 July. Members also visited the Ontario towns of London and St Thomas, speaking to a variety of representatives from shelters, police, and agencies, including some battered women. A number of women also gave in camera testimony at Queen's Park; their words were not reproduced in Hansard but some of their stories were transformed into anonymous case studies and appeared in the final report. Hearing and seeing the actual women and men who make up the living lineaments of the 'issue of abuse' had a significant impact on the committee.

In his opening comments the chairman of the standing committee, Yuri Shymko (High Park–Swansea, PC) referred to the background material prepared by the researcher. He encouraged the committee members to become familiar with the topics in order to 'save time and enhance the quality of the questioning.' In doing so, he was asking committee members to employ conceptual practices that already ordered and organized how the issue would be pursued. While discussing who should appropriately appear before the committee, he stated the mandate of the committee as he saw it: 'We are stressing battered wives and battered women, the whole focus of family, inter-family and intra-family violence, which is very large … It is impossible, in the time frame of two weeks, to cover the entire problem of family violence fully. It is not because we are in any way prejudicing battered children, who are part of family violence, but that is the decision … we have made. So could we follow one line of questioning along this particular subtopic of family violence?'[7] Already, then, it would seem that the chairman had accepted the focus on wife-battering rather than the more comprehensive spouse abuse he favoured in the preliminarry sessions. He determinedly located it within the broader category of inter- or intra-family violence (his own particular formulation). Apart from some information and a brief discussion of the funding of hostels provided by Dr Doris Guyatt from COMSOC, the committee's main presentations on the first day of the hearings came from the Ontario Association of

Interval and Transition Houses (OAITH) and the London [Ontario] Alternatives to Violence Project, in the morning and afternoon respectively.

ONTARIO ASSOCIATION OF INTERVAL AND TRANSITION HOUSES

OAITH was represented by its co-ordinator, Trudy Don, and by Joy Pyymaki, a member of its co-ordinating committee. Don described the history of the Toronto house, which opened in 1973,[8] and the discovery that many of the women who came to take advantage of the temporary accommodation being offered women and children were, in fact, being beaten and terrorized by husbands. She outlined the reasons for needing the number of houses then in existence (thirty-five by 1982, with nine more trying to open); the basic reason was that husbands cannot be legally kept away from their homes, so women need somewhere where their safety can be ensured. They need protection, accommodation, food, and emotional support in a time of pain and crisis, shelter for their children, and help in negotiating the system with regard to court orders, housing, employment, and so on. She formulated the problem as one of economic dependence, a second victimization by an unresponsive system, and of damage to children who see their mothers harmed while their fathers apparently incur no penalty; the men involved come from all walks of life and are violent only towards their wives, whom they view as possessions.

Don's presentation and answers to the committee's questions were solidly grounded in the history and experience of the women's movement's discovery that many women are beaten and abused by their menfolk and in the various attempts that had been made to get something done about it. It is clear that she saw the difficulties women face as battered wives and the difficulties faced by those working to help them as having a material basis in the situation of women in society as a whole, and particularly in their relation to family and work-place. Throughout her presentation the themes of economic dependence, lack of business skills and opportunities, and lack of accommodation for women alone and especially women with children reiterated the problems women face if they try to leave marriages in which they are being beaten.

A major difficulty that became obvious in working with battered women was the fragmentation and lack of co-ordination of such services as existed and the failure of any one aspect of the system to take responsibility for dealing with the situation. From this recognition then came recommendations, touched on in the presentation to the hearings but listed in full in the written brief given to the committee. OAITH insisted that services must be co-ordinated, legal sanctions enforced, and attitudes changed so that women would be given protection and the aid necessary to rebuild their lives. This co-ordination and work should be undertaken in conjunction with interval and transition house workers who understand the problem.

How these house workers 'understand the problem' was also discernible in Don's testimony. While she named the issue as one of male violence towards women, actionable under criminal law as assault, Don did not take up the language of the legal framework and referred throughout to 'women,' 'the women,' 'the husband,' 'the man,' never to 'perpetrators' or to 'victims'; there was no degendering of the issue in her language or approach. According to Don women do not provoke or deserve battering; alcohol, drugs, poverty, race, and general frustration or stress do not by themselves account for male violence. Not all children of violent homes grow up to batter or be beaten, but the cycle of violence from generation to generation is of concern, as is the cycle of abuse and reconciliation within a relationship. The overriding factor that makes it possible for any one of these features to be part of why men batter is, in Don's view, credited to her experience with the issue, the male attitude of dominance, authority, and right to treat a wife as a possession.

When presenting her material, Don often referred to studies for support, particularly to the recent doctoral dissertation produced locally by Kincaid and to the London Alternatives to Violence Project. She also located information on intergenerational cycles in 'studies,' sources unspecified. The information and understanding she brought before the committee had the authority of practical involvement and experience, backed up by reference to various aspects of the discourse. Don went in some detail into the work of the houses in providing services and the difficulties faced by women trying to leave their marriages. She identified a pattern of remorse and courtship on the part of the men that often persuades women that things will change. A feature of this is sometimes the promise, made by the men, to get help in the form of counselling. Using the list of those slated to appear before the committee as a reference point, Don supported the idea of counselling for batterers to break the pattern of repeated abuse, but pointed to the lack of available counselling groups and also made a plea for this not being seen as a substitute for transition houses. She also noted with approval the appearance before the committee of representatives of the police, with whom OAITH had no quarrel. The association did, however, have concerns because '[the] police have the attitude that a lot of males have, that in fact the women did something to provoke it ... They talk about a domestic dispute and that is always lowest on their list of priorities. It is not an important issue to them. They see themselves as the people who keep the peace, who reconcile, who smooth things over and will leave again.'[9]

The issue of police effectiveness and the laying of charges was an important one in Don's estimation. She credited the London experiment, in which the police laid charges in all cases where there were grounds to suspect that an assault had been committed, with making 'a tremendous improvement in the situation'[10] by delivering a statement to the effect that a police officer, as a representative of Canadians, did not condone the behaviour. A lot of the discussion in which Don had participated as a member of the Attorney General's liaison committee on family orders concerned the laying of charges. Restraining orders were also described as problematic; they appeared to be both invalid and ineffective, and particularly questionable in view of the need to go to the Supreme Court to obtain them.

In pulling together her statement, Don referred to the excitement with which OAITH viewed the recommendations of the federal report[11] and suggested that the standing committee might want to consider some of them. She highlighted public education and awareness of the unacceptability of wife-battering, the need for more houses in the short term, and the danger to women who are actually being killed while long-term solutions are being sought.

In response to questioning from various members, Don and Pyymaki acknowledged that long-range solutions involve tackling women's economic dependence and that the short term includes the need to intervene in the socialization of children from a very young age. Don credited the education work done by the houses with reducing the tendency of doctors to prescribe tranquillizers as a solution to battering. On the issue of mandatory reporting, Don expressed support for the idea but insisted that it must be the woman's choice, not something imposed as if she were a child. Questioning concerning formulae for funding elicited a detailed discussion of funding problems inherent in the per-diem method. Under this system, houses received funding from local government on a per-capita basis for women staying in the shelters. This funding did not provide for capital costs or for staffing for a range of necessary support services. Don suggested ways in which various departments of the federal and provincial governments should fund aspects of the necessary services, for example Central Mortgage and Housing in relation to capital funding for houses and assistance with second-stage housing, the Department of Justice in relation to advocacy and court-accompaniment programs. COMSOC, she suggested, should not bear the total weight, as a welfare matter, of an issue that is the responsibility of the whole community. The use of the General Welfare Assistance Act caused a variety of problems since women who were working or whose husbands were receiving welfare payments presumed to meet the requirements of the family were not eligible, even when in need.[12]

Don referred one questioner to Dr Guyatt, who she said often intervened with local administrators reluctant to fund women's stay in a house. More concerns about fund-raising and the time it takes away from research and service provision were raised. The relationship of houses to the Children's Aid Societies (CAS) was questioned by a committee member (a social worker and a former CAS employee). In discussing the relationship that the houses have with other services, Don expressed frustration that they were now forced to take women who were former psychiatric patients or prison inmates and had nowhere else to go. The whole issue of accommodation for women, 'second-stage' housing for women leaving interval houses, and the lack of protection under the Human Rights Code for women of colour and women with children against discrimination by landlords was discussed. Don entered a plea that interval and transition houses not be expected to solve all the drug, alcohol, and accommodation problems women face: 'It is not because our sympathies are not with them – they certainly are. But we cannot do it all. The problem is that we are often asked to be everything and then when we do it all, we are told we are too fragmented.'[13]

Many other problems that the interval and transition house movement faced in trying to meet the needs of battered women and make the system more responsive were revealed in the question-and-answer process. These touched on the attitudes of police and judges, lenient sentencing, priority given in police response to 'serious' crime such as armed robbery, the authoritarian attitudes of batterers who are righteous about their right to discipline members of their families (one was quoted as dismissing as ludicrous the idea that he might be arrested, by saying, 'It is only a family matter. Everybody laughs at these kinds of charges'),[14] the secretive nature of the family, and so on. Don noted that the London policing project showed that repeat calls diminished, and women did mostly show up as witnesses when police laid charges.

There was considerable discussion about the fact that wife-battering is a crime that is not treated like other crimes, the need for changes in legislation, and the responsibilities of the legal system. Don saw it as being a problem not with the Criminal Code itself, but with its interpretation. The London experiment provided hope but was an isolated situation; police training was improving but needed to be part of a broader strategy in which those working to provide services to battered women should be consulted so that lines of communication and responsibility are clear. Such was not initially the case for the Toronto domestic response team (another service scheduled to appear at the hearings).

The particular problem of rural women and the changes in the Family Law Reform Act were illustrated with reference to the experience of farm wives and other women. The questioning returned to the theme of police practices in rural areas and the whole issue of danger to the police in dealing with domestic disputes. Don was highly critical of the statistical basis for assessing the danger, based on one set of u.s. figures quoted time and again. The chairman cited Ottawa figures that state that 15 per cent of police deaths for 1961–73 occurred during domestic incidents. A question was raised about the other 85 per cent and whether this represented any more danger than that faced by fire-fighters or transition-house workers.

When asked for a definition of wife-battering, criteria for admission to shelters, and the organization and purpose of OAITH, Don stated: 'What we are generally talking about is physical battering ... the wilful use of power or force to hurt another person ... Assault with bodily harm under the Criminal Code ... is a very definite definition.'[15] Psychological and emotional abuse are often the result of fear that physical abuse will be repeated. Rather than being a criterion for admission to a house, physical abuse was seen as a priority, precedence being decided, where possible, on the degree of immediate danger involved.

Questioned about the causes of wife-battering, Don agreed that the stereotyping of welfare recipients and certain ethnic groupings and the notion of intergenerational modelling do not cover the situation. She suggested that the stress caused by economic cut-backs rather than actual income may be one of many contributing factors, but that the causes of wife-battering are still unknown. It is now accepted, Don said, that alcohol and drugs are not in themselves causes and that doing away with alcohol, drugs, poverty, and stress is not the answer: 'These are contributing factors. If there is a tendency toward that patronizing attitude – the attitude, "It is an okay thing for me to do; after all, I am the father of the family, this is my wife" – then these other factors would contribute ... That is where we are beginning to differentiate. Thank God for it, because we were not getting anywhere: we were looking at all these factors but we still were not solving any of the problems.'[16]

Don and Pyymaki spoke of the various ways in which women had gone about publicizing and seeking support for the work of the houses, particularly through the media and by speaking to all kinds of groups including traditional men's groups such as the Rotarians, and at church breakfasts and so on. In fact, problems arose when publicity led to too much response in terms of women seeking refuge in numbers that the houses could not handle, since they were only able to admit one in five applicants. More important was the need for education to change attitudes among the police, Crown attorneys, and the court system. A major concern was with the availability of funding: 'We will take money wherever it comes from,' Don said in response to questions about whether the province should participate in funding the association as well as transition houses. Don at that time was the sole paid staff member of OAITH, which functioned to co-ordinate, provide support, run training workshops and collect information on behalf of houses, and respond to the bombardment of requests for figures, statistics, research, and policy. It also lobbied on behalf of individual houses that, as non-profit organizations, were in danger of losing their charitable tax status if they engaged in overtly political activity. The association itself was turned down for funding by COMSOC, the Justice department, and the Attorney General, and finally got a year's funding from the federal government through the women's program of the Secretary of State. This provided no certain continuity or job security.

The OAITH presentation was more than a delivery of information, a finding of already existent facts; it was part of a process of exchange in which particular ways of defining, understanding, and coming to grips with the issue of abuse as represented by wife-battering were being put into place. Committee members questioned Don and Pyymaki about causes, definitions, difficulties, and directions. It is clear that members already had a variety of experience with the issue – Cooke (Windsor-Riverside, NDP) as a social worker with the Children's Aid Society, Cureatz (Durham East, PC, substituting on this occasion for another PC member) and McGuigan (Kent-Elgin, L) in their constituency work, and Bryden (Beaches-Woodbine, NDP) in relation to her private member's bill and other women's activities.[17] Members has also heard the positions put forward at the preliminary meetings. In fact, they had begun to develop a framework or way of understanding 'the issue of abuse,' which became even more apparent when they questioned the representatives from the London project.

THE LONDON ALTERNATIVES TO VIOLENCE PROJECT

The witnesses appearing before the committee in the afternoon of the first day were members of the London Alternatives to Violence Project: a parole officer, a probation and parole officer, a researcher (Dr Peter Jaffe, who appeared as an expert witness at the federal hearings and who brought the same studies and reports before this committee), and two members of a program for men who batter. The two parole officers were founders and facilitators of the therapy-group program for battering men and they started the proceedings by presenting some background information on the project, the program, and the problem. They described men who batter and the difficulties involved in getting these men to stop denying responsibility for the violence and controlling relationships by using violence.[18] In general, they suggested that they had found a workable method of treating those men they recruited for the group and recommended mandatory or 'forced therapy'[19] as one approach to engaging men in the program. The two battering men told the committee the story of their past experience as batterers and the effect the group had had on their understanding, behaviour, and relationships. Members of the committee questioned all four men at some length in order to clarify details and draw out further information. The final presentation was made by Jaffe; his material consisted of an authoritative exposition of the overall project, with which he had been involved since 1972 (though the focus on wife-battering per se was set in 1979), and a review of a range of literature and studies. It is clear that his work provided the basis for much of the information that had been advanced by the two parole officers. In his turn, he was questioned in some detail by members of the committee.

During this procedure the committee heard something of what battering men thought and felt about their problem. It gathered a good deal of factual information about 'family violence' as defined and dealt with in the London project. It also learned about how other agencies, particularly the police, the mental-health services, and the criminal-justice system, respond to the problem. The committee members and the professionals had obviously already come to share a way of seeing and making sense of the issue. Members referred to the common reading they had done in the area; the professionals referred to each other's findings and work and to studies done elsewhere. The presentations expanded on or reiterated this basic understanding, added new information, recommended courses of action. The questioning clarified, explored, or tested out suppositions against the experience and knowledge of the presenters.

The problem of family violence, domestic violence, spouse abuse, or wife abuse, as it was variously termed in this session, was defined at several levels. Most immediately, it is dangerous, both to the participants (40 per cent of all homicides in Canada, they were told, are 'domestic') and to the police who must intervene. It is both symptomatic of and contributory to a violent society, since it is intergenerational. This was variously described as 50 per cent of the men in the program having either been abused or witnessed abuse[20] or alternatively: 'Statistically ... most husbands who abuse their wives have witnessed similar occurrences in their own family. Most victims, especially those who do not take some sort of action in terms of calling the police, or going to court, usually have witnessed their mother being treated in a similar way or themselves being so treated by their fathers or brothers.'[21] This statement by Jaffe was not referenced in any way, so there was no way of telling from where he took his statistical inferences. The actions of both 'perpetrator' and 'victim' are seen as learned responses. He has been socialized to violence, she to 'learned helplessness.' The expression of violence is a function of stress, tension, suppressed feelings, frustration, inappropriate expression of anger and jealousy, low self-esteem, the changing roles of women, difficulty with intimate relationships, the devaluing of women, and the use or excuse of alcohol. It escalates in severity and frequency. Violent behaviour of many kinds is condoned by society, and wife abuse is condoned, ignored, or excused by the medical, social, and justice systems. The woman is often blamed for her own victimization.

Given the agreed nature of the problem, the proposed solutions followed logically. The witnesses proposed that violence towards wives and girl-friends be recognized and treated as criminal and some form of mandatory treatment provided as an alternative to jail, either at the discretion of the judge or by choice of the offender. This solution would involve ensuring a proper response from the justice system. As one of the parole officers put it: 'It is against the law to assault someone else. We should pay attention to that and encourage police, crown attorneys and judges to pay attention to the fact and do something about it.'[22] Evidence was also offered for the effectiveness of the criminal-justice system in reducing violence when it responded properly, that is, police laid charges and men were dealt with in court.

It was also seen as necessary to co-ordinate and synchronize the pertinent agencies and institutions such as police, justice, mental health, and social services. Mental-health professionals and social workers, in particular, must be brought up to date and induced to stop blaming women for the problem. Men, having been socialized in groups, need to be resocialized in group-treatment programs and taught to express their feelings and talk about them rather than resorting to violence. When families learn to reason things out, violence decreases.[23] Where necessary, however, women must be helped to get out of dangerous relationships and provided with shelter and services.

Jaffe's testimony appeared to have been particularly influential, judging by the number of references to his work that cropped up throughout the hearings and the several citations he received in the final report. What he presented is particularly significant in relation to the exploration of theoretical approaches and different frameworks for understanding the issue. He introduced himself as a psychologist who had 'been working in the area of family violence since 1972.'[24] This work involved creating a family consultant program in which five team members worked with the police round-the-clock to ensure an appropriate response to a range of family-crisis situations, including 'domestic disputes.'[25] This program was perceived as effective in that it reduced repeat calls and had been under the umbrella of police funding since 1976. Since 1980, London had received funding from the Solicitor General 'to focus particularly on wife abuse and trying to do more to co-ordinate the criminal justice system response to wife abuse.'[26]

The focus of Jaffe's earlier research was on follow-up and evaluation of the Family Consultant Program and the recent work, undertaken with Carol Ann Burris,[27] reviewed police and court files in over two hundred cases of wife abuse in the first half of 1979 and follow-up interviews with about thirty victims to get their views on how they had been served by the criminal-justice system. These procedures revealed severe deficiencies in the operation of the system, with women expressing particular dissatisfaction with Crown attorneys and justices of the peace. At present, 'London,' that is, the co-ordinating committee for the area, was working in several new areas as part of a move to better co-ordinate the 'criminal justice and mental health system.'[28]

First, the police were laying charges in all incidents of family violence. Second, a treatment program for batterers was being developed, members of which had just appeared before the committee. Third, an attempt was being made to develop a victim-advocacy service to help victims of family violence get proper assistance from the criminal-justice and social-service systems. The fourth initiative was in the area of education: 'to increase public awareness that family violence is very much a community problem and trying to reach out to lawyers, clergy, family doctors and potential victims to make sure anyone who needs protection and assistance is given it rather than being discriminated against.'[29]

All this can be recovered from the statements and questioning. A couple of committee members digressed by advancing their own theories and indicated that they had not quite 'got it' and still adhered to prior myths and formulations, but the others showed, by their questioning of the witnesses on features such as patterns of violence, history, family background, and availability and effectiveness of treatment, that they had formulated a consistent understanding of the issue in question.

A slightly different interaction took place with the men from the batterers' group. They themselves showed some recognition of the framework and system being described by the experts and talked in terms of past or prior lack of recognition and current acceptance of the dimensions of the problem and their part in it. With the questioning of committee members they engaged in a testing of suppositions and theories of cause and effect against experience and hazarded suggestions for what had been significant in changing both attitudes and behaviour. While both men gave most whole-hearted praise and support to the therapy-group program, recommending it as a personal solution for other violent men, they were not able to make their stories conform entirely to the explanations being sought by the committee. We learn what these men had in common, which was their use of physical force and intimidation to control the women with whom they had intimate relationships. They also had in common membership in the treatment group and the perspective that this group experience supplied. The way they told their stories was shaped by this perspective, but the stories they told contain some significant differences that somehow disappear in the way the framework operates to generalize their experience. The differences are very apparent in the transcript; perhaps a summary will convey something of the quality.

Bill was a professional who worked with children. He was at a loss to account for his 'violent experiences' with his wife and found it hard to fit his story into some aspects of the professional framework, though he was both familiar and comfortable with the terminology of family dynamics. He did not come from a violent home and was not violent with anyone else. During the four years that they had been together, the couple had sought professional help on three occasions. Each time the social workers concerned saw Bill's behaviour as so uncharacteristic of him that they felt it must have been provoked by his wife. The frequency of the 'incidents' increased but the scale of violence decreased, since the potential was sufficient to intimidate his wife. Her leaving him and an occasion when he shook his infant son precipitated some energetic efforts on his part to get help and he was now attending the group, seeing a psychiatrist, and in marital counselling with his wife.

When challenged on his euphemistic use of such terms as 'incidents' and 'experiences,' Bill admitted to being uncomfortable with the word 'assault.' He described causing injuries serious enough that on one occasion his wife required medical treatment as a result. In the course of the questioning, Bill speculated on the causes of his behaviour, largely in terms of frustration at his lack of skills in dealing with his feelings and being able to let them out only with someone he was as close to as his wife. He described their relationship as 'very intense and enmeshed' and his behaviour as possibly a result of inappropriate anger responses, socialization, being male, and not dealing with stress very well.[30]

There was some discussion between Bill, one of the parole officers, and a committee member about the changing roles of women, and Bill admitted that his wife's desire to break out of 'the traditional role model of being a mother-parent and a housekeeper-maid for her husband' and facing him 'with an increasing role, beside being a provider, of also taking a more active role as a father-parent and sharing the housekeeping duties' was a source of friction.[31] He supported such changes and saw a need to facilitate women's acceptance as whole individuals. All in all, Bill could only say that the group helped him pull together the other counselling he was getting and was very useful to him but that he was still working at understanding what the problem was all about and had not found an answer yet.

Dave, however, had no difficulty in describing what happened to him and what the group had done for him. Brought up in a tough neighbourhood, at the age of twelve he had decided to ignore his parents' injunctions to stay in the house and to avoid fighting, because he was always getting beaten up. From then on he lived a life of drinking and fighting that landed him with a criminal record and two jail sentences for 'assault causings' (bodily harm) for beating up women. Self-reflection came late, painfully, and relatively recently, during his last jail term. Here is how Dave told it:

Whenever I used to punch out my old lady and that, I always used to think it was just because I was drunk or had too much to drink or whatever. That is where I just used to lay the blame. During this last bit I did, one day I was sitting in my cell and I was thinking, 'You know, there are other people who go out and get drunk and that, and they don't go round beating people up and getting into fights in the hotel or whatever.' I am on parole now from my last bit. The first or second time I went to see my parole officer, he said that these two guys were starting a group for alternatives to violence. I have always been reasonably curious, but without really admitting to anybody, why it was always me who went around punching people out and other people did not. So I started going to the group and I really learned to deal with my problems.[32]

Dave talked about the futility of repeated jail sentences without rehabilitative options. He summed it up by saying: 'The reason I am here today is because I would like to see this group go someplace. I do not want to see anybody else go through the hell and the misery and the pain that I put my family and girlfriend through; and believe me, I have put myself through a lot of pain. It is not easy doing time and it is not easy looking at a person you really loved and seeing them all beat to ratshit, you know? That is why I am here today.'[33]

Dave saw the causes of his violence in two ways. One was his total inability to distinguish between different feelings or to explore their causes. His only means of expression was rage and lashing out. The second was his belief that women should be obedient and unquestioning, as his mother was to his father, and know without being told what his needs were or what annoyed him. If they did not he would 'just haul off and smack them in the mouth.'[34] Where he grew up, however, fighting with men was 'manly' but hitting a woman was not. He found it very difficult to admit to what he was doing. Instead, he would say his girl-friend was giving him a rough time so he put her in her place.[36]

Only over a process of seventeen weeks in the group, where he had learned to identify his feelings and talk out his frustrations, had he been able to come to the point of telling not only the group but also the standing committee about his life and his actions. He regarded the ability to deal differently with being upset or frustrated, along with the recognition that women are equal human beings and should be treated as such (which he described as one of the most valuable things he has learned in his life), as having transformed his relationship with his girl-friend and his life in general.

The framework that the committee and the professional witnesses were using generalized the experience of these men into apparent illustrations of the universality of wife-battering and family violence. That the system worked differently for middle- and working-class men, and that neither of the men grew up in a 'cradle of violence' where hitting women was commonplace, along with the many other differences that might dispute the framework, are thus obscured. What we see, then, is a view of wife-battering as firmly located within the framework of family violence and needing to be treated as a social problem, properly handled by the appropriate social-problem apparatus. This proper handling requires recognition of the nature of the problem as violence and co-ordination of the various institutional forms whose job it is to respond. The local interval house is just one of many social service resources, one that the police should be more aware of perhaps but not in any way different. While the criminal nature of wife abuse is accepted as a given, there is a very little analysis of what it represents. Jaffe acknowledged the impact and input of the feminist position and was obviously sympathetic to the plight of 'the victim' when forced to leave her own home while the 'assailant' remains. There is no doubt that he was aware of the gendered nature of the issue; when it was suggested to him that unsympathetic police attitudes might change with new procedures but stem from their being males, he noted: 'One of the members of our co-ordinating committee on family violence is a senior member of the London Status of Women Action Group, an ardent feminist. Certainly her position, with some justification, is that a lot of this problem is really a male-based problem in that men are in the front line responding to abused women and they have difficulty taking a hard stand against that; somehow the behaviour is condoned and it is part of our socialization as men.'[36] For him, however, the issue was one of family members learning to handle their problems more rationally and taking the proper consequences when they failed to do so – those consequences being legal sanctions and treatment designed to alter their interactions.

CONCLUSION

The two presentations from the first day of the hearings have been described in some detail, not only to give a sense of the texture and mood of the proceedings, but also to lay out the elements of the ways the frameworks had been modified. It became evident that the feminist framework had become to some degree professionalized, while the professional framework had incorporated aspects of the feminist critique.

On behalf of OAITH, Don offered a comprehensive analysis of what was needed to shape up the response of the social-problem apparatus. She skilfully avoided collapsing the issue into either of the lines of development. Instead, she used the concept of 'violence' as a strategy to organize the state by matching aspects of battered women's needs with different state jurisdictions. Women's anger and outrage, expressed in the pin-pointing of wife-battering as a criminal act to be counted as assault under the law, was initially focused as one of a number of strategies for action. It was, however, embedded in a position that contained the issue and formulated it in a way that meshes together a range of disparate definitions. We are shown wife-battering as the outcome of male violence, as a result of the dependence of women in the family, as the victimization of women and as the consequence of patriarchal attitudes, negative sex-role stereotypes, and unequal treatment of women under the law. In putting this definition in place, Don drew on some of the same professional discourse as Jaffe and even cited the London project's findings in a number of instances. She showed us in a number of ways how OAITH and the work of the women's movement on the issue in general were organized by the state and differentiated in relation to different aspects of the social-problem apparatus into expert, professionalized, service, research, and lobbying components. Wife-battering as an issue was not presented as a focus for mobilizing women. Rather, it had become an issue to be taken up by the state. At the same time, however, an appreciation of the overall objectives of the women's movement was present in her analysis of the totality of women's oppression.

The representatives of the London program, Jaffe in particular, demonstrated the impact of women's movement activities and the feminist position on the work of professionals in the city and in the area of 'the issue of abuse.' The project's original focus on child abuse had been amended to deal with spouse abuse; this had been conceptualized as a feature of family violence and such violence designated as criminal assault. Both the family-violence and the criminal-assault frames had been gendered; that is, spouse abuse had been recognized as predominantly wife-battering and the victims and perpetrators of assault had been accepted as being women and men, respectively. Within this framework, the focus of violence as assault was on the justice system and particularly on policing and court practices backed up by a co-ordinated network of social agencies, which included women's services such as the local transition house.

Thus we can see how the two lines of development have come to overlap. The discursive framework of violence, whether it be male violence or family violence, provides increasingly co-ordinated conceptual tools that give wife-battering a form that is both clinical and criminal in its organization. How this was further negotiated and developed is the subject of the next chapter.

9 Negotiating the Elements

In the session in which the members of OAITH appeared before the committee, it was evident that the issue of protection, police, and legal practices was only one, albeit a significant one, of the issues involved in the enterprise of ensuring appropriate institutional response to wife-battering. The London Alternatives to Violence Project, however, particularly in Jaffe's presentation, introduced a new emphasis to the committee's second session. While the co-ordination of a range of responses to the issue of the abuse, defined in particular ways within each framework, was a common concern in both sessions, it had a somewhat different character in each. In Don's presentations the issue was grounded in the fragmentation of options available to women and the range of difficulties this fragmentation presents for the women and for interval-house workers. In the case of the London project, the presentation was grounded in the institutional requirements for co-ordination of effective service delivery and the need to articulate police practices, court procedures, and the mental-health and social-service systems into a proper and effective professional response.

The feminist framework and that being subscribed to by the family-violence protagonists found common ground in the area of policing, police response, and police practices. The recognition of wife-battering as assault under the law co-ordinates conceptually an aspect of 'violence against women' with an aspect of 'family violence.' Co-ordinated policies call for state intervention through the criminal-justice system as well as through such other aspects of the social-problem apparatus as the mental-health and social-services systems. Representatives from the Attorney General's department had met with the committee as informants on the question of the justice system in the preliminary sessions in May. The shift of emphasis towards recommending changes in the justice system required the committee to extend its mandate to include the ministries of the Attorney General and Solicitor General. These ministers were subsequently asked to appear at the hearings.

The modified professional and feminist positions were represented or disputed in other presentations and became part of the ongoing conceptual work of the committee. This conceptual process included the development of a clinical-criminal conjunction designed to co-ordinate work on the issue by government departments, agencies, and 'community groups' (in which women's movement services were included). The cumulative effect of what the committee had heard was demonstrated by the reception given to the presentation made by the attorney general of the province on the last day on which witnesses appeared before the committee.

LEGAL DISCOURSE AND PRACTICE

The acceptance of wife assault as a criminal issue entered that aspect of family violence into the framework of law and order and the legal discourse, rendering the women and men involved into victims and assailants or perpetrators. While for Jaffe the issue was indubitably gendered and focused on wife abuse, in other testimony, such as that of the police officer from the Toronto domestic-response team, who appeared before the committee on the following day, gender-neutral terminology was used throughout. This witness, Staff Sergeant Collett, referred to victims and perpetrators throughout his appearance before the committee, with one revealing exception. When referring to the issue of laying charges, Collett described the procedure like this: 'If the officer felt he had no other recourse but to make an arrest, then he would do that and the party would be taken before the courts by the police force. In the minor assaults, the hope is to have the person lay his or her own charges. That frees the officer for some of his other responsibilities. At the same time it takes one of the responsibilities away from the officer, that of attempting to make a judgement decision, of taking one person's word over another ... Where there is an allegation of assault, where someone says, "He hit me," and there is no visible mark.'[1]

In the context of police practices, which did not include recording the gender or relationship of protagonists in assault cases[2] the neutralized and degendered features of the initial family-violence framework (where 'interspousal violent episodes' took place or 'violence broke out between couples') dovetails with the language of domestic disputes and their handling in the administrative practices of policing and the legal system. Both contain the same removal of the subject of the action, abstracted in the terms of the discourse to become 'the person,' 'the perpetrator,' 'the assailant,' or 'the complainant.' Indeed, Collett's language here may well only have become gendered in direct response to the fact that the question he was answering at that point was asked in these terms – that is, about the police laying charges on behalf of people rather than the victim laying *his* or *her* own charge. Here he moved logically from his general statements to an instance of the particular (the laying of charges) and it was at this point of contact with the actual activities in which people are engaged that gender appeared. When he became even more specific, we find that laying a charge involved 'someone' naming an action and an actor (he hit me). The police must make a judgment when 'there is no visible mark,' a judgment that either does or does not transform those involved into 'assailants' and 'victims.'

The effect of the fact that the framework of assault is not gendered is not only that we cannot discern who assaulted whom, but also to give the impression that, since in law men and women are treated equally, in the mind of the questioner and the police, they are equally likely to be the victims of assault in the case of family violence. The problem highlighted here is that gender-neutral language does not allow the specifically gendered character of the issue to be recognized and responded to appropriately by the criminal-justice system.

A suggestive sequencing is evident in the appearance before the committee of witnesses representing three areas of police intervention. On the first day the committee heard from the London Alternatives to Violence Project. An important part of that presentation was the focus by Jaffe on the research, data collection, and effectiveness of the changes in methods of police intervention in London. This testimony was offered under the rubric of the Co-ordinating Committee on Family Violence, incorporating 'wife assault' within the framework of family violence. The second day brought the testimony of Staff Sergeant Collett from the Metropolitan Toronto Police. He represented the police domestic-response team, attempting to link police and social services. The small-scale nature of the program, and the total lack of record-keeping and evaluation procedures, did not impress the committee. On the third day, members heard from Dr James Bannon, a deputy chief of police from Detroit and chairman of the Domestic Violence Prevention and Treatment Board for the State of Michigan.[3] Bannon put forward a model for dealing with the issue that was based on the Michigan experience of getting specific legislation in place and making it work to protect women. He illustrated, step by step, the process, which he initiated during his doctoral studies and continued to co-ordinate, of making the criminal-justice system properly responsive to wife-battering. The sequence illustrates the various contending postions within the legal discourse and the interplay between them.

Bannon's credentials and his comprehensive and articulate presentation make it worth giving his testimony some emphasis because its eventual impact on the committee's findings was considerable and complex; he tied together levels of discourse and courses of action. First of all, he grounded his approach in experience as a police officer, an experience that involved an alliance with 'feminist and activist groups ... in attempting to get redress for the victims of domestic violence.'[4] He credited 'the practitioners in the criminal justice system, and particularly the police,' with being very responsive to the confrontation represented by his indictment of the police, the judiciary, the 'prosecutorial branches,' and the u.s. Civil Rights Commission. He noted, however, that their first response was to go to the social-science discourse. This he perceived as a false start since it led to the notion that police officers should be psychologists and therapists with crisis-intervention skills, whereas, in Bannon's opinion, the role of police officers should be to enforce the law to protect women.

Police 'mispractice' and 'malfeasance' (to use Bannon's own terms) in failing to respond adequately to domestic-violence calls have often put women in the tragic position of taking the law into their own hands so that, while virtually all domestic-assault victims are women, 80 per cent of homicide victims in domestic cases in the United States are men. Women were, he believed, indicting society saying in effect: '"You share my guilt. I am guilty, yes, I killed him, but you did not do anything for me. But if he was a stranger and he assaulted me you would have done something for me. You tell me this prior consensual sexual act sets an economic interdependence that says to people that they are different somehow than in stranger-to-stranger crime." I think that is tragic and I think that is wrong.'[5]

Paradoxically, however, the legislation on domestic violence passed in Michigan in 1978 had eventually to be amended to create terms for understanding the special relation between victim and assailant in cases of domestic violence, though Bannon did not appear to see its implications in terms of the failure of the concept of assault to provide adequate support for women and children. When it came to exercising non-bondable imprisonment procedures in cases where injunctions, protective orders, and restraining orders had to be enforced, the definition of who was to be protected had to be amended from divorced or separated legal spouses to include 'a provision that the parties had to have co-habited or be at present cohabiting ... it could be an order issued any time, even if the cohabitation continued.'[6]

Bannon also indicted the education systems and the medical and the social-services systems for failing to recognize and deal with the issue. This negligence was sufficient justification, he felt, for leaving it to grass-roots activist experts to run shelters and other support programs and for requiring the police to enforce the law on assault to provide the necessary protection. This was the principle on which the program run by his board operated. Services were funded 40 per cent by the board and 60 per cent by other financial sources and community contributions, which included all volunteer labour in the fund-matching process. This funding procedure, Bannon suggested, was necessary to avoid institutionalization and professionalization processes which would undermine the effectiveness of shelter services. Additional services, such as second-stage housing and social-service support for job-training, should be taken up by the official social-service agencies. Counselling programs for assailants, four of which were originally funded by the board as pilot projects, were no longer funded because it was felt that the money was desperately needed by the women's services. Assailants' programs should, the board had decided, be run and funded by some part of the institutional apparatus, such as the corrections branch.

Despite his adherence to the 'assault is assault' position, Bannon set the entire issue within the framework of 'violence' as the generic problem for which the American home must be held responsible: 'The home is where we learn violence as being an appropriate male behaviour,' he remarked (to which Richard Johnston replied: 'I noticed that myself').[7] Police behaviour in the early days he considered to have been 'predicated on our own masculine images, our own belief in violence as an appropriate remedy for confrontation or conflict resolution. I have often said that probably if we want to teach that violence is an inappropriate remedy for conflict, then the police officer is the worst case to try and teach that. We are the personification of violence. We have guns, we have blackjacks, we have nightsticks and we have all these other appurtenances of violence.'[8] The long-term solution he offered was the complete re-education and resocialization of males (and females too).

Immediate needs included more money for programs and the involvement of other institutions, such as the medical profession, the education system, and the church, in efforts to combat the problem. In the short term, Bannon described the criminal-justice system as the only answer:

My conviction ... is that the only appropriate remedy for domestic violence assault cases is that they be treated as stranger-to-stranger crimes ... Society has only one remaining, virtually intact, social control mechanism and that is the criminal law, not the civil law, not tort law ... The criminal law is ... our way of saying what is inappropriate or appropriate behaviour in our society. As long as you persist in saying to people that domestic violence cases are different, you transmit the message that there is a special case, that this is not such bad behaviour, not nearly as bad as punching the stranger on the nose in the street. That is what we are doing when we make distinctions in domestic violence cases between criminal and civil.[9]

Different police approaches or responses are located in a work organization, which is in turn embedded in the larger structures of the legal system's operation.[10] Bannon noted that domestic-violence calls were the first that the Detroit police department screened out as part of a scheme to cut back in the face of overwhelming numbers of calls for service of all kinds. The police department's administration justified this decision in these terms: 'We do not know how to deal with domestic violence, so why waste our time? That is the same thing the prosecuting attorney's office and the bench has been saying for years. These cases are intractable. We do not know how to deal with them. They are not appropriately in the criminal justice system in the criminal courts.'[11] The subsequent move to train police officers in crisis intervention and counselling then make sense as attempts to provide the police with ways of dealing with these calls outside the criminal system. The inadequacy of this response in terms of either deterring men or protecting women, and the demands from women's groups that such protection be provided, then shifted the emphasis and definition of the issue back towards the criminal-justice system. This emphasis in turn made it possible for the police to act on it as a matter of law enforcement, rather than one of the maintenance of order or keeping the peace, once the issue was defined as assault. Bannon's testimony, among many other things, actually gave an overview of how this process happened in Michigan, and how it was part of a concerted action to locate wife-battering under the auspices of the criminal-justice system.

When it came to presenting definitions of wife-battering as assault, there was remarkable unanimity among women's groups, such as Support Services for Assaulted Women, appearing before the committee. This presentation in particular opened with a strong statement of the feminist position and a refuting of both prior formulations and the family-violence position: 'You will notice we use the term "wife assault" rather than "domestic violence." This is because we want to stress that wife assault is a crime, not merely family interaction gone wrong. We also believe that freedom from assault is every person's basic right and that wife assault is not family violence; it is violence against women. It is not caused by mental illness. Men beat their wives because they are permitted to, because our society has not given a clear message that this conduct is intolerable, and therefore there is confusion among those whose responsibility it is to deal with the crime.'[12] Even groups that clearly did not have a feminist approach most often included some reference to the criminal nature of assault even when, as for example in the testimony of the Hope Haven Homes, the problem was identified as the result of the effects of alcohol on the essential family unit. The director put it this way: 'No one has the right to assault another person in any way, shape or form. That is our law and that is what we believe at the Haven.'[13] She also suggested that the police and courts need to understand the problem and that Hamilton's experimental Unified Family Court Program should continue, since it supported family life. Proper protection and understanding were necessary but not sufficient, as the real cause of abuse must be recognized as being alcohol. In closing her statement, she raised these questions: 'Are there enough people in our court and police systems who really see the culprit as alcohol abuse, and who see it as the trigger in the vicious circle of family violence and eventual breakdown? ... Is not the strength of the family unit each member pulling positively together that makes for a more unified law system, that unifies society and brings about stable, contributing citizens? Without the family, what do we really have?'[14]

We can begin to see here how even the most family-violence oriented of approaches had incorporated the criminal nature of assault into its framework, in this case without altering the belief that remedies must be formulated with the intention of strengthening the family unit against breakdown. Individuals must be treated within the family system to restore both to full functioning. Few groups appearing before the committee had such an obviously integrated clinical-criminal position, which included all family members in the clinical treatment aspects, but a number, particularly from programs with a social-service base and social-work component, embraced the notion of criminal assault as the extreme definition of certain incidents of family violence. It became, within this framework, the most extreme and profound example of 'family interaction gone wrong' – short of actual murder, to which it may well lead. Prosecution for assault was thus constituted as a treatment strategy for dealing with the most serious manifestations.

THE SEARCH FOR RESOLUTION THROUGH CO-ORDINATION

The committee members, in their questioning of those who appeared before them, showed a particular interest in both short-term issues of shelter and protection for women and long-term issues of prevention through the changing of attitudes and practices that sanction abuse. The latter was presented by many witnesses as a matter of education rather than particular changes in legislation:[15] training of police, lawyers, and other professionals; public education and publicity campaigns; and attention in schools from preschool up, both to the effects on children's behaviour of being or seeing others abused and to the content of curricula that should emphasize changing sex roles and realistic views of family life.[16]

The committee heard from several projects – the London Family Consultants Program described by Jaffe, the Toronto Domestic Response teams, a Quebec program, and the proposed London Battered Women's Advocacy Clinic – that attempted to deal with the jurisdictional dilemma by providing services that link the two systems of criminal justice and social services using a clinical-criminal framework. None of these programs, however, directly linked the two state-based jurisdictions of justice and social services. In the London and Toronto projects, the social-service professionals who work with the police to provide back-up resources and referrals for various family-crisis situations were not employed directly by either department. They were drawn from Family Services Centres, other community agencies funded by United Way or private sources, and, in some cases, employed through purchase of service agreements with municipal departments of social services. These workers thus provided an external linkage between the major systems.

The proposed advocacy service in London was also designed specifically to address the gap in services represented by the lack of co-ordination between criminal justice and social service jurisdictions. As

Lorraine Greaves, representative of the board of directors engaged in opening the clinic, put it: 'If you can think of those systems as very separate entities, the clinic does not believe that they should stay separate. On the other hand, we are not advocating a merging of their administrative structures, but we are simply saying that networks have to be operationalized, activated, between them. That is not necessarily going to happen on its own. We feel that, on behalf of a specific population of victims, we can offer service that will in part activate those links between those systems.'[17]

It was Greaves's testimony that most clearly articulated the position that battered women, as victims of family violence, were in a unique position, unlike victims of other forms of assault. It was on the bases of these differences that the need to link the two systems was posited.[18] The difference articulated as being most profound was that of the economic dependence of victims on their assailants. This meant that any choices outside the marriage that a woman might make would 'often mean a considerable drop in her standard of living, or in fact, considerable pain and hardship for herself and her children.'[19] Women and children as victims of abuse are also emotionally tied to the assailant, and this emotional tie is invoked by people in general, and the system too, as the rationale for not intervening in the sacrosanct family unit.

If married, as Greaves pointed out, a woman is legally tied to her assailant and this status has ramifications. He is also the father of the children and may or may not batter them as well. The battered woman, Greaves suggested, is as susceptible as anyone else to the idea of keeping the family 'intact' and this goal is a major consideration in her decisions about the situation. She may also be living with her assailant, which exacerbates the difficulties involved in laying charges, as does the fact that she seldom has any social-support system because of the isolation imposed by the way abusers control any contact with friends or family. As a result of isolation and prolonged battering, the woman may be depressed and lacking in self-esteem. If she did seek help from one of the systems she may well have been made to feel as if she was at fault and was in fact the offender in the situation. As a result of these specific relational aspects of wife-battering in the context of the family there were gaps in services available to deal with the problem in both the criminal-justice and social-service systems. Even existing shelter services and the Family Consultant Unit in London were able to deal with only a small fraction of the calls made upon them.

The Advocacy Clinic was not envisioned as a new service in itself; it was to be a cost-effective marriage of information about the legal and social-service systems, located outside either, in the community, but with equal access to both. The support offered to women in the form of 'a service to victims of family violence'[20] was designed, Greaves stated, to create opportunities for women to make their own informed choices and help them to plan their actions, and to act as advocates for them where necessary. 'This may involve the initiation of criminal charges, the exercise of referral to social agencies, the establishment of marital, family or individual therapy and/or the placement of the client in job training: all of those addressing some of the characteristics of the victim that I mentioned earlier.'[21] The direct service to battered women was to happen in conjunction with 'community development' to encourage change in the community systems involved in the treatment of and response to battered women and battering men. This would increase public awareness and complement the clinics' prevention and education plans, proposals for curricular changes, and media campaigns.

In this part of the description, Greaves referred, in the space of three sentences, to battered women as the clients, the woman, and the client again. Victims of family violence became clients of the clinics. Elsewhere, however, she also articulated the issue as one of violence against women, part of a spectrum that includes 'incest against girls and women, sexual harassment, rape and pornography.'[22] Here Greaves made no bones about the gendered character of the issue: 'One thing we cannot ignore ... is that most of the perpetrators ... are male and most of the victims are female ... There is an ethic, if you will, that allows certain behaviour on the part of the male in our society and that has as its mirror the encouragement of a certain behaviour on the part of women, which is the acceptance of their victim role.'[23] It was in this testimony that the professionalization of the women's movement postion became fully apparent as the clinical framework is extended to women and children as victims and clients to be linked to health and social service as well as to criminal-justice systems by the work of the proposed advocacy clinic.

This merging of the family-violence and violence-against-women frameworks could be seen in a number of the statements made to the committee. It was a feature of an attempt at the conceptual co-ordination that must be accomplished if the practical and administrative co-ordination necessary to lodge the issue of wife-battering satisfactorily within the social-problem apparatus was to be achieved. What was being brought into the work of the committee through the presentations made at its hearings was part of a dynamic process of negotiation and development of ways to understand and act upon women's experiences, in which the 'issue of abuse' was being constructed as a phenomenon. As Greaves put it: 'All of those activities [wife-battering, incest, sexual harassment, rape, and pornography] promote a certain image of a male-female relationship. All of those activities have, until very recently, been received or been acknowledged by the community; and by that I mean the legal system, the social services system and what not, as something less than crime, something private; something not nice but something less than crime. I am pleased to say that in the last 10 years [the] definition of crime I talk about is being activated.'[24]

INDICTING THE JUSTICE SYSTEM

As witness after witness appeared before the standing committee, the testimony concerning the need to lodge wife-battering as assault under the provisions of criminal law either in its own right or as an aspect of family violence seems to have had a cumulative impact. As representatives from groups and services described the problems they faced in working to get something done about the situation of women who were being beaten, and as women and men themselves told the committee of their experiences of trying to get help and protection, the overriding message that the committee heard was that wife-battering must be properly handled as a criminal act, regardless of whether or not a treatment element needed to be contained within the definition. The corollary to this was that at the time it was not being handled as such, with the exception of a few isolated examples such as the London project and the Michigan legislation and program. The work practices of the police and the judiciary did not reflect this crucial understanding, nor did the training of police, lawyers, or other professionals who may come in contact with wife-battering in the course of their work.

The impact of the various testmonies concerning the inadequacy of the justice system's response to the issue and in particular the presentations of Jaffe, Collett, and Bannon could be seen when the attorney general of the province, the Hon. Roy McMurtry, addressed the committee on the penultimate day of the hearings. McMurtry testified for over two hours, which, the chairman noted, was the longest time any witness had spent before the committee and, in the chairman's words, 'points out the importance of [the] office and the role of our justice system in providing a resolution and ... in changing some of the attitudes as well as the procedures in the justice system to the victim.'[25] McMurtry was the only minister to testify, although it came out early in the session that there was a last-minute attempt part way through the hearings to get the solicitor general to appear once it became evident that the justice system was a major area of conern. Since the solicitor general had left on vacation, and McMurtry, in fact, had occupied that position for a number of years, the committee addressed its concerns regarding police training and procedures to him in addition to those in his own area of legal responsibility. Most of the time was spent in extensive and rigorous questioning by committee members clearly perturbed by the implications of what they had heard so far, particularly from battered women themselves, about the operation and function of the justice system at all levels.

The attorney general attempted to demonstrate the serious response his department was making in the face of a shortage of resources and a lack of straightforward resolutions. As with the earlier appearance of his representatives in the May sessions, it was evident that the problem for McMurtry was organized and understood as one of jurisdictional claims and unclear mandates. While McMurtry was prepared to acknowledge some flaws in police attitudes and some delays in the processing of cases before the courts, his major rationale for the failure of the police to treat wife-battering like other instances of assault, to which he returned again and again, was that women almost invariably press to withdraw charges once laid. He situated this 'fact' in his own experience as a young Crown attorney, insisted that nothing has changed, and could not be persuaded otherwise by committee members citing research figures from the London study.

His 'experience' was in itself indicative of how the lack of recognition of gender and gender relations in legal language rendered the situation of women invisible. The withdrawing of assault charges could be interpreted only as inconsistency or irresponsibility on the part of women, rather than possibily making good sense in the circumstances. It became obvious that McMurtry was still operating from the initial professional family-violence position and had not been briefed on the tenor of the previous sessions or submissions. He was also still bound by the assumption that assault charges must be brought by the victim rather than by the Crown.

One excerpt from the long testimony demonstrates both the development of the committee's own thinking in relation to defining the problem and the complexity of the structure of legal response when confronted with the dilemma of individual versus family rights. It also indicates a further piece of McMurtry's agenda which throughout appeared to be to avoid any commitment by the Attorney General's Office to fund or take responsibility for additional research or services that could be defined as being within the mandate of any other department. In this excerpt, McMurtry had just told the committee that in his recent dealings with a North Atlantic Treaty Organization conference on child abuse he found many member countries unconcerned with wife-battering as a public issue, although he felt they were 'similar problems in so far as the family structure is concerned.'[26] Alan Robinson (Scarborough-Ellesmere, PC) then asked:

MR ROBINSON: *With respect, recognizing that it is a public issue in Ontario, how is it that the judicial system has grown in such a way to protect stranger from stranger but not family member from family member with the same measure of equality?*

HON. MR MCMURTRY: *I do not want to create the impression it is my view that the judicial system is insensitive to this problem at all. I think the judicial system is sensitive to it but it is a much more complicated problem because of the nature of the family structure. To some extent, we deal with some of this in the paper that I circulated.*

The police, the courts and the social service agencies are often very concerned, as they should be, with the maintenance of the family unit. I have had discussions with social workers, very highly qualified people, who think most of these cases should be kept out of the courts and should be dealt with by different forms of counselling. There is a very wide variance of opinions among qualified people as to the role of the criminal justice system. Obviously, from what you have heard, many people believe that the role of the criminal justice system should be much greater, but we also hear from people who think it should be much less. That adds to the complexity of the situation.

We are talking about all sorts of diversion, victim, accused, reconciliation, concepts and whatnot.

MR ROBINSON: *Fair enough, but not debating whether or not it is pro or con, or it is more or less, but just taking your own words and recognizing that it is a complicated and complex problem, would it not seem reasonable that the judicial system in Ontario should devote more resources towards that aspect of assault or violence than, seemingly, less, as it does now?*

HON. MR MCMURTRY: *I would like to have more resources in every area. I have already said that it is my view the courts of this province, and indeed of this country, do not treat cases of violence generally with the degree of serious I believe is required.*

MS BRYDEN: *It still seems to me, Mr McMurtry, that the whole thrust of the present instructions to the police and to the crown attorneys seems to downgrade domestic assault in comparison to other forms of assault and I think this is something we will have to look at.*

HON. MR MCMURTRY: *I do not agree.*

MS BRYDEN: *The result has been, Mr Attorney General, that the victim is discouraged from lodging charges by the instructions that the police are given: not to discuss the seriousness of the crime, not to threaten arrest, and not to legalize unnecessarily – that is in the instructions for the Ontario Police College. So the victim is discouraged from laying charges, the police are not instructed to lay charges in all cases and, as a result, we get very few convictions, ridiculous sentences and no orders for treatment of the batterer so that this serious crime is being downgraded constantly by the instructions that are given both to the crown attorneys and to the police.*

Do you not feel that those instructions are stacked in that direction of defusing the whole issue and making this appear to be a less serious crime than any other assault?

HON. MR MCMURTRY: *No.*[27]

It is clear from this session that the justice system was being confronted with the issue of wife-battering on a number of fronts. For example, McMurtry explained that the Liaison Committee on the Enforcement of Family Orders was not set up to deal with family violence, yet the issue became part of its terms of reference. Trudy Don from OAITH reported that she sat on that committee, and had obviously had an impact on its concerns. The complexity of the legal structures, both in terms of the law itself and in terms of the organization of its administration through legal and police practices, was such that the work of dealing with family violence was not easy to accommodate. What McMurtry experienced as a function of women's 'unwillingness' to follow through on laying charges can be seen, as Bryden proposed, as a culmination of responses to police training (which directly instructed, in its 1982 manual, that police attempt to dissuade 'the complainant' from laying charges),[28] to inadequate support in the court process, and to more general pressures from a society that abdicates responsibility for the situation as a 'public issue.'

The chairman closed the session with a statement that showed how far his own thinking had developed since his early equivocation:

If there is anything I would like to point out of a commonality between the report of the federal task force and this report that will be coming, it is in stressing the importance that wife battering should be treated as a criminal activity, which we all share, and that wife beatings should be regularly processed by the criminal justice system, in other words, the criminal division.

If there is any hope, it is that the shift will change from the onus being on the victim to the charge being laid by the police and perhaps in the standard procedure which at present is that the family court division treats these victims, the exception being the criminal court division. Our hope is that if there is any change at the provincial level, the criminal court division will be the focus of these cases for victims and that the exception perhaps will be the family court, when a choice is given to the victim.

If there is any reference I thought symbolic, it is that the term 'complainant' is always used for the battered wife. Very often in the reports that we have, we tend to see them not as complainants, but as victims of criminal violence.[29]

CONCLUSION

In considering the July 1982 hearings before the Standing Committee on Social Development of the Ontario Legislature I did not attempt to summarize or represent the entire process or the many individuals and groups who took part. Instead I have tried to show how particular ways of looking at and conceptualizing the 'issue of abuse' were put forward and negotiated so that a compromise definition was arrived at. Wife-battering as a criminal act was accepted as being an outcome of the violence of society, both manifested and manufactured in the family. This definition came to predominate and organize the work of the committee.

The process identified so far set up a framework to contain the many facets of the problem and suggested a range of possible solutions for bridging the gap in jurisdictions which the presentations revealed. These involve various arrangements, particularly in relation to the justice system and social services, that would link or co-ordinate their work. In some cases, additional programs, such as the various police and social-work crisis services, already performed the function. Co-ordinating agencies such as the proposed advocacy clinic in London and the one at Hiatus House, a Windsor transition house that operates a similar legal clinic, were described as filling real gaps in services. Multi-representative co-ordinating committees such as those in Michigan and London were proposed, along with public and professional education campaigns. Witnesses such as Bannon and Don put forward suggestions that involved the criminal-justice system and women's shelters in dealing with the immediate issue, leaving the professions and institutions the role of long-term program providers and support services. For them, the priority was protecting women. Others, such as Jaffe, looked to the criminal-justice system to mandate treatment for assailants, or to provide sentencing that acknowledges the criminal nature of the problem. This would involve measures such as prison terms, which could be served on evenings and weekends without affecting the family's income. The London group had received funding from the Solicitor General to co-ordinate the responses of aspects of the justice system and now intended to move towards co-ordination with the mental-health system. Co-ordination was to operate in relation to victims as well as perpetrators of violence, since too much police time was seen to be taken up by dealing with problems more appropriate to the mental-health mandate.

As far as the Criminal Code went, Don and other witnesses indicated that the problem lay not in its content, but in its administration. The testimony of battered women and women who worked in the shelters showed that the problem manifests itself not in the law but in women's lives. It is women's experience of battering that requires the linkage of 'services,' 'protection,' and legal codes, which are not linked in actuality. Initially family violence as a conceptual practice for making that link had the problems already identified in previous chapters: it did not allow for protection, nor did it lead to effective ways of stopping the problem. Introducing the definition of certain acts as assault under the Criminal Code did provide the possibility of protection but had its own disadvantages. Wife-battering, treated as an equivalent to stranger-to-stranger assault, did not deal with dependence and the need for shelter and support for women and children. When assault as a category was merged with family violence as a subset of deviant behaviour, the dilemma was, to some degree at least, resolved. The definition pathologized certain aspects of gender relations and made them amenable to various treatment strategies without attacking the structures that determine them. The state thus became further involved in the management of family relations, no longer seen as fully private, as the co-ordination of its various organizational and institutional forms was engineered and articulated at the conceptual level. What this looks like in its documentary form is the subject of chapter 10.

10 Reporting for Action

SETTING UP THE REPORT

The process of public hearings culminated in the production of a report and recommendations that brought together the deliberations of the committee; the accounts, positions, and information put before it by witnesses; and the knowledge generated in other discursive forms, available in texts such as briefs, books, reports, articles, and films. At the end of the afternoon of 29 July and during the session on the following morning, the committee directed its attention to this, the final task of this stage of its activities. It was decided, after discussion, that these deliberations would continue to be held in public and transcripts for Hansard kept in order so that the principle of public accessibility would be maintained as far as possible. It was also felt that members of the committee had shown themselves able to work co-operatively and had conducted themselves in such a way that there was no need to provide a private forum for acrimonious debate or in order to avoid partisan 'grandstanding' or 'government bashing' in the closing session.[1] As Alan Robinson (Scarborough-Ellesmere, PC) put it: 'We are agreed on some very fundamental principles that have been brought to light in recurrent themes. I think probably the most strident comments ... were likely those made to the Attorney General this morning.'[2]

Two aspects of the timing of the production of the report were considered initially: the strategic necessity of presenting it to the legislature for debate before the December adjournment, and the consequent need to set up a timetable for its drafting. In this discussion the process for writing the report was laid out though the specifics were dealt with in some detail later. It was a documentary process in which the researcher was to develop a first draft to be discussed by the committee at a later date.[3] He would do this using work already prepared by the research service (a compilation of all recommendations submitted by participants and other concerned individuals and groups), the tapes or transcripts of sessions, any documents tabled with the committee, and background material on legislation, funding, and court procedures.

When the committee reassembled on the morning of 30 July, they dealt with the 'fundamental principles' and 'recurrent themes,' identifying them and negotiating the order of priority to be given to each. Several people advanced their sense of a consensus of concerns put before them by various groups, some taking their cue from the compilation provided by the research staff.[4]

Robinson and Richard Johnston (Scarborough West, NDP) proposed that violence be emphasized as the predominant factor for consideration. Johnston commented on the profound impact that the hearings and readings had on his recognition of the 'enormity of the socialization that has taken place in our acceptance of violence and the way that impacts in so many different ways on our lives.'[5] He hoped that the report could provide a framework that would acknowledge the gravity of the problem and avoid a repetition of the trivialized way in which the federal report was greeted. Sheila Copps (Hamilton Centre, L) and Marion Bryden (Beaches-Woodbine, NDP) debated with Don Boudria (Prescott-Russell, L) and Jim McGuigan (Kent-Elgin, L) on the priority of transition-house funding problems or the primacy of concerns with the criminal-justice system in relation to policing and court procedures. Only Andy Watson (Chatham-Kent, PC) demurred on the priority of the justice system, suggesting that non-judicial alternatives such as counselling had been inadequately discussed. He suggested that the committee might not be entirely behind an earlier statement made by the chairman that the criminal division was the appropriate site for all assault charges, and requested more information on family-court options.

Eventually seven areas of concern were delineated by the chairman. Starting with 'the victim,' and followed by the police, the judicial system or courts, shelters (emergency and second-stage), treatment and programs, publicity, and education, and with the addition of a category to be called 'research and statistics,' these became the organizing format for the report. Other areas such as the economic and emotional dependence of women, persistently raised by Boudria, were discussed and agreed to. Bryden was anxious that shelters and their funding needs should be number two, after 'the victim,' as a key part of the problem, and made a point of the importance of this. Federal and provinical concerns were broached as a separate topic.

Areas of disagreement identified by the chairman as needing further discussion were: funding mechanisms, mandatory reporting, holding a wife-abuse register, the appropriateness of family-court procedures, and the whole question of sponsorship in relation to the Immigrant Act. The work of the researcher in sorting all this out was laid down as the production of a draft that would make a general introductory statement about the importance of the problem, its criminality, and the need for such things as better training for police, followed by material and recommendations in some form of priority, such as the categories delineated above.

Johnston made a number of decisive organizational points; this was a further example of his key role. Throughout the proceedings he exercised considerable leadership in planning, marshalling resources, and introducing information gained from both his contact with the Ontario Association of Interval and Transition Houses and his extensive reading of material from the general discourse. At various times in this session he emphasized violence as the crucial underlying concern, reminded the committee that its task was to present its report to the legislature, who would be advised by its content and recommendations, and worked with the researcher and the planning subcommittee to elucidate a number of points that emerged from the committee's deliberation. It was Johnston who suggested the eventual organization of the report, which was described by the chairman as follows: 'That there be a strong introductory statement; that case studies be included; that there be a direction in the future in terms of the whole topic of inter and intra family violence and what this committee should be doing or what further recommendations would be needed; and finally that the recommendations be geared in a visible way towards specific ministries that would be implementing these recommendations.'[6] Johnston's suggestions were all directed at moving the report into place as the avenue for a proposed range of courses of action that, it was to be hoped, particular departments within the government would take. It was not to be presented as merely a summary of the committee's deliberations and recommendations. Since the meetings in which the final report was approved were not public, it is possible to judge what the committee finally agreed upon only from the report itself. In a later interview, however, Johnston confirmed that it reflected the areas of consensus and disagreement accurately and put forward options when the committee felt unable to come to a decision in any area.[7]

THE WORK OF THE REPORT

At the most straightforward level, the report documents the work of the committee in taking up the task appointed it by the legislature. It collects and orders the recommendations made (many by representatives of groups who appeared as witnesses before the committee) and apportions them to the appropriate ministries. It knits together themes, links institutions and agencies, and attempts to establish responsibility for taking action within the existing structures of government. Thus it gives the reader – and in this case the implied reader is the government – a way to recognize and conceptualize the problem being put before it so that the solutions offered can be seen as comprehensive, viable, and urgent.

Behind the seemingly straightforward surface nature of the document, a more complex process can be seen. The report puts together and presents a framework for identifying and understanding the phenomenon being addressed. This understanding in turn is part of what makes it possible to take certain courses of action. These put in place, strengthen, co-ordinate, or try to create the proper correlation between the problem and the work of solving it through the appropriate institutional forms and administrative procedures for its resolution. The framework designates who and what is to be included in or excluded from the understanding being put forward and which features are to be given more and which less weight. By rationalizing the tensions, contradictions, and inconsistencies contained both in the framework itself and in the process of the hearings, it gives the government a way to take up issues, even where the committee and its informants were undecided or in disagreement. An example is the consideration of the best options for funding shelter services and the ambivalence with regard to mandatory reporting of instances of wife-battering.

It makes sense, then, to examine the report to see how it tells the government to think about and deal with the problem being put before it. First and foremost – in fact, literally on the cover of the report – the reader is constrained to recognize wife-battering as a serious social problem, an act of intolerable criminal violence to which the government and society must respond by changing attitudes so that it is no longer condoned. A statement to this effect is set prominently in a boxed format directly under the title of the document, *Standing Committee on Social Development, First Report on Family Violence: Wife Battering*.[8] The title, therefore, names this intolerable criminal act of wife-battering as a feature of family violence. The title-page alone shows how the 'issue of abuse' has been taken up and developed from where the committee started its deliberations to an the overall and inclusive position contained in the title and the highlighted statement.

These shifts can be traced at the level of language throughout the report. Women are very much present, as battered, assaulted, and abused women, wives, but also as individuals with rights and as economically disadvantaged members of society. Men appear as batterers, but also as culpable in general terms for incorrect and harmful attitudes towards women and for the inappropriate use of violence. Though 'family violence' and 'domestic violence' tend to be used interchangeably, 'spouse abuse' virtually disappears, and there is no discussion of battered husbands.

THE REPORT

The report can be examined to discover how the frame is shaped – its nature, dimensions, priorities, and 'reading,' that is, how to think about it – in order to place recommendations within the appropriate institutional contexts in which action can be taken. The recommendations then suggest what work is to be done, lining up the problem or features of the problem with the relevancies and existing bureaucratic and administrative imperatives and exigencies of the ministry, institution, agency, or department concerned. In order to see how this is done, I have analysed the document section by section, as it is organized, in terms of the significance of each in achieving institutional co-ordination by absorbing and articulating the concerns and positions put before the committee.

Preface and Introduction
Both the preface and introduction are important in setting up the framework in which the report is to be read. The preface describes and systematizes the history of the proceedings being reported upon. The time frame and organizational forms in which the work of the committee took place are described and the contribution of support staff and particular witnesses, namely Dr Doris Guyatt from the Ministry of Community and Social Services (comsoc) and Ms Trudy Don from the

Ontario Association of Interval and Transition Houses (OAITH), is acknowledged. The committee thanks and commends the witnesses who appeared before it, and credits the testimony of victims and batterers with shocking committee members and shattering widespread myths concerning family violence. These presentations 'reinforce this committee's conclusion that wife battering must be treated as a crime.'[9] Wife-battering is defined as 'any form of physical assault perpetrated by an adult male against an adult female, presently or previously living together. The definition is extended to marital and common law relationships.'[10]

The ministries of the Attorney General, the Solicitor General, Community and Social Services, and Education are singled out as the primary recipients of the recommendations in the report, which, though not legally binding, are offered in the 'hope that they will be discussed and implemented.'[11] In relation to institutional contexts named as the police, public education, and government legislation regarding the operation of transition houses, the recommendations are declared to have a major underlying principle: 'the need to affirm the criminality of wife battering.'[12] Finally, the preface places the report in the context of the work of the committee on the issue of family violence. It delineates as potential subjects for subsequent hearings child abuse and/or incest, abuse of the elderly, and causes of family violence in general.[13]

The introduction opens with a statement of the place of criminal law in Canadian society. Criminal law serves to underline fundamental values so that criminal acts that seriously violate important values demand a response; society must speak out and reaffirm those values. Wife-battering is defined as such an act, contravening an essential value, that of 'the inviolability of the person.'[14] Having reaffirmed the criminality of wife-battering, the introduction then names a variety of incorrect attitudes that must be remedied, through public condemnation. These include its being a private family dispute, a personal problem, the symptom of marital difficulties, and the result of provocation or overheated argument. It must be understood that 'an assault, as defined in the Criminal Code, is no less an assault because the assailant and victim are husband and wife.'[15]

When it comes to accounting for the causes of wife-battering, the introduction tells us that the evidence before the committee points to traditional male attitudes towards women as property, inferiors, and subordinates as being a major contributing factor. The words of one of the men from the treatment group who appeared at the hearings are used to illustrate these attitudes and to confirm that alcohol alone is not a causal factor. Neither, it is suggested, is mental illness in the batterer, who tends to be violent only in 'the family setting.'[16] The committee admits to some trouble with a purely intergenerational explanation for the 'cycle of violence' theory, which does not account either for the fact that some children who grow up in violent homes become neither abusers nor abused, or for those who abuse without a violent history. More research is necessary into this aspect of causality and into the societal acceptance of force as appropriate behaviour for men and submission as an appropriate response for women: 'The concept of violent behavior being "macho," of symbolizing the "real man" in our culture, whether in sports, in the school yard, or in the neighborhood bar, and the relationship between this concept and wife assault, require investigation.'[17]

The first recommendation arises from this concern and directs the ministries of the Attorney General, the Solicitor General, Community and Social Services, and Education to fund research into the causes and means of preventing wife-battering. The committee expresses its anxiety, however, that research not be used as an excuse for delaying the implementation of the recommendations that follow or as a tactic to maintain the status quo.

The preface and introduction demonstrate the success of witnesses such as Guyatt, Don, and members of other women's groups in making wife-battering a public issue to be addressed by the state. Its gendered features are clearly presented but the framework transforms any possible structural implications. The issue appears as one of individual rights under the law being abridged by men's violent behaviour and proprietary attitudes. 'Violence' in general, and 'male violence' in particular, are taken up as a matter of socialization into dysfunctional stereotypic roles. These then become the focus of intervention by realigned and co-ordinated components of the social-problem apparatus. The extension of the definition of wife-battering to include common-law relationships allows for state intervention into personal relationships beyond marriage.

The Victim
After this general overview of how wife-battering is to be understood, the report moves on to consider, first, under the subheading 'The Victim,' what constitutes wife-battering, who suffers it, and the effects on the recipients. The forms of physical and psychological abuse are

detailed, facts regarding its incidence presented as a problem because of its hidden nature, and the parameters of the framework delineated. We are told that all classes and cultures, across income and educational levels, are affected. Batterers come from all walks of life and women may experience economic and emotional dependence regardless of the socio-economic level of the family. Though the concept of 'learned helplessness' applies to some women's experience, it is not common to all. The specific though sometimes overlapping problems of immigrant, native, rural, and francophone victims in obtaining services are de-scribed for each circumstance. Children are also characterized as victims, since they suffer as a consequence, but their needs are to be dealt with in a later section of the report.

When the particulars of who fits in the framework and for what reasons have been laid down, the resolutions follow in logical sequence, articulating each aspect of the problem to the institution designated as most appropriate to respond. Recommendations 2, 4, and 7 are made directly to the Ministry of Community and Social Services. Recommen-dation 2 concerns the need for a policy directive to municipal welfare administrators regarding the correct handling of applications for assis-tance from immigrant women. Similarly, recommendation 4 asks comsoc to establish twenty-four-hour toll-free multilingual counselling lines for battered women. Recommendations 5 and 6 deal with the need for interpreters and services within shelters to recognize and respond to the needs of francophones, immigrants, and native women. These, too, are to be funded by comsoc. Recommendation 7 asks comsoc to encourage community groups to establish shelters for immigrant women where needed. The Ministry of Education is to expand the number of English as a Second Language classes for immigrant women (recommendation 3). Finally, in recommendation 8, the federal govern-ment is asked to review the Immigration Act and the practices of Employment and Immigration Canada 'to ensure that a sponsored immigrant woman cannot be deported if (1) she has left her husband-sponsor because of his battering and (2) the separation from the sponsor has led to the severing of the sponsorship.'[18]

In this section the report's framework allows for an acknowledgment of women's dependence within the family as something that operates across classes and races. At the same time it reduces the many positions and needs put forward by witnesses into the category of 'victims' and gathers up a variety of concerns and recommendations from a wide range of groups into a formulation designed to justify the aim of providing proper services from different agencies and institutions. A further aspect of this organization of the problem is posed in a response to the report put forward by OAITH after its publication. The authors of the OAITH response note that the emphasis on immigrant, native, rural, and francophone 'victims' and their needs, coming so early in the report, gives the impression that these groups are more frequently 'victimized' than other women. This incorrect assumption would be rectified, the OAITH response suggests, by including these groups in the section on transition houses where arguments for increased funding and services would be bolstered.[19]

Police

Having delineated what constitutes wife-battering and who qualifies as its victims, the report takes up the issue of who responds to the immediate circumstances. The first agent of the criminal-justice system, and the one most often called upon for help, is the police force. People logically look to the police for protection, and they are available on a twenty-four-hour emergency basis.[20] Facts from the 1979 London study are cited to show the then-pertaining level of police response to domestic calls with regard to laying assault charges: 'Police laid charges in only three percent of the cases, yet they advised 20 percent of the women to get medical treatment and 60 percent to lay their own charges; victims had been assaulted an average of 35 times before they called the police.'[21] From this we can understand that, although women had clearly been assaulted within the definition of the Criminal Code to the degree of obviously needing medical treatment and having a case deserving of charges, police officers did not intervene in the manner that might be expected.

How, then, do members of the committee account for the problems with the existing institutional response from the first rank of the criminal-justice system targeted as bearing prime responsibility for dealing with wife-battering as a crime? A number of reasons are suggested to explain why the police are reluctant to lay charges. First and foremost, officers hold the same societal attitudes concerning the privacy of the family unit as have been indicated in the introduction as being all too common. They do not regard assault between husband and wife as assault to the same degree as that between strangers, and believe that interspousal problems should be solved without police interven-tion, or at least with the help of social-service agencies who are deemed to be better suited to the handling of family matters. Combined with such attitudes is the inadequacy of police training and the actual misinformation given police concerning their ability to lay charges in the case of common assault. They may also hesitate to lay charges because of the perception that the victim will want the charges withdrawn later. In fact, where charges have routinely been laid by police, in the London experiment, only 19 per cent were subsequently withdrawn.[22]

This latter finding, along with others from the London study, is used to put forward a rationale for the response desired from the police in order to properly locate the problem as a criminal matter to be dealt with as such. Courts are seen as treating charges laid by the police more seriously than those laid by women themselves, giving more serious sentences. Going through the court procedure and receiving a conviction and sentence appears to decrease the likelihood of violence recurring. The committee would like to see further research on the effects of various court dispositions on violence in the family and notes that since the hearings the attorney general has written to Crown prosecutors requesting that every effort be made to encourage police to lay appropriate charges when grounds exist for doing so.

Family Consultant Programs
Next, the report turns to what it calls 'Family Consultant Programs,' a section that describes three different mechanisms whereby a 'close working relationship between the police and social agencies can bring an element of immediacy to family crisis intervention.'[23] Programs in London, Toronto, and Quebec offer models for liaison between police and social-service consultants with mental-health and social-services training. These consultants act either as a team or in sequence to respond to the crisis at the time of police intervention and link 'the family' or the victim to necessary follow-up services: 'Whenever appropriate, the consultant [in the London program] will facilitate contact with community resources, such as a social service agency, family physician, lawyer, justice of the peace, or a psychiatrist.'[24]

This section of the report concludes by reviewing the inadequacies of police record-keeping and the need to produce statistics as data on which decisions about responses can be based. Police training and its inadequacies also come in for criticism and comment. Despite some questions having been raised in the course of the hearings concerning the veracity of the reports of danger to the police resulting from intervention in 'domestic disputes,' this 'fact' is presented as one rationale for proper police training. The meagre nature of the training received and its misleading aspects are noted: 'Current training de-emphasizes the criminality of wife abuse. An Ontario Police College manual categorizes incidents of wife assault as part of an officer's "non-criminal order maintenance duties" (*Family Crisis Intervention*, pp. 1–2). Family violence is not perceived as a law enforcement issue.'[25]

This lack of proper training and instruction leads directly to the kind of police response that fails to appreciate the needs of the victim and is ignorant of the resources available to her. Nor are police familiar with their powers with regard to court orders such as restraining orders, orders for exclusive possession of the matrimonial home, and peace bonds. They need more information on how to proceed in this regard.

The recommendations following this section of the report all relate to aspects of police response and methods of obtaining kinds of action deemed necessary and appropriate. Recommendation 9 deals with the responsibility of the Ministry of the Solicitor General, through the Ontario Police Commission, to instruct municipal and provincial police forces to lay charges when they 'have reasonable and probable grounds to believe an assault has taken place'[26] and lays out the conditions for charging. A joint meeting of the various bodies responsible for policing in Ontario and the Crown Attorney's Association should be called to ensure recognition of the urgency of implementing this policy.

Research into the effectiveness of police-family consultant programs in reducing the recurrence and level of violence should, according to recommendation 10, be funded by the ministries of the Attorney General and Solicitor General, and should include a project to co-ordinate OPP police work and social work in rural areas. In recommendation 11, the Ontario Police Commission is directed to instruct police forces to record all instances of wife-battering and to indicate the relationship between victim and assailant in all assault charges. Recommendations 12 and 13 deal with the need for more extensive formal training, both for new recruits and for veteran officers, and with the need for revision of the Police College training manual. The non-criminal designation of wife assault must be eliminated and officers properly instructed in the means and circumstances for the laying of charges. These revisions should be undertaken after consultations between the Ministry of the Solicitor General and the London Co-ordinating Committee on Family Violence.

This section of the report contains the crux of the framework's organization and emphasis in carrying forward the enterprise of lodging wife-battering in the system. The recommendations are directed at shaping up police practices and linking them to social-service provisions. It is evident that, for the police, wife-battering is not yet a fully public issue. This view is demonstrated in their response and reporting procedures and in their traditional attitudes towards the family unit. The family-support programs described are fully professional, and transition-house services are barely mentioned. It is possible to see, in the description of the work of the programs, that, in fact, a police response, even when adequate, does not totally provide a solution to the problem of wife-battering by treating it as assault. The circumstances frequently require some further form of support and service to the victim. When no family-consultant program is available, police may defuse the situation and leave, persuade the man to leave, or recommend or take the woman and her children to a transition house. There is no mention of transition houses as an option offered by the social-service workers, but the section on police training notes that a London survey determined that only 5 per cent of all victims were referred by police to emergency shelters.

Recommendations for revisions in police procedures suggest that these be made in consultation with the London Co-ordinating Committee. The local transition house thus appears as only one service provider among professional bodies. The influence of the presentation made by Peter Jaffe and the London group is evident throughout the report, and a great many of their recommendations, most of which concern police, court, and co-ordination procedures, are taken up and incorporated into those made by the standing committee. James Bannon's views are also evident in the areas of training, data-collection, and record-keeping, but his insistence that grass-roots women's groups should be the main focus of intervention and services is not incorporated into the body of the text or the recommendations.

The Judicial System

The section of the report that addresses the judicial system deals with a number of complex legal issues. It does so in a way that indicates that the fiat of declaring wife-battering to be assault like any other assault does not mean it is easily integrated into the criminal-justice system. Key roles in responding to the problem are taken by justices of the peace, Crown attorneys, and judges, each of whom is seen to be reluctant to treat wife assault as a crime. Justices of the peace are often unwilling to accept charges from women, presumably hoping that a 'cool-off' period will reduce chances of their laying charges and thus relieve the court system of an additional burden on its case-loads. It might also reduce the likelihood of charges being laid and then withdrawn at a later date. The attorney general is reported as agreeing that Crown attorneys do not have sufficient time with victims prior to court hearings, and that this is particularly unsatisfactory in cases of assault that have a 'high emotional component, such as domestic violence, sexual assault.'[27]

Domestic-related criminal charges are generally processed through the Provincial Court, Family Court Division. Police officers and justices of the peace refer complainants to Family Court. Those who favour the handling of wife-battering by the Family Court system point to the advantages offered. It is seen as desirable that all civil and criminal proceedings regarding the same family be dealt with in one court. The Criminal Division does not have jurisdiction over a battered women's claim for shelter or financial support, nor does it have the auxiliary support services for counselling and conciliation that are available in Family Court. By handling domestic assault cases in a different court, 'the criminal justice system is recognizing the uniqueness of the victim-offender relationship. Most abused women are emotionally and legally attached to their assailants; they may still be living together.'[28]

Opponents of the use of Family Court in cases of wife-battering point out certain inherent disadvantages. Non-criminal court suggests a non-criminal offence, of the same nature as failure to pay support. The less-formal atmosphere and the possibility of counselling and conciliation services reinforce the notion of a family problem rather than a crime. There are few full-time Crown attorneys attached to Family Court, and prosecution of the case may be left to the woman's lawyer, or if she does not have one, to the woman herself. There also may be delays in getting cases heard since courts do not sit daily outside major urban areas.

The committee is undecided as to how to solve the problem. The successful police program in London involved directives requiring the police to lay charges in Family Court when 'the assault occurs between members living together in the same dwelling unit as a family.'[29] All other assault charges or wounding charges involving the use of a weapon are laid in Criminal Court. The committee concludes that whichever court exercises jurisdiction over assault charges, it is crucial that the criminality of assault must be emphasized. Beyond this, it recommends that the Ministry of the Attorney General 'investigate Provincial Court procedures to determine if domestic violence cases should be prosecuted in Criminal Court instead of Family Court.'[30]

With regard to sentencing, the committee sees the safety of the victim as the prime consideration. Such is not currently the emphasis in sentencing procedures, and judges are inclined to treat domestic assault as 'the sign of a troubled marriage, rather than a public crime.'[31] Judges express concern that prison sentences eliminate the victim's source of income, do nothing to rehabilitate the offender, and may provoke a vengeful response. The report notes that these concerns apply to the sentencing of any offender; incarceration of the breadwinner removes his family's source of income, even though it may not be the wife who is the victim of the crime. Conditional discharges to 'keep the peace' are not sufficient; probation orders should specify conditions such as keeping away from the victim, having no direct or indirect contact, and undergoing counselling. These conditions should be strictly enforced by the police. The committee supports the idea of court-ordered group therapy, where such groups exist (since it appears to be more effective in curtailing violence than individual or family therapy), and favours a province-wide expansion of such groups. The imposition of fines is equated by the committee with 'a licence fee to continue the battering,'[32] but members agree with options such as those suggested by the attorney general concerning intermittent sentencing, which confines the offender at night and during the weekends, but allows him to maintain his job and support his family.

The committee recognizes the need of victims of wife abuse for some form of advice and information regarding the operation of the criminal-justice system. Women are, for the most part, unaware of their legal rights and their options under the Compensation for the Victims of Crime Act and the Family Law Reform Act. The proposed London Battered Women's Advocacy Clinic and the Hiatus House Complainants Support Program are described, and their work in providing services and information is endorsed by the committee, which supports the extension of such services throughout the province 'as one means of making the criminal and civil justice systems more accessible to the victim.'[33]

The recommendations following this section are designed to ensure a better fit between wife-battering, defined as assault, and the justice system designated to respond. Recommendations 14 to 17 are directed to the Ministry of the Attorney General and deal with: the proper instruction of justices of the peace on the ciminality of wife-battering; proper assistance to Crown attorneys in preparing cases in consultation with victims; and investigation and review of the whole issue of Family

Court, Criminal Court, and the Unified Family Court as proper venues for dealing with the various aspects of domestic assault. Probation orders are dealt with in recommendation 19 and mention is made of the committee's need for further information on the sentencing issue. Research comparing the effects on family violence of different court dispositions is requested. The Ministry of Correctional Services is charged in recommendation 20 with funding the operation and evaluation of group counselling programs for batterers. Victim-advocacy clinics, according to recommendation 21, should be funded by the federal Department of Health and Welfare,[34] the Department of Justice, and the provincial Ministry of the Attorney General. The duties of an advocate are specified in some detail. The need for a federal-provincial conference on the subject of wife-battering, focusing particularly on issues such as the consequences of Supreme Court decisions concerning section 6 of the Family Relations Act and other legal and jursidictional matters, is the subject of recommendation 18.

What comes to light in this section are the anomalies and inconsistencies in the judicial system when it comes to dealing with wife-battering as a crime. Under some aspects of the law, the family is treated as a unit. The individuals within the unit must be separated if they are to fit the basis of individual rights and the 'inviolability of the person' upon which much of the criminal-justice system is based. The committee is not certain how to make this separation work in the case of 'domestic assault,' where the individuals concerned are not separate in the sense that strangers are separate, but are tied in social, economic, and legal relationship to each other. The recommendations suggest that the government, through the various ministries and departments, must decide how the issue should be properly shaped so that appropriate action can be taken. Treatment for battering men is delegated to the Ministry of Corrections, whereas the role of advocacy clinics for women, at least in the case of the London project, is designed to link the provincial Justice department and the social-services system (while requiring federal funding). Though the committee does not incorporate the recommendation from the federal report that the victim be made a compellable witness against her husband at the option of the Crown in prosecuting wife-assault cases, this is in fact the implication of its recommendations 14–17. The ironic outcome of the Crown laying charges is that a woman refusing to testify against her husband can be charged with contempt of court, thus making her doubly the 'victim.'

The discussion of the debate over Family Court or Criminal Court as the proper venue for the disposition of 'domestic-related criminal charges'[35] makes clear some of the dimensions of the difficulties that arise from treating wife-battering as assault. The dual court systems appear to be set up, at least in some respects, to deal with aspects of social life as separate and discrete. Under this system, matters relating to the family are dealt with in the realm of civil law concerning contracts, property relations, maintenance obligations, and so on. Such matters, if not exactly private, are at least not criminal. There is clearly a degree of tension or slippage when it comes to managing personal, familial relations through the criminal-court system. The framework of the report addresses this disjunction in an effort to co-ordinate the justice and social-service aspects of the social-problem apparatus by setting wife assault within the definition of family violence. The range of testimony on legal procedures and the necessity of a response that takes into account the needs of women and children for adequate support has not provided the committee with any immediate answers to the jurisdictional problems evident in the legal structures of the court system. The concerns and positions put forward by the women's movement are translated, in this debate, into technical problems with the administration of legal codes.

Transition Houses
The section of the report dealing with transition houses starts with a preamble, under the heading 'Need for Shelter,' that justifies the existence of such houses in terms of women's need for safety and protection from further assaults while seeking some kind of legal remedy for the situation. It is pointed out that she may have to leave her home, belongings, and even children if the circumstances are sufficiently dangerous, and needs somewhere to go. This need, the report suggests, might be satisfied by other accommodation, but since many victims are financially dependent on their husbands, they cannot afford alternative housing. Though it would be logical to remove the husband from the situation, this cannot be done because no legal mechanisms exist for short-term restraint, and the legal protection processes that do exist take time and require court proceedings. 'The shelter allows the woman to re-establish herself, with her children and then apply for some kind of public assistance, if she is unable to find work.'[36] The report continues with 'the facts' about the services: number of houses, number of women and children serviced, information from the COMSOC report on hostels, and so on. It acknowledges but does not

emphasize the report that Interval House in Toronto is able to admit 'only one in six families seeking emergency shelter.'[37] A quotation from the OAITH presentation describes the approach used in the houses, which offers support in decision-making and the recognition of shared experience.

At this stage, the promise of further reference to the needs of children is fulfilled in a paragraph describing the trauma and disruption suffered by children who have witnessed or experienced violence. Transition-house staff report that children 'act out' destructively or 'withdraw,' 'internalizing their own hurt.'[38] In addition to recreational programs, the report suggests these children should have individual and group counselling services available to them.

Under the headings, 'Funding and Standards: Description' and 'Funding and Standards: Options,' the report puts forward a comprehensive review of the problems with methods of funding. It details possible alternatives reviewed by the committee: revisions in the General Welfare Act, funding under the Charitable Institutions Act, or new legislation concerning family violence. Following the Michigan model, such new legislation would formulate a statute for Ontario under which a domestic-violence prevention and treatment board would be located within the Ministry of Community and Social Services.[39]

The committee opts for item 3, new legislation, as being more adaptable to need than the existing statutes, notes the urgency with which it should be initiated, then suggests interim block funding and an increase in the ceiling of the per-diem rate paid to houses. These options form the basis of recommendations 22 to 25, with the Ministry of Community and Social Services being nominated as the department that should introduce new legislation. Recommendations 26 and 27 ask that the Ontario Housing Corporation revise its point-rating system for admission to rental housing units to give preference to victims of wife assault and its policy for transferring tenants to other housing units to include wife assault as grounds for transfer. The final recommendation in this section (28) asks that the federal government encourage the Canada Mortgage and Housing Corporation to set aside additional subsidized units 'for use as housing for battered women and their children.'[40]

It is possible to see in this section the ways in which the problem of wife-battering, as taken up in the work of the women who built the transition-house movement, does not fit with existing administrative and organizational structures. Particularly it does not conform to the category provided by the hostel program under the General Welfare Assistance Act, which would have to be considerably amended to accommodate the needs of transition houses and the women who make use of them. New legislation would reorganize the means of co-ordinating response to the problem. By making it the responsibility of the Ministry of Community and Social Services, however, the reorganization would retain its social-service orientation rather than the justice-system orientation that would accrue to it if the ministries of the Attorney General and Solicitor General were to take charge. This option may reflect the Michigan model,[41] or result from the wish to continue the existing location of funding and responsibility within COMSOC as the ministry responsible for the regulation of services to families and for the implementation of most of what is known as 'family policy.' In its deliberations on this issue, the committee was engaged in exploring ways to better co-ordinate the existing organizational structures, including COMSOC, the Ontario Housing Corporation, and Canada Mortgage and Housing, and make them more flexible and responsive, but also was clearly concerned with instituting better control, regulation, and supervision of transition houses.

The preamble to this section is rather equivocal, suggesting support for transition houses only as dire necessity dictates. It in no way acknowledges the pioneering work of the transition-house movement in bringing the whole issue to light and developing a network of refuges and other services in attempts to do something about it in the face of systematic institutional indifference. Wife-battering remains a welfare issue under policies that hitherto treated the family as a unit; new legislation would provide increased funding to enable COMSOC to establish and maintain shelters, train 'persons' to deal with 'domestic violence,' and provide treatment to 'victims,' in this case both women and children. This approach is professional and clinical and knits together a number of demands from women's groups and recommendations from social-service providers into an administrative whole, with transition houses as the crisis-management component.

Health-Care and Social-Service Professionals
The report next looks at health-care and social-service professionals, crediting their mistaken attitudes towards wife assault as having led them to avoid the problem or treat it in a superficial manner. This view, the report insists, amounts to a secondary victimization of assaulted

women at the hands of professionals. Traditional attitudes towards the privacy of the family and lack of formal training on the issue of family violence are named as the basis of the inadequacy of professional response from the medical, mental-health, and social-service systems. This contention is supported by illustrations from the experience or testimony of a number of witnesses.

Some time is spent in detailing the argument concerning mandatory reporting as a possible response to wife abuse, but the committee reaches no consensus on the issue, though the majority are opposed to mandatory reporting. These members suggest the possibility of reviewing the issue if other recommendations contained in the report are implemented but fail to significantly reduce the incidence of wife-battering. All agree, however, that doctors, nurses, psychiatrists, lawyers, counsellors, social workers, and clergy members 'should listen to the victim more carefully and make it clear that she does not have to put up with the abuse. Alternatives should be presented. She should be made aware of community services for battered women, including the location of any transition houses.'[42]

Co-ordinating Committees on Family Violence
Finally, in this section on health-care and social-service professionals, the report looks at co-ordinating committees on family violence, citing the London committee as an example. This co-ordinating committee is made up of representatives from the police, the Family Consultant Service, the transition house, the Status of Women group, the Provincial Court, Adult Probation and Parole, and criminal and family lawyers. It has assisted in research and reviewing data, is currently monitoring the impact of changes in police procedures, and is involved in increasing public awareness of the crime of wife-battering. The co-ordinating committee works to ensure that victims and professionals are familiar with available resources, and also to implement the advocacy program and the operation of the group-therapy program for batterers. The activities of such co-ordinating committees are seen as worthy of support, and the report, in recommendation 30, suggests that other municipalities should undertake their formation to bring together members representing local criminal-justice, medical, mental-health, and social-service systems to 'discuss ways of preventing family violence and promote an integrated community response to the problem.'[43]

The other recommendation (29) is directed to professional faculties, governing bodies, and associations that are charged with ensuring that their students and members have an understanding of wife assault as 'unacceptable criminal behavior.'[44] Bodies affected by this recommendation include the College of Physicians and Surgeons of Ontario, the Ontario Medical Association, the College of Nurses of Ontario, the Ontario Nurses' Association, the Canadian Psychiatric Association, the Law Society of Upper Canada, the Canadian Bar Association (Ontario Branch), and the Ontario Association of Professional Social Workers.

Thus the committee uses its framework to put forward ways in which aspects of the existing institutional structure should be aligned and co-ordinated in their various responses. Some members are not comfortable with the use of the psychological concept of 'learned helplessness' to present the victim as unable to act on her own behalf and a majority resist proposals to control 'the facts of the matter' through mandated reporting, even for the sake of data collection. There is some resistance to so mandatory a method of state intervention into the organization of personal relations within the family. If, however, the other methods they are recommending do not properly dispose of the problem, they see that further insertion of state practices may be necessary. Co-ordinating committees at the local level provide a way of ensuring that the conceptual reorganization demanded of professional training and authorization is put into practice in the everyday work of the institutions and bodies concerned with responding to the problem.

In this process and its attendant recommendations, we see that prior formulations held by professionals are to be refuted or updated through education and training. The framework allows for co-ordination of all agencies and institutions to link legal, health-care and social-service approaches at the municipal level. The influence of the standing committee's visit to the London setting and the testimony of Jaffe and the London Alternatives to Violence group can be seen to have resulted in a strategic position that provides for the co-ordination of the social-problem apparatus and the local state.

Education
When it comes to considering education as a topic, the report divides its concerns between the aspects of public education and formal schooling. Public education is seen as necessary to combat the myths about wife-battering that have been repeatedly drawn to the committee's attention. Myths that pervade society concern the nature of wife-battering and its perpetrators, who are often thought to be, in the words

of one witness, 'these weirdos out there who are doing it. It is people who do not work, or it is immigrants or it is a different culture. Everybody thinks it is somebody else.'[45] Public education must challenge the various myths that exist by: informing people of the extent of the problem and its criminal nature, informing batterers that their behaviour is illegal and intolerable, and informing women of their right to assistance and where they can get it. The committee supports the kind of work being done by Support Services for Assaulted Women, which receives no provincial funding and has had to restrict its services as a consequence.

The school system is seen as needing to respond at several levels. The curriculum should encompass classes to help young people develop awareness of the crime of wife-battering, its possible causes, and society's responses to violence. Such information should be presented 'in the context of male-female relationships in the family and in society in general.'[46] 'Socialization' within schools should be directed towards students learning that self-defence is the only justification for violence. Teachers and other educators should also receive professional-development education that would acquaint them with the problems faced by children from violent homes and the kinds of behaviour such children may manifest. The special needs of children living in transition houses should be attended to, both in terms of their own emotional responses to the situation and in terms of their safety from retaliation by hostile fathers.

Two main concerns underlie this section. First is the need to integrate the framework of family violence into a general shared understanding of the problem. This integration can be achieved by eliminating myths and wrongly held attitudes through a course of action using a variety of educational and media methods. The second concern relates to the recognition of both the preventative possibilities of curriculum additions in the schools and the intervention possibilities inherent in bringing existing problems to light. Both prevention and intervention have practical consequences for the work of teachers who must learn about the problem so as to present the correct understanding in the classroom and be able to deal with the results of children's experience as manifested in school behaviour or in direct appeals for help. In addition, teachers must deal with the practical difficulty of integrating children from transition houses into the everyday routine of the classroom.

The recommendations attached to this section break down into the same divisions. Numbers 31 and 32 deal with various public-education devices, such as multilingual materials, posters, brochures, and radio and television messages, that could be provided by community groups funded by the Ministry of Community and Social Services. Recommendations 33 to 35 are directed to the Ministry of Education and concern the development of curricula such as guide-lines for a mandatory Life Skill course on the topic of the roles of men and women in society and the family, parenting skills, constructive problem-solving, conflict management, and anger control. School-boards should be encouraged to incorporate topics such as husband-wife violence and sex roles and violence into existing courses. Family Studies and Physical Health and Education would be appropriate examples. The last three recommendations (36 to 38) deal with the needs of children in schools serving shelters. They concern the setting up of liaison committees with shelter staff, the designation of teachers responsible for the integration of children from shelters, and the need for staff training for educators on the needs of children from violent homes.

The framework operates at two levels in relation to education. The first level addresses long-term solutions by offering corrective information and socialization with regard to violence, sex-roles, and anger control both to 'the public' and to schoolchildren. Though somewhat buried in the body of the report, this strategy is, in fact, key, arising from the overall position on wife-battering as family violence put forward in the introductory and concluding statements that frame the entire report. The work of the feminist group Support Services for Assaulted Women is endorsed as important and influential in this regard, but no direct-funding recommendation is forthcoming. In the short term, the committee recommends policies for dealing with violence as it affects the operation of schools and the work of teachers in order to properly articulate this part of the social-problem apparatus to the issue.

Federal-Provincial Conference
The final section of the report deals with the need for a federal-provincial conference as suggested in a recommendation of the House of Commons Standing Committee on Health, Welfare and Social Affairs in their report to the federal government. The federal recommendation, however, stipulates that the conference deal solely with the enforcement and administration of criminal law, which is not deemed satisfactory for the purposes of the provincial committee. The bounds of the proposed conference are extended by a number of further recommendations. These are suggested as agenda items, some of which have appeared

elsewhere in the report as recommendations in specific sections. They basically reiterate the recommendations concerning various aspects of the co-ordination of the delivery of justice between the two levels of government, but add in concerns about immigration laws affecting battered women, the need for joint federal-provincial research, and the conducting of joint public-education programs. It is also suggested that the conference review: a proposal to register all current criminal orders on a province-wide and country-wide computer system; a proposal that a breach of such orders should lead to arrest; a proposal with respect to the development of uniform sentencing in wife-battering cases; and a proposal concerning the formal training of police on the problem of wife-battering, to include, at minimum, members of the RCMP who act as provincial or territorial police and all provincial and municipal police officers.

Recommendations 40 to 47, some of which are duplicates of earlier ones, provide an agenda, not intended to be exhaustive, that points to the areas where the committee sees a need to consider, organize, amend, and reorganize the internal work processes, procedures, policies, and practices of different levels and departments of government. They deal with the jurisdictional problems that must be addressed in order to co-ordinate the response to and disposition of wife-battering if it is to be recognized as a criminal act.

The Report's Conclusion
The conclusion of the report is presented here in full:

This Committee has been deeply disturbed by what we have seen and heard. A fundamental value of our society – the inviolability of the person – is infringed and, yet, the criminal justice, medical, mental health, and social service systems tend not to see that infringement. They are preoccupied with other values – in particular, the privacy of the family unit and the desirability of preserving that unit.

This Committee respects the privacy of the family. We consider the family to play an important role in helping individuals to grow to their full potential. Nevertheless, society's obligation to protect each of its members from harm must be supreme. Above all else, including the maintenance of the family, a battered woman must be given protection. The message should be clear to the victim – 'you do not have to put up with the violence.' As for the batterer, he must know that any assault is a crime. Society must no longer tolerate violence within the family.[47]

In summarizing the views and concerns of the committee, it contains within it the contradictions inherent in the framework of wife-battering as criminal assault in the context of the family, developed during the course of the hearings and put forward in its report. It also speaks to the necessity of aligning the report with the strong ideological commitment to 'traditional family values' emphasized in the speech from the throne and cited in the Minister of Community and Social Services' introduction to his annual report, which was put before the committee at the beginning of this process.

This concluding section is followed by a series of vignettes in which the experiences of women and men are placed within the professional format of the case-study. Two long ones, one taken from one of the briefs presented to the committee[48] and one developed from the story of a witness who met with committee, both concern women unable to obtain adequate protection from police or courts. Three short ones detail a variety of abusive situations and the severity of the attacks against the women involved. The battering men who appeared before the committee also appear here as anonymous case-studies. The report ends with a complete list of recommendations, as they are ordered in the body of the text, and a list of the 72 individuals or groups who either appeared before the committee or submitted written material.

The committee and its researcher produced a readable and coherent report. To some extent, at least, this is its purpose; all the wide-ranging diversity of information and opinion that was brought to the committee and all the many positions that its own members held on approaching the 'issue of abuse' have been sifted, included or excluded, ordered, and made rational, logical, and functional in terms of action to be taken. The report is designed to be read as a whole or section by section by those to whom the recommendations apply. Though it does not pretend to be comprehensive and puts forward several areas where more research, more facts, are necessary, the report does present a way both to see and to act on the problem. Wife-battering is presented as assault, which, though it takes place within the family, must be treated as a criminal matter. As a symptom of family violence, it is a serious social problem requiring a properly co-ordinated, informed social-problem apparatus to handle it. The framework reads as the way to see and act in relation to the issue, thus laying the basis for the necessary co-ordination at the conceptual level and organizing the relations of all parties to the problem, to the action to be taken, and to each other. Thus we can see a documentary process that presents a rational plan for co-ordination and alerts the reader – that is, the government – to unresolved anomalies in policy and legislation. The coherent internal frame locates the relations and tasks of all parties – government departments and ministries, professionals, grass-roots activists, and battered women themselves ('the victims') – and seemingly equalizes the relations between them with a message that suggests that, if everybody co-operated and did their job properly, the problem would be at least ameliorated in the short term while long-term educational strategies take effect. By the same token, any other position on the issue or possibility for action is obscured.

CONCLUSION

The report of the standing committee can be seen as a measure of the distance the committee came in its thinking from the time when it was first asked to consider 'the issue of abuse.' The achievements of the women's movement representatives were considerable. Their testimony had a substantial impact on how the issue was taken up and dealt with by the committee, revealing its gendered nature and the seriousness of its dimensions and consequences. The ideological circle of the professional formulation of family violence was breached and the concept extended to include a great deal of knowledge about the situation and needs of battered women. Presentations made to the committee by women's organizations convinced it of the inadequacy of existing state responses to wife-battering at many levels, resulting in recommendations with the potential for providing a range of mechanisms that would make that response more equitable and effective.

Nevertheless, in the committee's report, a possible 'political' focus that would provide for a way of seeing the many different forms and locations of oppression in the lives of women is eclipsed by the general picture of violence towards women in the context of the family. Such violence is presented as a social problem that can be addressed, if not solved, by the criminal-justice, social-service, mental-health, and educational systems working together and in conjunction with 'the community,' and co-ordinated by the provincial government.

This organization of the relations of the parties to the problem in fact not only marginalizes the work of women as activists and service providers, who become just one of many interested parties now to be professionally co-ordinated. It also transforms women who are beaten and their abusers into abstract victims and perpetrators, members of 'the violent family' that must be helped to handle 'its' violence. The larger issues of women's subordination and the response to them represented by the women's movement are thus managed and contained within a framework in which the work of women's movement activists in this field becomes a movement of services to 'battered women,' not a movement *of* women who are beaten and abused. The terrain of the struggle against women's oppression becomes reorganized into a struggle by women's movement experts, including feminist professionals, against the malfunctioning of the social-problem apparatus.

The framework produced by the enterprise of conceptual co-ordination achieved in the report provides for the lodging of the issue within the administrative processes of the state. In doing so it implicates the work of the women's movement in producing a generalized account and engaging in strategies for action concerning wife-battering as assault. This allows for its absorption as an issue of the movement into a social-problem apparatus designed to intervene in the problems faced by individual women within their families and intimate relationships.

11 Action and Reaction

Having looked at the report of the Standing Committee on Social Development in its own terms, we can look briefly at what it achieved in relation to the work of the committee and what it provided for by way of government action. At the same time, it is possible to see what the process of constructing the report excluded from the final presentation and thus to explore the transformative nature of the procedures under examination. We have seen that reaching this point has been part of a process of struggle to get the issue of wife-battering considered. This struggle necessitated addressing the existing institutional divisions and departments within the state and developing a conceptual framework that begins to co-ordinate the various aspects of the social-problem apparatus so that the issue can be properly lodged within the system. The report of the standing committee provided such a moment in this third stage of the process of institutional absorption.

In providing a brief assessment of the report and its consequences, I consider first what the groups appearing before the committee asked for and their success in achieving it. The achievements and limitations represented by the report are considered in the light of subsequent government action. My purpose here is not to draw firm conclusions about the impact of the report. Rather, I support my argument about the concerted concept of 'family violence,' developed in the work of the women's movement and the committee, by embedding the report in an ongoing process. The report moves the issue one step farther in the enterprise of getting it lodged in state processes and procedures. The framework for action provided by defining wife-battering as a subset of 'family violence,' at the same time identifying it as a criminal offence, allows for a range of government responses that correlate the work of different departments and jurisdictions but maintain the focus on the family unit. The framework then operates as an 'ordering procedure' for assembling and emphasis in both the body of the text and the recommendations put forward.

THE RECOMMENDATIONS RE-EXAMINED

An examination of the compilation of all recommendations put before the committee[1] shows that women's groups, overwhelmingly, asked for control of the issue through properly funded services and consultative procedures that would acknowledge and use their expertise in the area. Such procedures would involve back-up from police and the court system and support from social-service and other government departments. What the report actually proposes is an emphasis on the criminal-justice system, allied with the Ministry of Community and Social Services (COMSOC) as the sponsor of legislation on funding, and co-ordinated with other departments and professional groups. Interval and transition houses become part of the back-up support and crisis service network.

Reading the report with the objective of analysing what it contains and what it discards shows how the emphasis of the recommendations has been transformed. The narrative is persuasive; the jumble of demands has been turned into a rational plan that co-ordinates responses and alerts the governmental reader to areas of unresolved anomaly. What the government should do is clear: it must apportion responsibility and define mandates within departments; introduce legislation to provide adequate funding, standards, and control; and, above all, state its unequivocal position on the unacceptability and criminality of violence within the family as elsewhere. This latter point is presented as vital in the battle to change attitudes among professionals, legislators, and the public including perpetrators and victims. The effort to co-ordinate women's concerns so that they can be lodged within appropriate departments appears relatively successful.

A review of the recommendations in their entirety, however, shows that some of those presented to the committee were assimilated in their original form, some adapted in various ways, and some omitted altogether. This treatment is an indication of the weight the committee assigned to the various positions put before it. Those recommendations adopted as they stood or in virtually identical form were mainly taken directly from the federal committee's report on wife-battering and concerned the co-ordination and disposition of criminal orders that prevent a man from harassing his wife. Others stemmed from areas where the committee reached agreement on proposals relating to the police, the justice system, services to victims of violence, education, and professional responsibility. This ordering and emphasis is significant here, since it show a process of correlation and co-ordination between different levels of government, the priorities being readily accepted once the conceptual framework was in place.

A second category of recommendations includes those where the content is largely the same in the original compilation and in the report, but the responsibility for action has been assigned to different actors. This reassignment is largely a case of apportioning action to specific ministries and departments when the original recommendations were framed in general terms, In some cases, however, the streamlining alters or eliminates aspects of the original intention, as for example in recommendation 12, which deals at some length with police training, amalgamating a number of recommendations from different groups and organizations but leaving out one from Kingston Interval House that asks that 'police training programs should be required to use community expertise in educating recruits and members about issues of wife assault and the role of shelters.'[2] Recommendation 30, in contrast, is based on considerable discussion in the hearings but on only one specific recommendation (from Peter Jaffe, chairman of the London Committee on Family Violence) that 'professionals should talk to other professionals in the area, e.g., with doctors, with social workers, with police, etc.'[3] The resulting recommendation in the report is a full-blown directive to municipalities to form co-ordinating committees representing the local criminal-justice, medical, mental-health, and social-service systems. There is no mention of local shelters or women's services, although these are indeed represented on the London Co-ordinating Committee, nor did any of the shelters ask for such a committee. Shelters become just one of a range of services and interested parties, and by no means the most crucial or authoritative one. Municipalities rather than ad hoc or non-governmental agencies such as the United Way are seen as the appropriate site for such committees; they become official state bodies charged with a major co-ordinating function in relation to the social-problem apparatus.

Another recommendation in this category addresses the jurisdictional issue of whose financial responsibility services for battered women should be. A range of funding proposals concerning higher per-diem rates and other sources of income are made by various women's groups without being assigned to particular funding bodies, though COMSOC is implied in those that relate to the per-diem issue. The Ontario Association of Interval and Transition Houses' brief, however, in keeping with remarks by co-ordinator Trudy Don during the hearing, recommends that 'an Interministerial Committee shoud be formed composed of representatives of those ministries under whose jurisdiction the various programs are provided by the Transition Houses would fall: and that this Committee would recommend funding to the Transition Houses from the Ministries for those programs.'[4] This attempt to diversify jurisdiction from COMSOC alone and lodge the issue in different aspects of the social-problem apparatus is not picked up and COMSOC is designated as responsible for funding measures, albeit in consultation with OAITH.[5] The exception is one recommendation with regard to the funding of group-treatment programs for batterers, which names the Ministry of Corrections. Thus services to battered women and their children remain a 'welfare problem.'

Several recommendations that criticize the organization and ideology of power relations between men and women in 'the family' and society in general are transformed into recommendations for 'life-skills,' 'conflict management,' and 'anger control' training as part of the school curriculum. This list puts together practical suggestions from several groups regarding education programs with recommendations from the Social Services department, City of Thunder Bay, which are actually addressed to the provision of counselling services in the area of parent-effectiveness training, pre-marital counselling, and so on.[6] This transformation is more than a mere toning down of language. It is a process whereby the controversial and political aspects of some recommendations are eliminated. They are replaced by the subject-free terminology of violence and the designation of professional services designed to maintain wife-battering as an interactive, relational problem to be treated through education, socialization, and counselling. Questioning 'the family' has been transformed into deploring 'violence.'

One recommendation included in the report in relation to shelter funding comes not from the many funding proposals contained in presentations and briefs, but from discussion with Doris Guyatt from COMSOC during the hearings. In considering possible funding mechanisms, such as changes in the legislative basis for per-diem payments to shelters, the issue of enforcing standards of safety, fire regulations, and staffing was raised. The consequent recommendation for new government legislation to deal with wife-battering, which directs that the bill should 'ensure that the capital and operating cost of transition houses for battered women and their children, including the cost of support services, are adequately funded,' contains the final proviso 'Standards for the houses should be prescribed.'[7] What arose as part of the women's groups' enterprise of getting adequate funding for their services becomes, in this process, a potential issue of control and licensing, extending beyond physical plant to the hiring and credentials of staff. This issue has obvious implications for the ability of women's shelters to hire staff and deliver services within a non-professional framework.

Close to one hundred recommendations put before the committee did not appear in any recognizable form in the report. The majority of these relate to proposals for funding for shelters, programs, facilities, and services. The wife-battering framework adopted in the report allowed for the elimination of any presentations and recommendations that opposed treating wife assault as a matter for the criminal courts. Recommendations that supported funding purely clinical approaches or reduced the issue to the need for alcohol-abuse treatment services were not adopted. The framework also, however, excluded many recommendations that addressed the needs of women who come to shelters, needs that relate to the generally oppressive conditions of women's lives, particularly those of immigrant, native, francophone, and rural women. These are transformed into needs for special services in the areas of language training, interpreters, special facilities, transportation, and so on.

In contrast, the way the framework operated to emphasize the justice system allowed for almost all recommendations put forward concerning policing, court procedures, and judicial practices to be included. Nineteen of the report's forty-five proposals (two recommendations are listed twice in separate categories) concern the justice system in some way, and some, such as recommendation 9, contain more than one recommended change. There are only seven recommendations dealing with the funding of shelters and related services, and three of these are, in fact, interim proposals to take effect while the major recommendations for new legislation are being implemented. The actual ordering of the report places the police and justice-system sections and many of the attendant recommendations before the discussion of transition houses and funding needs. The sequence and the number of recommendations reinforce the importance of addressing the assault aspects of the issue.

To examine the report and note the way in which the 'issue of abuse' is contained by the framework it provides and the recommendations made is not to negate its achievements. Much of the credit for its strengths must go to Richard Johnston, who steered the issue and the process throughout with skill and perseverance. The presence throughout the hearings of Marion Bryden, whose insistence first mounted the initiatives, did much to support the feminist position. Trudy Don and the member groups of OAITH were skilful, moving, and persuasive. Doris Guyatt's bureaucratic acumen and obvious concern for the situation of battered women made her a key participant. The women and men who admitted to being beaten or batterers brought the reality of their experiences before the committee.

Nevertheless, there is a clear element of transformation and compromise in the final product that maintains wife-battering within the family-violence framework, and places an emphasis on the justice system and the co-ordination of aspects of the social-problem apparatus. It also introduces mechanisms for controlling the standards of transition-house accommodation and service provision. The central concern with the functioning of the justice system and the proposed new legislation to be put forward by COMSOC may address women's demands for stable and adequate funding and the necessary protection of women.

It does so, however, at the expense of their repeated demands for control of the issue as one to which they can contribute the most knowledge and expertise. Even more important it does so at the expense of a broader understanding of the dimensions and particulars of oppression in women's lives and the part played in this by the organization of family relations. Some of the consequences can be judged from the government's response to the report, tabled in the Ontario legislature in December 1982.

THE GOVERNMENT'S RESPONSE

In terms of the enterprise of co-ordinating and locating the 'issue of abuse,' the report's immediate impact on the government of the time may seem to be limited and somewhat ambiguous. When we look beyond the issue of direct correspondence, however, it is noticeable that the report is an identifiable part of a considerable change of social consciousness and that a social consensus about the nature and seriousness of wife-battering has been reached within government circles, among professionals, and by 'the public' at large. The report provides a reference point, not only in future government undertakings such as the federal/provincial/territorial meetings of the Ministers Responsible for the the Status of Women that took place in 1984,[8] and later moves to hold the government accountable for progress in the area,[9] but also for professionals and other interested parties seeking a way to grapple with the problem. It provides a framework to relate things to when it comes to publicity and public-education campaigns and so on. This framework may, in fact, be its chief strength and the major achievement of the work done in and through the committee by the women's movement.

When the report was presented to the provincial legislature, no one laughed, which might be seen as an improvement on the reception given to the federal report by Parliament earlier the same year. The minister of Community and Social Services, however, seemed by all accounts to have had what amounts to a tantrum. The brunt of his complaint of extreme disappointment in the work of the committee was directed at the report's endorsement of COMSOC responsibility for funding support and shelter for battered women. His response took the form of a diatribe against men who beat their wives and remain in the family home while women and children are forced to leave and become the responsibility of the taxpayer – his responsibility, in this case. The minister, Frank Drea, refuted facts and figures in the report, called it a rehash of old ground, stated that the recommendations did not go far enough, and accused the committee of writing from a male perspective that 'lets the wife beater off absolutely scot-free.'[10] COMSOC commissioned an internal study at this point to pin-point and specify what aspects of the issue could be rightfully seen as COMSOC's responsibility and what could be rejected as belonging elsewhere, particularly within the jurisdictions of the Justice and Health ministries.[11]

The remaining government members accepted the report more stoically; indeed the various Justice departments had already begun to issue directives to police and courts during the hearings and before the report even came out. The cabinet, however, did not appear anxious to act on its other recommendations and might have shelved the report but for pressure from the two Tory women in the cabinet.[12] In June 1983, Drea announced a new $1.68 million program for assisting women who were victims of family violence in isolated communities in northern Ontario. This was an attempt to capitalize on some residual monies in another program designed to provide construction-industry jobs. It was strictly slated for new buildings, not for the renovation or support of existing services. The information package announcing this program contained more than twenty pages of blueprints, construction requirements, and administrative plans, and fewer than three and a half pages on the provision of services. The buildings were designated as family crisis centres, twelve eight-bed homes (eight in municipalities, four on reserves), designed to serve a target population of abused women and their children, or single mothers, elderly women, and native women in crisis situations. Staffing was to be both minimal and paid at minimum wage, augmented by volunteers. The church was named as first choice for providing this service, with existing women's groups as second choice. No consultation with existing women's groups was undertaken, and negotiations for the project were underway in several communities before the end of the summer.

In October 1983, the deputy premier (minister responsible for women's issues) and the provincial secretary for Justice introduced a platform of government initiatives on family violence: wife battering.[13] These included: the family resource centres already underway; the appointment of a co-ordinator within COMSOC to develop an umbrella program dealing with prevention, protection, and public education concerned with wife abuse, child abuse, and abuse of the elderly; and the appointment of a provincial co-ordinator to bring together and disseminate information on the initiatives and liaise with government departments, non-governmental groups, and policy makers. A steering committee with representatives from Justice, Municipal Affairs, Housing, the Ontario Women's Directorate, and 'Social Policy ministries' was reported as being established to assist the co-ordinator.[14] Also announced were a variety of other measures in relation to public education; standardized protocols for physicians, clergy, police, social workers, and other service providers; and long-term prevention strategies; along with initiatives already taken with regard to police and court procedures. The preamble to the statement of initiatives acknowledged the Canadian Advisory Council on the Status of Women's book, *Wife Battering in Canada: The Vicious Circle*, and several other reports as providing additional impetus for government action, denying that the initiatives were a direct response to the report alone.

The Government Initiatives document, as the main response, shows some of the dangers integral to the problem of locating wife-battering within the framework of family violence, even when defined as assault. It completely ignores the work of women's groups other than the federally appointed advisory council and stresses the dimensions of criminal justice and family support, making men firmly the responsibility of the legal system, while women remain a welfare problem as regards subsistence, but one reduced to victims requiring victim-assistance services when it comes to law. Any suggestion of new legislation is rejected; presumably it is one of the areas where there is, as the document states, 'some divergence of opinion between the Standing Committee and the Ministries of the Ontario Government, on the best way to meet some specific needs of battered wives.'[15] Many recommendations are dismissed as being already covered by ongoing government undertakings such as the development of victim-assistance programs and the expansion of Adult Basic Education and English as a Second Language programs. Proposed stabilization funding for transition houses turned out to be administered in an ad hoc manner, which eventually benefited some houses at the expense of others.[16] The family resources centres have in several instances undercut the existing work of women's groups in the community and provided for services based on traditional social-service lines. The rejection of the committee's omnibus recommendation on legislative change wiped out in one move a whole range of funding requests and options, and left the issue wide open to piecemeal absorption and appropriation, which indeed happened later with the endorsement of the setting up of privatized and volunteer services such as 'safe houses' that provide individualized shelter for individual women and children with none of the supports offered by transition houses.[17]

Despite the equivocal nature of the provincial government's more immediate response to the report, the work of the standing committee encouraged an ongoing commitment to acting on the issue of wife-battering. In 1983, all the provincial ministers responsible for the status of women requested that a report on the situation in regard to wife-battering country-wide be prepared for their 1984 meeting. This report acknowledged the importance of the work of the women's movement, quoted the standing committee's report from Ontario, used a comparable framework in its preamble, and cited, in sections on Ontario, responses and initiatives in indirect but recognizable relation to the standing committee's recommendations.

The issue of wife-battering had been set on the public agenda. Changes had been made in the administrative and policy procedures of the Justice department. The social-problem apparatus at both the federal and the provinical levels had gone through some reorganization in order to accommodate and co-ordinate the issue and the standing committee itself was strengthened in the process of carrying out its task. According to Richard Johnston,[18] the experience of working in a collective non-partisan manner, in a way which made some impact, led to a strengthening of the committee's position. The experience of this committee reflected the climate of the time when not only Ontario but also the federal government and the Parliament at Westminster were actively considering how to expand and strengthen the function of the committee system in the parliamentary process. Johnston suggested that the committee became more influential from that time on and developed a reputation as a powerful force that took on 'heavy-duty issues.' With the election of the minority Liberal government in 1985, Johnston himself became the chair of the committee and felt that the collaborative model produced a good and effective working structure. He suggested to me in a 1987 interview that his 'threat' of bringing the issue of wife-battering back before the committee for review may have been instrumental in precipitating the Liberal government's announcement of a $7 million program for dealing with wife assault in the spring of that year.

OAITH was later called upon to consult with the Ministry of Community and Social Services on a new funding formula for interval and transition houses, only to have one introduced unilaterally in 1988 in the midst of the consultation process. The role assigned to OAITH in the new proposal required the organization to act as mediator between the government and funding to shelters. It was asked to provide the criteria for distributing $1.4 million (according to OAITH a 'mere pittance' in the overall family-violence budget), thus potentially becoming a quasi government funding body without control of the amount allotted to the shelter sector. The funding formula gives the ministry the power to define core services, optimum staffing levels, maximum length of stay for women in the houses, and a number of other items. The formula does not include any permanent investment through capital expenditure and maintains a hostel model for staffing needs.

Working with this formula means that transition, interval house, and family resource centre staff must all focus on residential and crisis components of the service. A staff member from one shelter reports that the result is the undercutting of the staff's ability, operating under severely constrained staffing levels and a lack of financial resources, to provide what they regard as the essential components of a political movement. Advocacy, court support, outreach, and follow-up organizing; public education; and non-residential support – all of which allow for some measure of movement building – fall outside the funding definition. In addition, residence requirements, which vary from a few days to six weeks, militate against long-term changes in women's lives and precipitate the return of many women to abusive husbands.[19]

The point in this review has not been to prove or disprove the exact effect of the work of the standing committee and its report on the actions of the Ontario government in the provision of solutions to the 'issue of abuse,' now conceptualized as wife assault. The report stimulated administrative co-ordination between departments and levels of government, some adjustment in the procedures of the justice system, a legitimization of the problem and its nature, the rejection of prior formulations as 'myths,' and a 'correction' of attitudes. It organized the relationship between agencies and institutions at the local level to government policies and procedures, designating transition houses as one of many necessary solutions and OAITH and other shelter workers as expert consultants. It also allowed some reorganization of the committee's position and some shift of internal power balance within the provincial government in this regard.

The total impact on what the provincial government did and continues to do is important, but is part of an ongoing political process that continues beyond the events researched in this study. The argument here has concerned how the issue was raised and how it was transformed in the existing political process, even by individuals and a committee generally sympathetic to and concerned about the situation of battered women. In seeing how it came to take on a particular ideological character that made it part of the ruling process of aligning issues to a social-problem apparatus, we see the transformation in action in the practical activities of the participants. These activities, in turn, were part of a social relation involving the development of a discourse on wife-battering and family violence constructed elsewhere but available to the committee through the work of its informants and researchers. In this process, the 'issue of abuse' came to be understood as one of faulty or outdated attitudes and institutions, inappropriate socialization, anachronistic sex-role stereotypes, pathological masculinity, passive femininity, and unequal treatment under the law in a society given to 'violence.'

The state was then prepared to concede that 'violence' is wrong in any context except self-defence, even, or perhaps especially, in the intimate relationships of family life. The potential of all men to be violent is represented in the 10 per cent or so who are presumed to engage in wife-battering and they must be seen as committing acts of criminal assault that should be prosecuted, so that such 'behaviour' can be eliminated at best, or at least managed. Here feminist strategy meets ruling strategy and provides the state with a new population of individuals to work on. Individual women's right to protection by law as expressed in the principle of 'the inviolability of the person' can thus come to have precedence over men's right to assert their authority in the family by means of force. Family relations are no longer private matters; child-welfare legislation has long superseded the right of parents to absolute power over their children. The framework of wife assault as a subset of family violence begins to introduce mechanisms for state intervention into the activities of men in what has heretofore in this regard been the mostly private domain of the family. Although such intervention may provide some recognition and support for individual women who must leave violent men and care for their children on their own, the fundamental organization of 'the family' in a capitalist and patriarchal society remains untouched.

CONCLUSION

This chapter considered the impact of the report and looked at what it allowed for as different ways of lodging wife-battering in various locations within the social-problem apparatus. The key concepts that have been shown to form the framework adopted in the report are features of the transformative process that emerges from an examination of the report. 'Wife-battering' defined as 'assault' and designated as a subset of 'family violence' provides for a reorganization of relations, a redistribution of tasks, and a differentiated division of labour when it comes to the work of the women's movement, professional agencies, and the state. The result is a further depoliticization of the issue from one that potentially mobilizes women to challenge procedures, practices, and structures that are oppressive into an abstracted mode in which a hitherto unacknowledged aspect of 'violence' must be controlled by the state. The issue is thus transformed into a matter of individual rights and the equitable administration of the law, backed up by and co-ordinated with a range of social-service supports.

This formulation of the issue is the end-product of a particular instance of the generalizing relation being traced in this study. In the case of the hearings before the Ontario legislature's Standing Committee on Social Development, a manoeuvre to get the provincial government to address the issue directly became a process of conceptual co-ordination that provided for some changes in state practices. The changes include some commitment to a concerted approach through the creation of departmental and interdepartmental positions within the bureaucracy with responsibility for initiating and co-ordinating government response. While government action did take up some of the concerns advanced by OAITH in its attempts to pressure MPPs and ministers, it did so in ways that eventually undercut the work of women's movement organizations. Neither secure and adequate funding nor control of the issue by women's movement experts have proved to be the long-term outcomes of the enterprise. This realization returns us to the debate in which my initial dilemma was grounded and sets up the contradiction once again. How is it that in the women's movement we seem to get what we want, we achieve some measure of success, we appear to make some impact, yet we find that the process that advances our cause also incorporates it into the very institutions against which we struggle? Control slips away and what we get turns out not to be what we wanted after all. The concluding chapter draws together some of the themes that emerged from the analysis of the process studied here and raised questions about aspects of our own practices that, in Morgan's words, 'keep us on a treadmill of ineffective organizing.'[20]

12 Conceptual Practices and the Relations of Ruling

In this study I looked at one aspect of the dilemmas and contradictions women face as feminists when they seek to enter into the political process in order to redress the difficulties and dangers in their lives. I began my introduction to the book by locating my work in a process of reviewing the activities of the women's movement and the relationship of women to the state. I set out to address the analytic gap that Morgan proposes as a crucial site for analysis of the organizing practices of social movements and the ruling practices of the state (understood here as a set of social relations). Addressing this gap commits us to analysing both the internal contraditions within social movements and the actual processes of state action.[1] These processes, which Morgan identifies as bureaucratization, individualization, and professionalization, can be seen in operation in the relations studied here. They are processes that fragment class and structural issues into single issues, creating artificial categories that can then be reconstructed into the problems of a 'mass of individuals.' They also impose hierarchical stratification on collective 'non-capitalist' forms of organizing by appropriating knowledge and monopolizing the power to define and provide for those in need.[2]

In the case in point, such processes have operated to frame wife-battering as a problem of the individual rights of women to protection from the violent acts of individual men. Their needs are segmented and entered into the legal system for protection; the welfare system for financial support; the mental-health system for counselling; the education system for job training, language training, and so on. Women become 'battered wives,' men 'wife-batterers.' Formulations such as 'deindividuated violence' or 'male violence' perform the function of reconstructing the problem as one involving a mass of individuals.

Feminist organizations struggle to maintain collective structures and the control of definitions of the problem in the face of professional reformulations of 'family violence' and state regulation of funding and licensing procedures. Oppositional discourses are incorporated into the academic and policy discourses that family violence references.

Morgan's characterization of the contradictions within the women's movement as those between humanist and political goals is useful in charting the strategies that allowed feminists with different and conflicting positions to put forward the issue in a way that established its legitimacy. In doing so, they evoked the moral claim of women and children in danger to crisis services providing shelter and support. Her characterization does not, however, fully capture the complexity of the struggles within the movement, but rather converts them into a matter of competition between abstract philosophies and goals. The events studied here indicate a process arising partly from the ferment within the movement over how to account for women's experience and men's actions and partly from attempts to present the issue in differentiated forms both to gain resources from the state and to demand changes in state procedures and practices.

ORGANIZING THEMES

In bringing forward the analytic task Morgan identifies, I have attempted to extend her enquiry by looking both at the contradictions within the women's movement and at the state's institutional and administrative procedures as they interact in a process of institutional absorption.

The stages of the process and its conceptual organization, development, and reorganization were not self-evident when I embarked on this enquiry. The transcripts of the Ontario hearings, the preliminary sessions that led up to them, and the report could have provided the basis for many possible arguments and analyses. Finding the focus that illuminated the particular social relation explicating the involvement of women's organizations, their input into and their impact on the outcome in relation to the Ontario government, was a process of elimination. To assemble the elements that would contextualize the hearings within the generalizing relation as it applies to the absorption of this particular issue of the women's movement, I used my own experience and prior efforts at analysing the various events that became the entry point for the study. I also used a wealth of material that made up the current discourse of family violence and the oppositional discourse of violence against women. The extreme confusion I experienced in trying to make sense of these procedures, knowledge-making practices and activities, some of which I had taken part in, seemed at first like a problem of my own intellectual limitations. As the work of investigation proceeded, however, it proved to be a feature of the opaque nature of ideological practices and the equivocal role of the professional in the social construction of knowledge. In reviewing the themes as they arise in the study, therefore, I will draw attention to them as building-blocks in my understanding of the process being traced.

Chapter 1, setting up the problematic for the study and the method used, identified professional practices of knowledge-making as implicated in the relations of ruling. Being thus implicated poses a dilemma for activists concerned with changing these relations when they must introduce their own knowledge and practices into the channels that the state legitimizes as avenues for change. Three stages in the development of the process of absorption of a women's issue into the institutional procedures of the state mark the conceptual shifts that are the major themes of the study.

Chapter 2 looked at the struggle within the women's movement to find a way to think about and account for the situation of women being beaten and brutalized in their homes, in order to make sense of it in the context of the ferment of positions concerning the overall determinates of women's oppression. This struggle took place, in Vancouver at least, in concert with one against professionals attempting to address the issue in terms of the responsibility of social-service and legal institutions to respond to an emerging social problem. The work of the United Way carried the issue forward from the grass-roots work of women's organizations into the sphere of professional agencies and institutions. The recommendations of its task force report provided a framework for understanding family violence and locating it in institutional and administrative procedures. These were very similar to those recommended later by the Ontario legislature's standing committee, but the location of the United Way as mediator between community and local state was not articulated fully into the legislative process or the social-problem apparatus and its impact was restricted to local agencies in Vancouver and other parts of the country.

The events described in chapter 3 show the work of assembling concerted conceptual positions that are being translated to the purview of the state at the federal level. The generalizing relation was mediated by the work of the Canadian Advisory Council on the Status of Women and in subsequent developments in the work of women's organizations. Though an oppositional discourse on wife-battering was being developed in the women's movement, it was already being modified and differentiated by being aligned with the various sites within the state that could be pressured to respond. As we formulated and reformulated the procedures for putting our voice forward, a line of development onto the terrain of the state marked by defining wife-battering as assault, aligned the issue with various aspects of the criminal-justice system.

Chapter 4 examined what can be learned from an analysis of some of the documentary processes contained in two reports that demonstrated a second line of development on the terrain of the state. This development initially made family violence the responsibility of the social-service, health-care, mental-health, and education divisions of the state's social-problem apparatus. A third report, that of the Federal Standing Committee on Health, Welfare and Social Affairs, shows how subsequent work by women's movement organizations resulted in a modification and the beginnings of a merging of the two lines of development. This report contains a recognition of the gendered aspects of family violence, a focus on wife-battering, and a determination of the issue as one of assault requiring improved legal sanctions to protect individuals within the family.

The conceptual frameworks that both develop from and contribute to this process of merging can be discovered in the social-science discourses of family violence and wife-battering produced by the work practices of academics. Chapter 5 theorizes the process whereby existing discourse was reworked to incorporate the oppositional discourse provided by feminist knowledge and critiques of prior formulations. The forms of existing discourse, however, also determined the approach of a number of feminist scholars. These two forms of determination and appropriation contribute much of the confusion experienced by scholars and researchers trying to make sense of the process of knowledge-making in relation to the issue.

Chapter 6 recapitulates and draws together the conceptual aspects of the process studied so far. In it, I identify the key role of the concept of 'violence' in two major processes of redefinition with regard to the lines of development identified previously. The first occurred within the women's movement and marked the emergence of 'violence against women' or 'male violence' as a central theme and organizing force in the movement. The second involves recognizing the technical, administrative properties of the concept of 'family violence' in organizing the state's response to pressure to deal with wife-battering as a problem identified as stemming from violence within the family. The interaction established by the acceptance of the definition of wife assault as a criminal act set up 'violence' as the crucial issue to be addressed and controlled. For the women's movement, controlling violence meant changing power relations between women and men by punishing men for enforcing dominance by violent acts. For the state, it meant punishing men who break laws designed to uphold the state's monopoly over the use of force.

The second part of the book considers how these elements both raised and limited the possibilities for action when the issue, as it had been generalized at the federal level, was brought forward to be acted on by the government of Ontario. This level has jurisdiction over the major sites in which possibilities for lodging the issue exist. Chapter 7 describes the strategies used by the Ontario Association of Interval and Transition Houses to pressure members of the government to consider wife-battering and how one of the opposition parties took up 'the issue of abuse' and had it referred to the legislature's all-party Standing Committee on Social Development. As a result of these manoeuvres the committee decided to set up public hearings. It called on members of the ministries of Community and Social Service and the Attorney General for information, defined the parameters of the issue to be addressed as spouse abuse, and heard evidence of the inadequacies of existing institutional responses. The committee was introduced to the discourse on wife-battering and the work of women's movement organizations by one of the comsoc representatives, who was instrumental in framing the issue as one of wife-battering in the context of violence in the family. In this process the committee began to develop the conceptual tools needed to come to grips with the issue.

With the advent of the public hearings themselves, described in chapters 8 and 9, the elements of a framework for eliciting government response were put in place in a process of conceptual co-ordination. Chapter 8 concentrated on two presentations in which the already modified lines of development were further integrated to support a framework in which the committee could come to terms with the issue. The presentation by the representative of OAITH avoided any one particular definition and put forward information that carefully matched the range of needs of battered women, their children, and their abusers with different areas within the social-problem apparatus. The second presentation from the London Alternatives to Violence Project set up a framework for understanding men's violence in the family as a matter for criminal sanctions and clinical treatment. In this presentation the role of the police and the courts was specified as the laying of charges, prosecution by the Crown, and adequate sentencing procedures, including mandatory treatment where therapy groups are available. The needs of women and children are to be met by a network of social services, including emergency shelters. These services are co-ordinated with the work of the justice system in order to relieve the police of tasks more appropriate to the mandate of mental-health and social-service professionals. The testimony considered in chapter 9 displayed the suggestions put before the committee concerning how the different elements of the framework of wife-battering as assault under the law should be prioritized and co-ordinated. The impact of this testimony can be judged by the way in which the committee members questioned the actions of the province's attorney general and insisted that his department and that of the solicitor general take action to improve and co-ordinate the handling of cases of wife assault.

The work of the committee and its witnesses culminated in the production of a report, an analysis of which is undertaken in chapter 10. In it can be seen the results of the process of presenting, modifying, transforming, and containing the issue of abuse. The framework developed in the process of the initial meetings and the public hearings operated to organize the content and emphasis of the material it contained. This material was shaped to legitimate specific recommendations to different government departments as to how they should be responding to the issue. The central definition of wife assault as a subset of family violence provided the conceptual co-ordination that correlated different aspects of the social-problem apparatus with each other and with the problem.

In chapter 10 and in the discussion that follows in chapter 11, the report is treated as a part of the social relation being explicated in this study. The process of generalization moved the issue from local 'support services,' in the context of the mobilization of a women's movement committed to struggling to end women's oppression, to a full-blown social problem to be addressed by the provision of integrated and co-ordinated services to victims of violence. The resulting government initiatives provided for some services to be professionally controlled and others to be offered on a privatized, minimally funded or volunteer basis. Policies proposed fall far short of a serious challenge to the organization of 'the family' and indeed reinforce unified family services while failing to expand shelters in a feminist direction. Aspects of the issue are addressed, but the bases of women's oppression remain unchallenged.

ANALYSING CONCEPTS AND RULING PRACTICES

The study shows some of the practices of the women's movement as it struggled to put forward this particular aspect of women's experience. Part of this process involved the development of conceptual tools that would grapple with the ways in which the state operates to handle problems when they are raised as public issues. I have been concerned with the ways in which our thinking had to be organized so that the state, through its social-problem apparatus, could be induced, shamed, or pressured to respond. Wife-battering was first linked with 'family violence' to provide a connection with existing family policies and service agencies. The struggle to include wife assault introduced the possibility that sanctions already existing in the Criminal Code could be invoked. In the process of articulating government agencies and institutions, however, aspects of the mobilization of a movement for political change got lost. The work done with battered women has become, in many cases, the site for professional and voluntary service provision, which overrides the consciousness-raising elements of link-ages with a fully mobilized women's movement and the other issues involved in the struggle against women's oppression. Working in women's shelters becomes, for some, part of a career process in which to develop experience and expertise as social-service workers or use existing skills to provide services. This focus is not in itself negative or culpable, but it is assimilative. It operates as part of the way in which women's movement representatives come to be professionalized as experts speaking for and about battered women.

The contradiction embodied in this process of professionalization lies in the fact that its very success eliminates the possibility of a more radical critique. This is not a new problem, or one confined to the 'battered women's movement' or the 'shelter movement,' or what is more commonly known in Canada as the 'transition house movement.' The professionalization and attendant insitutionalization of social move-ments have a long history that can be traced in the roots of aspects of social work, education (particularly adult education), labour and popular health movements, and the initiatives of the previous wave of feminist organizing. They raise issues of the reproduction of class relations in a division of labour and the place in these processes of state practices. The extent to which what is shown here has class implications is revealed in the fact that the conceptually co-ordinated organization of state responses to wife-battering creates divisions between volunteer and paid-staff working shelters while making women using transition houses a welfare problem. Indeed, an informant suggested to me that shelters have become the new 'poorhouses,' with all the attendant stigma that word implies. The emphasis on the criminal-justice system specifically obscures the different experiences and locations in the social structure of black, minority, native, and immigrant women and also white working-class women. The very clear class differences between the men who appear before the committee as batterers cannot be accounted for, except in ideological terms set up by the framework that designates family violence as crossing all cultures and classes. The implications of criminalization and its clinical correlates as a protective and 'preventive' strategy for different segments of the population are hidden from view, let alone discussion.

CONCLUSION

The clinical dimension of the concept of violence links together the two lines of development of family violence and male violence to give them a particular character. What is important in the process studied here is not the specifics of the recommendations to a particular provincial government, which may or may not have been acted on, but the framework for action that has been set up. The process gathers up local and particular threads, homogenizes and co-ordinates them, and then allows for the reapplication of the definition or diagnosis and standardized solutions to the local level through appropriate divisions of the social-problem apparatus. The particular dimension of situations that may relate to gender, class location, racial or ethnic background, the abuse of alcohol, or any other way in which we might understand what is going on are eliminated. Violence as a concept becomes the actor or motivator, allowing for the development of methodologies by means of which it can be studied as a single phenomenon and theories formed, regardless of context or consequences. A wide range of actions can be treated as comparable and ranked accordingly. As a result data can be produced that make claims that women are in fact more violent than men.[3] Feminist concerns about the coercion and abuse of women and children in the context of oppression and inequality are subsumed under theories of a sick society in which individuals can be prosecuted but basically need treatment and cure.

As I write the final revisions to this study, people across the country are recoiling in shock and horror from news of the killing of fourteen women and the wounding of a number of other women and men at the University of Montreal. As we seek to make sense of this seemingly senseless act, concepts of violence come into play. Some politicians and editorial writers hasten to deplore random violence and the delinquency of 'youth,' calling for tighter gun controls and security measures. Other voices, among them some who speak for the women's movement, have been quick to name the tragedy as manifestation of women's ongoing scapegoating and victimization as objects of men's hatred and violence. Both positions generalize and abstract the event in ways that divert our attention from the particular circumstances and context. Still other feminists have clearly identified these murders as a political act. It appears from available reports that an enraged young man specifically selected as his target women studying in a department of engineering to which he had been refused admission. He shot them, these analysts point out, not just because they were women but because they were women who had stepped out of their place. As such, they were, in his eyes, feminists, and responsible for his failure and despair. This analysis makes it clear that lack of acknowledgment of the specific context and target of this horrifying act allows us to deplore it as violence but does not provide any way of holding accountable the activities of the state and the media over the years in trivializing, marginalizing, and increasingly (to use Michele Landsberg's term) 'demonizing' feminism.[4]

Feminism and struggles for women's rights have been scapegoated and discredited many times in the past. After both world wars, for example, 'sex antagonism' and a focus on women's demands were characterized as selfish and unpatriotic impediments to the building of a brave new world. Careful historical work in the United States by both Pleck and Gordon argues that previous campaigns and crusades for the relief of women and children being cruelly treated by their male relatives were defeated and dispersed by forces upholding the patriarchal family. Pleck sees the Victorian wave of feminist organizing on the issue faltering on the rocks of divorce, which was too threatening a barrier even for feminist supporters. Both she and Gordon see the next wave of crusaders as being betrayed and undermined by professionals, particularly psychiatrists and social workers, who transformed existing criminal explanations of men's behaviour into sophisticated victim-blaming theories of female masochism and seduction.[5] Morgan insists that the current struggle in the United States has been appropriated into a different range of professional interventions from the social-problem apparatus in the form of court diversion programs; welfare provisions; and alcohol, drug, and family treatment programs.[6] In Canada feminists working in the areas of wife-battering, rape, and incest have had some success in restoring earlier definitions of 'crimes against women,' evoking societal sanctions of violence as assault. The clinical focus adopted by professionals, however, is now directed towards men, not as brutish by nature but as unable to handle their feelings and themselves victims of cycles of violence, violent families, and a violent society.

Family violence as ideology operates to turn away the feminist focus on the gendered organization of power relations in the family. Far from 'engendering violence,' as de Lauretis suggests,[7] it degenders it. A recent example of this in operation took place in the federal government's consultation 'Working Together: 1989 National Forum on Family Violence.' Billed as a 'working' forum for family-violence experts, its promotional material made it clear that these experts represent some 'special needs' groups. The word 'women' appears only once in a list of populations with special concerns. The word 'men' does not appear at all, nor is there any mention of shelters or the work of the women's movement. Accounts from participants describe the organization of the forum as preventing dialogue between presenters and participants. The workshops in which new strategies and directions were to be developed were specifically composed of a selected range of people working in different areas, such as wife assault, child abuse, elder abuse, child sexual abuse, and rape. This organization made it structurally impossible to find a common ground on which to 'work together.' Participants from other areas were disgruntled with what they perceived to be 'too much emphasis on wife assault,' and one participant reported afterwards that her group was instructed 'not to let the feminists have it all their own way.' Eventually feminist caucuses were set up by women withdrawing from the main agenda, and they protested against the format, emphasis, and artificial structure. Yet again the struggle was enjoined between the movement and the state; the role of family violence as an organizing concept in the struggle was evident.[8]

I want to emphasize that setting in place an analysis of the social relation explicating conceptual practices implicated in the process of ruling is not a matter of moral judgment. I am not saying that mobilizing women's movement strategies around issues of 'violence' was in some way reprehensible. It is a matter of a particular division of labour among aspects of the work, so that different pieces of the problem can be addressed. It is also a matter of seeing how social relations are socially constructed. In tracing these social relations, I attempt not to proceed ideologically, by starting with concepts to be defined and discovered, but to discover instead how concepts are themselves organized, as part of a social relation. In this context concepts are technical work processes that organize both phenomena and courses of action, and thus their construction is integral to social relations. Categories and concepts of ideologies *substitute* the expression of a textually mediated discourse for actual relations (actual practices, work processes, and the organization of practical knowledge of actual individuals). Thus an examination of the actual relations, practices, and processes, and the discursive forms substituted for them, reveals the ideological features of social organization.

The commitment to working with the women who came to transition houses and other women's projects did not stem from humanist goals alone, nor was it only professionally oriented 'liberal' feminists or anti-professional 'radical' feminists who took on the work and struggled with one another over how to do it. It came directly from an understanding of the connection of the personal and the political and a commitment to work with the most personal and intimate forms of oppression while trying to change the broader structures in which they arise. The sheer pressure of the demands for shelter led to a situation in which the same women could not work at both levels at the same time and resulted in a division of labour that eventually became a division between 'services' and 'service providers' and those doing more 'political' work, lobbying and representing women's shelters and organizations. The work of the women's movement is atomized as women work in transition houses, in victim-assistance programs, in advocacy clinics, and so on.

I have not found it useful, in exploring the instance of incorporation and absorption described in this book, to talk about the rifts, divisions, and battles within the women's movement in terms of the categories of feminist theory. The struggles that took place could be reconceptualized in terms of liberal, Marxist/socialist or radical-feminist positions. Such reconceptualizing would, I suggest, impose an ideological organization on our actual experiences and practices, generalizing the particular in relation to political divisions that correspond to organized political structures outside the movement. Many of the divisions we now characterize in this manner were not how we thought about the situation then, and themselves arise out of or were organized by the different strategies available for taking up our 'issues.'

Women became involved in often bitter struggles over whom we could or could not work with and how the work should proceed. Conflicting analyses and strategies came out of the different skills, experience, and understanding women brought into the movement and those that were developed as we worked, struggled, and changed. Often women with professional training attempted to put aside practices that created power differentials between women but, as the demand intensified and the work became overburdening, women tended to take on the tasks that they knew how to do. Entering the political process brings us together to work for change, yet at the same time provides for a dispersal, a division of labour, a fragmentation of our political, mobilizing force. That sets up the contradictions; they are not merely a matter of attitudes, power plays, personal ambition, and so on.

To see the work done by women as taking on some of the characteristics of a career path, however, is descriptive rather than judgmental. My own experience of seeking to use my training and skills to develop ways of working as a feminist that would avoid the process of professionalization has highlighted the dilemma for me. The division of labour takes on a further aspect when those of us who are academics and researchers situate our work at the level of analysis. Riddington, writing about the delivery of feminist 'services,'[9] suggests that, as feminism develops increasingly complex analytic positions, we can no longer identify with women who come into contact with the movement for the first time. These women need the basic consciousness-raising experiences that were common to us all in the early stages.

An aspect of the dilemma being raised can then be seen as one of maintaining the grounding of movement women in the everyday oppression that is shared by women in all its different locations of class and race. 'Issue politics,' formulated in relation to state practices, provides for the creation of isolated organizations. Ideological constructs such as 'the battered wife' have lifted the experience of women who are beaten and abused out of the general experiences of women and made wife-battering available as an issue to be absorbed into the social-problem apparatus. The task of relocating it in the broader structures of the reproduction of relations of domination and control, which are the relations of ruling, forces the women's movement to address the relation of knowledge and power as one of a range of ways in which we are incorporated into them.

Recently I talked about my study with one of the women who was a key participant in the events being analysed. She was excited by the possibility of finding ways to recover the potential for political mobilization eroded away by processes such as those addressed here. Talking about her years in the transition-house movement, she wondered whether we had achieved anything beyond creating a lot of (poorly paid) jobs for feminists in transition houses. 'Sometimes,' she said, 'we seem to have come a long way. But when I think about what a woman faces when she leaves a transition house, what her options are, I think things are if anything, worse. There is little available low-cost housing, the gap between women's and men's wages is increasing in many areas, there are few decent jobs, no affordable day care – nothing.'

While I think she was underestimating the enormous impact on the lives of women who are battered of the heightened awareness created by the work of the women's movement, and indeed the number of women's lives saved by shelters over the years, I recognize as central the dilemma she raises. This book does not resolve it, but attempts to move our efforts forward by uncovering for our understanding a feature of how our work comes to be organized against us by the processes we engage in. The development of strategies for political action to change the oppressive conditions of women's lives, without being appropriated through our interactions with the ruling apparatus and participation in the relations of ruling, is the task that confronts the women's movement as it moves into the 1990s.

Notes

CHAPTER 1: The Women's Movement and the Relations of Ruling

1 See, for example, publications such as *Resources for Feminist Research*, Vol. 15, No. 1 (March 1986), entitled 'Issue of the Decade: Feminists and State Processes.' The exploration of the impact of state practices on women's lives has also been integrated into scholarship taking up issues of state formation, particularly by Marxists and neo-Marxists: M. McIntosh, 'The State and the Oppression of Women,' M. Barrett, *Women's Oppression Today: Problems in Marxist Feminist Analysis*, E. Wilson, *Women and the Welfare State*, J. Jenson, 'Gender and Reproduction: Or, Babies and the State,' C.A. MacKinnon, 'Feminism, Marxism, Method, and the State: Toward Feminist Jurisprudence,' and Z. Eisenstein, *The Radical Future of Liberal Feminism*, have all contributed to the debate, as have many others.
2 A. Schreader, 'Professionalism and Its Implications for Women'; S. Findlay, 'The Politics of the Women's Movement: Lobbying Our Way to the Revolution' and 'Facing the State: The Politics of the Women's Movement Reconsidered'
3 Working Group on Sexual Violence, *Feminist Manifesto*; J. Barnsley, *Feminist Action, Institutional Reaction: Responses to Wife Assault*; S. Findlay, 'The Politics of the Women's Movement,' 'Struggles within the State: The Feminist Challenge to Hegemony,' and 'Defining the Political: Creeping Pluralism and the Decline of the State/Capital Imperative'
4 See, for example, sessions organized by myself and Roxana Ng at the Canadian Anthropology and Sociology Association Meetings in 1984, 1985, and 1986.
5 See, for example, E. Wilson and A. Weir, *Hidden Agendas: Theory, Politics, and Experience in the Women's Movement*; L. Segal, *Is the Future Female?*

Troubled Thoughts on Contemporary Feminism; A. Oakley and J. Mitchell, eds., *What Is Feminism?: A Re-examination*; R. Hamilton and M. Barrett, *The Politics of Diversity: Feminism, Marxism and Nationalism.*

6 D.E. Smith, *The Everyday World as Problematic: A Feminist Sociology*, p. 93

7 D.E. Smith, 'Women and Psychiatry' and 'Women and the Politics of Professionalism'; E. Wilson, *Women and the Welfare State* and 'Feminism and Social Work'

8 R. Ng, 'Immigrant Women and the State: Toward an Analytic Framework'

9 R. Ng, *The Politics of Community Services* and 'Immigrant Women and the State: A Study in the Social Organization of Knowledge'; M.L. Campbell, 'Information Systems and Management of Hospital Nursing: A Study in Social Organization of Knowledge'; A. Griffith, 'Ideology, Education and Single Parent Families: The Normative Ordering of Families through Schooling'; A. Mueller, 'Peasants and Professionals: The Social Organization of Women in Development Knowledge'

10 K.J. Tierney, 'The Battered Woman Movement and the Creation of the Wife Beating Problem'; S. Schechter, *Women and Male Violence: The Visions and Struggles of the Battered Women's Movement*; P. Morgan, 'From Battered Wife to Program Client: The State's Shaping of Social Problems'

11 See, particularly, Morgan, 'From Battered Wife to Program Client,' and Schechter, *Women and Male Violence.*

12 Schechter, *Women and Male Violence*, has done an excellent and comprehensive job of such an historical analysis in relation to the u.s. experience.

13 Tierney, 'The Battered Woman Movement,' uses such a framework to describe the fate of the feminist activist approach in the United States.

14 Morgan, 'From Battered Wife to Program Client,' p. 17

15 Ibid., p. 18

16 Ng, 'Immigrant Women and the State,' p. 1

17 Ibid.

18 Ibid., p. 2

19 Morgan, 'From Battered Wife to Program Client,' p. 19

20 Ng, *The Politics of Community Services*

21 Mueller, '*Presents and Professionals*'

22 D.E. Smith, 'The Social Construction of Documentary Reality,' 'The Ideological Practice of Sociology,' 'Institutional Ethnography: A Method of Sociology for Women,' 'No One Commits Suicide: Textual Analysis of Ideological Practices,' 'Textually-Mediated Social Organization,' 'Institutional Ethnography: A Feminist Method'

23 K. Marx and F. Engels, *The German Ideology*

24 D.E. Smith, 'Feminity as Discourse' and 'Institutional Ethnography: A Feminist Method'

25 Smith, *The Everyday World as Problematic* p. 3
26 Marx and Engels, *The German Ideology*
27 Schreader, 'Professionalism and Its Implications for Women,' p. 1
28 A. Gramsci, *Prison Note Books*
29 Smith, 'The Social Construction of Documentary Reality' and 'Women and Psychiatry'
30 D.E. Smith, 'A Peculiar Eclipsing: Women's Exclusion from Men's Culture,' p. 282
31 J. Kelly-Gadol, 'The Social Relations of the Sexes: Methodological Implications of Women's History'
32 Smith, 'Women and the Politics of Professionalism,' p. 12
33 Smith, 'Institutional Ethnography: A method of Sociology for Women,' p. 171
34 Smith, 'Women and the Politics of Professionalism,' p. 19
35 'A cosmetic quibble' is how a leading bureaucrat described to me the objections raised by women and men concerned with the terminology and title of the Canadian Association of Social Workers' Task Force on Spouse Abuse.
36 M. Selucky, 'Police Response to Wife Battering,' pp. 23–4
37 Cited in A. Griffith, 'Single Parent Families: The Category as Ideology,' p. 7
38 Adele Mueller, personal communication, 1986
39 Smith, 'Institutional Ethnography: A Feminist method,' p. 8
40 Ibid.
41 Ibid.
42 Ibid.
43 Ibid.
44 Ibid.
45 Ibid.
46 Ibid.
47 Ontario Association of Interval and Transition Houses, *Press Release*, 16 April 1987
48 See, for example, M. Roy, *Battered Women: A Psychosocial Study of Domestic Violence*, and E. Hilberman and K. Munson, 'Sixty Battered Women.'
49 Morgan, 'From Battered Wife to Program Client,' p. 19

CHAPTER 2: The Entry Point: Raising the Issue of 'Wife-Battering'

1 P. Morgan, 'From Battered Wife to Program Client: The State's Shaping of Social Problems,' p. 19
2 J. Barnsley, *Feminist Action, Institutional Reaction: Responses to Wife Assault*, p. 19

3 Cited in Barnsley, ibid.

4 J. Downey and J. Howell, *Wife Battering: A Review and Preliminary Enquiry into Local Incidence, Needs, and Resources*, p. 93

5 Ibid.

6 Barnsley, *Feminist Action, Institutional Reaction*, p. 21

7 Ibid.

8 Organizations such as the United Way function to gather up new populations; designate them as deserving of services; and connect them with appropriate government funding, either directly or through local agencies funded by United Way and various other sources, including joint funding arrangements with local social-welfare departments.

9 Professor of Social Work and member of the planning committee, W. Nichols, private conversation, 1980

10 M.A. Straus, 'A General Systems Theory Approach to a Theory of Violence between Family Members,' 'Leveling, Civility and Violence in the Family,' and 'Sexual Inequality, Cultural Norms, and Wife Beating'

11 Barnsley, *Feminist Action, Institutional Reaction*, p. 25

12 G. Errington, 'Family Violence – Is It a Women's Problem?'

13 The work of this task force has been analysed in some detail by me and by Barnsley in an attempt to understand the interaction between the women's movement and various institutional representatives. Here I will just try to summarize how the experience appeared at the time to those of us involved, leaving an analysis of its significance to a later point.

14 Barnsley, *Feminist Action, Institutional Reaction*, p. 51; G.A. Walker, 'Doing it the United Way: A Preliminary Look at the Dilemma of Women and Professionalism in Action,' p. 25. The co-ordinator told me at one time that one of the major feminist participants 'only has one spiel and we don't want to hear it again.'

15 E. Pizzey, *Scream Quietly or the Neighbours Will Hear*

16 For this distinction, see Diana Russel's introduction to Del Martin's *Battered Wives*.

CHAPTER 3: Translating the Issue to the Purview of the State

1 For a description of this and a specific history of the movement to that point, see Lynn Teather, 'The Feminist Mosaic.'

2 G. Matheson, ed., *Women in the Canadian Mosaic*; Canadian Women's Educational Press, *Women Unite*; M. Stephenson, ed., *Women in Canada*

3 The texts cited above regarding the developing discourse of the early 1970s make no mention of rape, incest, sexual harassment, or wife-battering as

part of women's experience or as areas of concern to the movement.

4 This account of the federal government's plan of action is taken from the proceedings reported in L. MacLeod, *Wife Battering Is Everywoman's Issue: A Summary Report of the CACSW Consultation on Wife Battering*, p. 19

5 L. MacLeod, *Wife Battering in Canada: The Vicious Circle*, p. 1

6 MacLeod, *Wife Battering Is Everywoman's Issue*, p. 1

7 Ibid., p. 2

8 Ibid., p. 37

9 Ibid., p. 1

10 Ibid., p. 2

11 Ibid., frontispiece, cited from a presentation by Joyce Hayden, Trudy Don, and Connie Chapman, 7 March 1980

12 Ibid., p. 3

13 Ibid.

14 Ibid.

15 Ibid, pp. 21 and 24

16 Our efforts to present and analyse the United Way experience were not well received by other task force members, particularly the co-ordinator. The consultation itself had created considerable conflict among movement women in Quebec. Participants later received a letter written by women from several transition houses and other groups, objecting to the selection process and challenging the representativeness of those who attended the consultation from Quebec.

17 MacLeod, *Wife Battering Is Everywoman's Issue*, p. 37

18 MacLeod, *Wife Battering in Canada*, pp. 61–3

19 Since their appearance before the hearings, the group has renamed itself 'Education Wife Assault.' We in Vancouver were in contact with this group from its early days and exchanged brochures, information, and ideas.

20 MacLeod, *Wife Battering Is Everywoman's Issue*, Addendum

21 Cited in F. Macleod, ed., *Report of the Task Force on Family Violence*, Appendix III, p. 1

22 See, for example, the Task Force on Spouse Abuse set up by the Canadian Association of Social Workers, in 1980–1.

23 House of Commons, Standing Committee on Health, Welfare and Social Affairs, *Report on Violence in the Family: Wife Battering*, p. 3

24 *Hansard*, 28 January 1982, p. 9

25 Ibid., p. 10

26 *Hansard*, 11 February 1982, p. 4

27 *Hansard*, 18 February 1982, p. 9

28 Ibid., p. 31

CHAPTER 4: Documents as Organizers

1 J. Downey and J. Howell, *Wife Battering: A Review and Preliminary Enquiry into Local Incidence, Needs, and Resources*
2 Ibid., p. 1
3 Ibid., p. 2
4 Ibid., p. 3
5 Ibid., p. 4
6 Barnsley says on last report that some 15,000 had been printed and distributed. See J. Barnsley, *Feminist Action, Institutional Reaction: Responses to Wife Assault.*
7 MacLeod, personal communication, 1981
8 D.E. Smith, 'No One Commits Suicide: Textual Analysis of Ideological Practices'
9 F. MacLeod, ed., *Report of the Task Force on Family Violence*, p. 2
10 Ibid.
11 Ibid., p. 3
12 D.E. Smith, 'Women and the Politics of Professionalism,' p. 22
13 G.A. Walker, 'Doing it the United Way: A Preliminary Look at the Dilemma of Women and Professionalism in Action,' pp. 11–20
14 Even the ubiquitous 'grounding assumptions' had not identified family violence as more than marginally problematic in terms of the normative understanding of the family that it implied and the need to name men as the main perpetrators, but were concerned to critique 'the family' as socially constructed.
15 Walker, 'Doing It the United Way'
16 M. Bograd, 'Women and Family Therapy: Thoughts on Theory and Practice'
17 House of Commons: Standing Committee on Health, Welfare and Social Affairs, *Report on Violence in the Family: Wife Battering*, p. 7
18 Ibid., p. 15
19 Ibid.
20 Ibid., p. 17
21 Ibid., p. 19
22 Ibid.
23 G. Smith, 'Policing the Gay Community: An Inquiry into Textually-Mediated Social Relations'

CHAPTER 5: Discourse as Dilemma

1 D.E. Smith, 'Where There Is Oppression There Is Resistance'

2 The work of U.S. activist Betsy Warrior, psychiatric researchers Hilberman and Munson's 'Sixty Battered Women,' and feminist consultant Jennifer Baker Fleming's comprehensive manual *Stopping Wife Abuse: A Guide to the Emotional, Psychological, and Legal Implications for the Abused Woman and Those Helping Her* were added to E. Pizzey's important British text, *Scream Quietly or the Neighbours Will Hear* and D. Martin's *Battered Wives* as sources of description, information, and legitimation.

3 As I have recounted the process in earlier chapters, I have shown that we also opposed Steinmetz and Straus's position on family violence. The same applied to later work done by Dutton et al., which promoted psychological premises such as 'trauma bonding' and 'de-individuated violence.' See S.K. Steinmetz and M.A. Straus, 'The Family as a Cradle of Violence'; S.K. Steinmetz and M.A. Straus, eds., *Violence in the Family*; D.G. Dutton, 'An Ecologically Nested Theory of Male Violence toward Intimates'; D. Dutton and S.L. Painter, with D. Patterson and C. Taylor, '*Male Domestic Violence and Its Effects on the Victim*'; S.L. Painter and D. Dutton, 'Patterns of Emotional Bonding in Battered Women: Traumatic Bonding.' The two journal references, though dated 1985, refer to work produced and available in 1980 but published later in journal form.

4 P. Johnston, 'Abused Wives: Their Perceptions of the Help Offered by Mental Health Professionals'

5 M. Amir, *Patterns in Forcible Rape*; J.J. Gayford, 'Battered Wives'; I. Gillman, 'An Object-Relations Approach to the Phenomenon and treatment of Battered wives'; R. Goodstein and A. Rage, 'Battered Wife Syndrome: Overview of Dynamics and Treatment'; E. Pizzey and J. Shapiro, 'Choosing a Violent Relationship'; N. Shainess, 'Vulnerability to Violence: Masochism as Process'; J. Snell, R. Rosenwald, and A. Robey, 'The Wife-Beater's Wife'; B. Starr, 'Comparing Battered and Non-battered Women'

6 Lunbeck notes that both Pleck and Gordon, in their recent historical work on family violence in the United States, trace the subversion and defeat of a previous campaign against the abuse of women and children to the elaboration of clinical theories of seduction, masochism, and victim blame developed by psychiatrists, psychologists, and social workers. This adds a significant and ironic dimension to the context of current struggles against existing formulations of the issue. E. Lunbeck, 'Centuries of Cruelty,' p. 3

7 P.S. Penfold and G.A. Walker, *Women and the Psychiatric Paradox*

8 Johnston, 'Abused Wives'; J. Meade-Ramrattan, M. Cerre, and M. Porto, 'Physically Abused Women: Satisfaction with Sources of Help'

9 Gayford, 'Battered Wives'; R.J. Gelles, *The Violent Home: A Study of Physical Aggression between Husbands and Wives*; R. Peterson, 'Social Class,

Social Learning and Wife Abuse'; M.A. Straus, 'Sexual Inequality, Cultural Norms, and Wife Beating'; M.A. Straus, R. Gelles, and S.K. Steinmetz, *Behind Closed Doors: Violence in the American Family*; L. Walker, *The Battered Woman*

10 Johnston, 'Abused Wives,' p. 16
11 Straus, 'Sexual Inequality'; M.A. Straus and G. Hotaling, *The Social Causes of Husband-Wife Violence*
12 Straus, 'Sexual Inequality,' p. 54, cited in Johnston, 'Abused Wives,' p. 19
13 Straus, Gelles, and Steinmetz, *Behind Closed Doors*; Steinmetz and Straus, 'The Family as a Cradle of Violence'; Steinmetz and Straus, *Violence in the Family*
14 Straus, Gelles, and Steinmetz, *Behind Closed Doors*
15 W. Breines and L. Gordon, 'The New Scholarship on Family Violence,' p. 500
16 R.J. Gelles, 'The Myth of Battered Husbands'
17 Ibid., p. 71
18 R.P. Dobash and R.E. Dobash, 'The Context Specific Approach,' p. 265
19 Johnston, 'Abused Wives,' p. 21
20 Straus, Gelles, and Steinmetz, *Behind Closed Doors*, p. 44
21 J. Giles-Sims, *Wife Battering: A Systems Theory Approach*; M. Roy, *Battered Women: A Psychosocial Study of Domestic Violence*; L. Walker, *The Battered Woman*
22 J. Barnsley, *Feminist Action, Institutional Reaction: Responses to Wife Assault*; G. Errington, 'Family Violence – Is It a Women's Problem?'; S. Schechter, *Women and Male Violence: The Visions and Struggles of the Battered Women's Movement*; D.E. Smith, 'Women and the Politics of Professionalism'; G.A. Walker, 'Doing It the United Way: A Preliminary Look at the Dilemma of Women and Professionalism in Action' and 'Women's Work and the State: Professionalism and the Organization of Class Relations'
23 Breines and Gordon, 'The New Scholarship on Family Violence'
24 Ibid., pp. 519 and 511, cited in T. de Lauretis *Technologies of Gender*, pp. 33–44
25 Ibid., p. 507
26 Pizzey and Shapiro, 'Choosing a Violent Relationship'
27 L. Walker, *The Battered Woman*
28 Johnston, 'Abused Wives,' p. 5
29 Ibid., p. 24
30 Ibid., p. 32
31 R.E. Dobash and R.P. Dobash, *Violence against Wives: A Case against the Patriarchy*, p. 434; Fleming, *Stopping Wife Abuse*; Martin, *Battered Wives*;

Schechter, *Women and Male Violence*; E. Stark and A. Flitcraft, 'Social Knowledge, Social Policy and the Abuse of Women: The Case against Patriarchal Benevolence'; L. Walker, *The Battered Woman*

32 Johnston, 'Abused Wives,' p. 26

33 J. Barnsley, Vancouver Women's Research centre, and Vancouver Transition House, *Battered and Blamed*; Dobash and Dobash, *Violence against Wives*; Martin, *Battered Wives*; E. Pleck et al., 'The Battered Data Syndrome: A Comment on Steinmetz' Article'; S.E. Small, *Wife Assault: An Overview of the Problem in Canada*; Schechter, *Women and Male Violence*

34 Schechter, *Women and Male Violence*, p. 107

35 I am referring here to the various methodological strategies developed in feminist research such as that put forward by D.E. Smith, 'Institutional Ethnography: A Feminist Method'; M. Mies, 'Toward a Methodology for Feminist Research'; H. Roberts, ed., *Doing Feminist Research*; and L. Stanley and S. Wise, *Breaking Out: Feminist Consciousness and Feminist Research*, and put into practice in relation to this particular topic by the Vancouver Women's Research Centre, among others.

36 Pizzey, *Scream Quietly*

37 Dobash and Dobash, *Violence against Wives*

38 Schechter, *Women and Male Violence*

39 Barnsley et al., *Battered and Blamed*

40 Martin, *Battered Wives*

41 L. Walker, *The Battered Woman*

42 Martin, *Battered Wives*, p. 8

43 Ibid., p. xiv

44 Ibid., p. xvi

45 Ibid., p. 8

46 L. MacLeod, *Wife Battering in Canada: The Vicious Circle*

47 L. Walker, *The Battered Woman*, p. xi

48 This concept derives from a range of material from studies of depression and 'locus of control,' and mostly stems from Seligman's work on the behavioural reactions of dogs that were unable to take action to avoid pain even when the conditions that had previously constrained them in the face of adverse stimuli had been removed. The animals had learned that nothing they could do would make any difference to their suffering, or have any impact on their circumstances. They then became unable to remove themselves from painful conditions, even when free to do so, and had to be dragged through the escape route over and over again before they would act. L. Walker (*The Battered Woman*) suggests that women's sex-role socialization to compliance and passivity, coupled with the lack of response

to their plight from possible sources of assistance, creates a situation in which women believe they have no control over their environment, their relationship, or the battering.

49 L. Walker, *The Battered Woman*, p. xi
50 Roy, *Battered Women*
51 D. Frinkelhor, R. Gelles, and G.T. Hotaling, eds., *The Dark Side of Families*
52 Ibid., p. 11
53 Ibid.
54 Dobash and Dobash, 'The Context Specific Approach'
55 Stark and Flitcraft, 'Social Knowledge, Social Policy, and the Abuse of Women'
56 Martin, *Battered Wives*, 2d ed., p. 271
57 Ibid., pp. 273–4, emphasis in original
58 L. Walker, *The Battered Woman*; Dobash and Dobash, *Violence against Wives*; M.D. Pagelow, *Woman-Battering: Victims and Their Experience*
59 Martin, *Battered Wives*, 2d ed., p. 279
60 Ibid.
61 Ibid.
62 Ibid.
63 Ibid.
64 Schechter, *Women and Male Violence*; P. Morgan, 'From Battered Wife to Program Client: The State's Shaping of Social Problems'
65 M. Roy, not incidentally, performs a similar service for men in her *The Abusive Partner: An Analysis of Domestic Battering*, which is, despite its degendered title, actually about violent men. It posits a 'spouse abuse syndrome,' juxtaposing papers by 'experts' from every likely discipline who write about theories of aggression and male violence to give substance to the clinical criminal organization of the issue (p. 249).

CHAPTER 6: The Concept of Violence

1 D.E. Smith, 'Using the Oppressor's Language'
2 See E.H. Newberger and R. Bourne, 'The Medicalization and Legalization of Child Abuse,' for a critical appraisal of the medicalization of child abuse.
3 E. Pizzey, *Scream Quietly or the Neighbours Will Hear*, p. 46
4 D. Martin, *Battered Wives*, p. ix
5 D. Martin, *Battered Wives*, 2d ed., p. 279
6 Flora MacCloud, personal communications, 1981
7 D.E. Smith, 'The Ideological Practice of Sociology,' p. 53

8 D.E. Smith, *Feminism and Marxism – A Place to Begin, a Way to Go,* 'Women and the Politics of Professionalism,' and 'Where There Is Oppression There Is Resistance'

9 Smith, 'Where There Is Oppression,' p. 13

10 See L. Segal, *Is the Future Female? Troubled Thoughts on Contemporary Feminism.*

11 See, for example, D.E. Smith, 'Women, the Family and Corporate Capitalism,' 'Women and the Politics of Professionalism,' and 'Institutional Ethnography: A Method of Sociology for Women'; A. Griffith, 'Ideology, Education and Single Parent Families: The Normative Ordering of Families through Schooling'; M. Barrett and M. McIntosh, *The Anti-Social Family;* B. Thorne and M. Yalom, eds., *Rethinking the Family: Some Feminist Questions;* Segal, *Is the Future Female?*

12 Smith, 'The Ideological Practice of Sociology'

13 Ibid., p. 53

14 Dorothy E. Smith, Lecture, Faculty of Social Work, University of Toronto, Fall 1986

15 Newberger and Bourne, 'The Medicalization and Legalization of Child Abuse'

16 L. Gordon, *Heroes of Their Own Lives: The Politics and History of Family Violence, Boston 1880–1960;* E. Pleck, 'Feminist Response to "Crimes against Women", 1868–1896' and *Domestic Tyranny: The Making of American Social Policy against Family Violence from Colonial Times to the Present;* C. Bauer and L. Ritt, ' "A Husband Is a Beating Animal": Frances Power Cobbe Confronts the Wife Abuse Problem in Victorian England' and 'Wife Abuse, Late Victorian English Feminists, and the Legacy of Frances Power Cobbe'

17 J.Q. Wilson, 'Violence,' p. 23, cited in Smith, 'The Ideological Practice of Sociology,' p. 53

18 D. Dutton and S.L. Painter, with D. Patterson and C. Taylor, 'Male Domestic Violence and Its Effects on the Victim'; S.L. Painter and D. Dutton, 'Patterns of Emotional Bonding in Battered Women: Traumatic Bonding'

19 D.Martin, *Battered Wives,* 2d ed.

20 I am grateful to Ian Taylor for making this point in comments on an earlier paper, and for drawing my attention to the news release from the Department of Justice, Ottawa, 21 December 1983.

21 C. Brown, 'Mothers, Fathers and Children: From Private to Public Patriarchy'

CHAPTER 7: Particularizing the General

1 Ontario Association of Interval and Transition Houses, *Report on the Hear-*

ings of the Standing Committee on Social Development, 'Family Violence,' Toronto, July 19–July 30, 1982, Queen's Park

2 Leglislature of Ontario: Standing Committee on Social Development, *First Report on Family Violence: Wife Battering*, p. i

3 Bryden also tabled a Private Member's motion asking that an all-party committee be formed to look at the issues raised by the Ontario Association of Interval and Transition Houses (OAITH).

4 Interview, April 1986, with Lynn Mellor, Clerk of the Standing Committee from late 1982 until early 1986. The clerk at the time under study here was Graham White. The committee also had available to it as resources staff people from the ministries and the Department of Research. I am grateful to Valerie Watson for conducting the interview for me. I am also grateful to my research assistant Beth Mairs and the staff of MLA Richard Johnston's office for providing documents and transcripts that informed my analysis of the initial stages of the Ontario events.

5 Legislature of Ontario, *Hansard*, 4 May 1982, p. 2

6 Ibid.

7 Richard Johnston, Interview, February 1987

8 M. Madisso, Letter (7 June 1982); M. Madisso, Memorandum (17 June 1982)

9 *Hansard*, 4 May 1982, p. 2

10 *Hansard*, 12 May 1982, p. 8

11 See, for example, *Hansard* 10 May 1982, p. 19, and 12 May 1982, p. 4.

12 *Hansard*, 4 May 1982, p. 8; 10 May 1982, p. 20; 12 May 1982, p. 4

13 Interview, August 1984, with a consultant engaged in work with the Ministry of Community and Social Services at this time

14 Johnston, interview, 1987

15 A good deal of discussion of how to be 'fair' without having to listen to every potential interest group in the province took place in these sessions. See, for example, *Hansard*, 4 May 1982, pp. 4–5, 11.

16 *Hansard*, 10 May 1982, p. 11

17 D.E. Smith, 'The Active Text: A Textual Analysis of the Social Relations of Public Textual Discourse', p. 8

18 *Hansard*, 10 May 1982, p. 13; 11 May 1982, p. 7

19 *Hansard*, 10 May 1982, pp. 25, 30, 40

20 Ibid., pp. 19, 20; 11 May 1982, p. 3

21 *Hansard*, 10 May 1982, p. 11

22 Ibid., p. 18

23 Ibid., p. 19

24 A senior bureaucrat characterized the objections raised by women and men concerned with the implications of the title 'The Canadian Association of

Social Workers' Task Force on Spouse Abuse' as a 'cosmetic quibble' in discussion with the author in Ottawa in 1982. It was self-evident to her that the spouses being abused were women and she was unable to appreciate the significance of the gender-neutral term.

25 *Hansard*, 4 May 1982, p. 12
26 *Hansard*, 10 May 1982, p. 20
27 *Hansard*, 4 May 1982, p. 4. Johnston suggests here that the Vancouver report on the protection of battered women and the Advisory Council on the Status of Women's publications cover spouse abuse. The question of abuse of the elderly, he states, has been less fully covered than child abuse or spouse battering, but he notes that there is a federal u.s. report that might be useful.
28 *Hansard*, 4 May 1982, p. 9
29 Ibid., p. 10
30 Ibid., p. 16
31 Ibid., p. 13
32 Ibid., p. 3
33 Ibid., p. 14
34 Ibid., p. 26
35 Ibid., p. 23
36 Ibid., p. 20
37 The comsoc report for 1981 refers in some detail to and quotes from the Speech from the Throne of that year, which strongly emphasizes the Ontario government's commitment to the family. The comsoc report itself does not contain any reference at all to family violence, violence in the family, victims of violence, or indeed women (with the exception of one reference to sole-support mothers). Reports for the years 1979, 1980, and 1981 (there is some disagreement in the hearings as to which report was actually 'referred out') have sections of varying length describing the ministry's actions with regard to child abuse and the development of a child-abuse registry, but nowhere is this highlighted in the minister's reports or summaries as being of particular significance or concern. Johnston confirmed that it was the 1981 report in question, but that its contents per se had no bearing on the tactic, which was to provide a forum for the issue and get it to committee (interview, 1987).
38 *Hansard*, 10 May 1982, p. 20
39 Johnston, interview, 1987
40 *Hansard*, 10 May 1982, p. 11
41 Ibid., p. 10
42 Ibid., p. 13

43 Ibid., p. 17
44 Included in Madisso, Memorandum
45 *Hansard*, 10 May 1982, p. 19
46 Ibid., p. 11
47 *Hansard*, 11 May 1982, p. 14
48 *Hansard*, 10 May 1982, p. 20
49 Ibid., p. 37
50 Ibid., p. 29
51 Ibid., p. 31
52 Ibid., p. 32
53 Ibid., p. 33
54 Ibid., p. 19
55 Question Period, Session on Wife Battering in the 1983 Conference of the Canadian Association of Schools of Social Work, Vancouver, BC
56 *Hansard*, 10 May 1982, p. 33
57 *Hansard*, 11 May 1982, p. 3

CHAPTER 8: Hearing the Issue

1 M. Madisso, Letter (7 June 1982); M. Madisso, Memorandum (17 June 1982)
2 P.J. Kincaid, 'The Omitted Reality: Husband-Wife Violence in Ontario and Policy Implications for Education'
3 Madisso, Memorandum
4 L. Grayson, *Final Summary of Recommendations re: Family Violence*
5 Madisso, Memorandum
6 *Hansard*, 19 July 1982, pp. 3–4
7 Ibid., p. 2
8 The first in North America, according to the Interval House brief submitted to the committee: a letter, case study, and list of recommendations, dated 19 July 1982
9 *Hansard*, 19 July 1982, p. 9
10 Ibid.
11 Ibid.
12 Ibid., p. 16
13 Ibid., p. 42
14 Ibid., p. 20
15 Ibid., p. 15
16 Ibid., p. 25
17 Bryden, though not a member of the Standing Committee, sat in on all its

public hearing sessions and took an active part in deliberations throughout.

18 *Hansard*, 19 July 1982, p. 3
19 Ibid.
20 Ibid., p. 4
21 Ibid., p. 46
22 Ibid., p. 21
23 Ibid., p. 37
24 Ibid.
25 Ibid.
26 Ibid.
27 P. Jaffe and C.A. Burriss, 'Wife Abuse as a Crime; The Impact of Police Laying Charges'
28 *Hansard*, 19 July 1982, p. 38
29 Ibid.
30 Ibid., p. 16
31 Ibid., p. 24
32 Ibid., pp. 11–12
33 Ibid., p. 30
34 Ibid., p. 18
35 Ibid.
36 Ibid.

CHAPTER 9: Negotiating the Elements

1 *Hansard*, 20 July 1982, pp. 28–9
2 Ibid., p. 23
3 Bannon we have already encountered as rating a positive mention in Del Martin's 1981 postscript to her 1976 book, *Battered Wives*.
4 *Hansard*, 21 July 1982, p. 2
5 Ibid., p. 3
6 Ibid., p. 5
7 Ibid., p. 18
8 Ibid., p. 3
9 Ibid., p. 11
10 M. Selucky, 'Police Response to Wife Battering'
11 *Hansard*, 21 July 1982, p. 8
12 Ibid., p. 27
13 *Hansard*, 23 July 1982, p. 47
14 Ibid., p. 49

15 Some groups and individuals do suggest legislative changes but most insist that existing legislation would suffice, if properly enforced.
16 For a summary of all the recommendations put before the committee, see L. Grayson, *Final Summary of Recommendations re: Family Violence.*
17 *Hansard,* 23 July 1982, p. 4
18 Ibid.
19 Ibid.
20 Ibid., p. 7
21 Ibid., p. 8
22 Ibid., p. 6
23 Ibid., p. 7
24 Ibid., p. 6
25 *Hansard,* 29 July, 1982, p. 37
26 Ibid., p. 2
27 Ibid., pp. 23–4.
28 Ibid., p. 7
29 Ibid., pp. 37–8

CHAPTER 10: Reporting for Action

1 *Hansard,* 29 July 1982, pp. 69–71
2 Ibid., p. 71
3 This committee has had a number of research staff during these sessions; by this stage the researcher was Philip Kaye.
4 L. Grayson, *Final Summary of Recommendations re: Family Violence*
5 *Hansard,* 30 July 1982, p. 9
6 Ibid., p. 19
7 Johnston, interview, 1987
8 Legislature of Ontario: Standing Committee on Social Development, *First Report on Family Violence: Wife Battering*
9 Ibid., pp. i–ii
10 Ibid., p. i
11 Ibid., p. ii
12 Ibid.
13 Ibid., p. iii
14 Ibid., p. 1
15 Ibid.
16 Ibid., p. 2
17 Ibid., p. 3
18 Ibid., p. 9

19 Ontario Association of Interval and Transition Houses, *Response to the Standing Committee on Social Development on 'Wife Battering Report'*
20 It is interesting to note here that in this section the problem is referred to as domestic violence for the first time in the report. Domestic violence or 'domestics' is the category that the police assign to disturbances in households and between neighbours or kin.
21 Legislature of Ontario, *First Report on Family Violence*, p. 10
22 Ibid., p. 11
23 Ibid., p. 12
24 Ibid., p. 13
25 Ibid., p. 15
26 Ibid., p. 16
27 Ibid., p. 19
28 Ibid.
29 Ibid., p. 20
30 Ibid.
31 Ibid., p. 22
32 Ibid., p. 22
33 Ibid., p. 24
34 No rationale is given for involving the Department of Health and Welfare, which at that time housed the recently established National Clearing House for Family Violence (later transferred to Justice). An informant has since suggested that the London Advocacy Clinic's eventual funding, through the Health and Welfare demonstration grant program, came about largely because of a keen personal interest in the issue on the part of Freda Paltiel, a high-ranking official in the department. There was a good deal of dispute between the federal and provincial governments over who should be funding such projects, with neither level wanting to take on the continuing costs. In this context it is not surprising that the province should recommend the federal department for ongoing funding of this aspect.
35 Leglislature of Ontario, *First Report on Family Violence*, pp. 19–20
36 Ibid., p. 27
37 Ibid., p. 28
38 Ibid., p. 29
39 The use of the term 'domestic violence' here seems to occur in connection with the consideration of the Michigan model, which has the same title as that proposed here. Bannon introduced this model in his testimony and it reflects the police focus of his orientation.
40 Legislature of Ontario, *First Report on Family Violence*, p. 37

41 It is not clear from Bannon's account to the committee how the legislation in Michigan locates the board in question, though he is its chair and most of his presentation concerned the relationship between legislation, policing, and the shelter movement.
42 Legislature of Ontario, *First Report on Family Violence*, pp. 40–1
43 Ibid., p. 42
44 Ibid.
45 Ibid., p. 43. Quotation drawn from a presentation to the committee by Leslie Lawlor, Support Services for Assaulted Women, 21 July 1982
46 Ibid., p. 44
47 Ibid., p. 49
48 This case study was adapted from the brief presented by the Thunder Bay Social Services Department and discussed in the hearings: *Hansard*, 26 July 1982, pp. 25–6.

CHAPTER 11: Action and Reaction

1 Much of the material used in my analysis of the recommendations was categorized by Valerie Watson, my research assistant in 1985–6. I am grateful for her help with this task.
2 L. Grayson, *Final Summary of Recommendations re: Family Violence*, p. 53
3 Ibid., p. 9
4 Ibid., p. 22
5 Legislature of Ontario: Standing Committee on Social Development, *First Report on Family Violence: Wife Battering*, Recommendation No. 24
6 Grayson, *Final Summary*, pp. 46, 59
7 Legislature of Ontario, *First Report on Family Violence*, Recommendation 24, pp. 48, 60
8 See the report prepared for this conference and published by the Ministry of Supply and Services in 1984, especially pp. 2, 187, and 398.
9 Richard Johnston, personal interview, February 1987
10 Nick Martin, 'Wife Beating Study Called Great Disappointment'
11 Interview with informed sources, 1984
12 Ibid.
13 Legislature of Ontario: Standing Committee on Social Development, *Family Violence: Wife Battering. Ontario Government Initiatives*
14 Ibid., p. 5. My informed source reported that the co-ordinator was chosen because she was 'clean to the issue,' that is, she had no prior knowledge or experience of family violence or women's issues and would therefore be 'objective.'

15 Ibid., p. 1

16 For a further discussion of this and other aspects of the Ontario government's initiatives, see T. Crowe, 'Stealing the Fire.'

17 Perhaps a small but telling cameo of the way in which the issue can and has
been appropriated can be seen in one of the advertisements put out as a
result of public education and pressure on professional groups in the wake
of the report. It appeared widely in the print media in 1986, and even on
public transit. The public-service announcement (it can hardly be called an
advertisement) shows a line-drawing of a shapely and naked young
woman with black eyes and bruises on her face. The drawing of her very
pregnant belly is cross-sectioned to show the curled fetus and placenta.
Accompanying this picture is text that highlights family violence as a health
issue. It draws attention to the dangers of the family-violence cycle, its
unacceptability, and what steps need to be taken to protect our children
from it. The last few lines, before a recommendation to contact the local
shelter or Interval or Transition House, suggest that failure to break the
vicious circle of abuse will result in the child growing up with its mother's eyes or its father's fists. At no point is the pain, suffering, or situation of
the woman herself acknowledged. The announcement was put out by
the Ontario Medical Association.

18 Interview, February 1987

19 I am grateful to Jude James and Trudy Don for information on the current
situation and implications with regard to the shelter funding and the
funding of family-violence services in general.

20 P. Morgan, 'From Battered Wife to Program Client: The State's Shaping of
Social Problems,' p. 18

CHAPTER 12: Conceptual Practices and the Relations of Ruling

1 P. Morgan, 'From Battered Wife to Program Client: The State's Shaping of
Social Problems,' p. 17

2 Ibid., p. 19

3 E. Pleck et al., 'The Battered Data Syndrome: A Comment on Steinmetz'
Article'; R.L. McNeely and G. Robinson-Simpson, 'The Truth about Domestic Violence: A Falsely Framed Issue'

4 The term 'demonization' of feminism was used by Michele Landsberg in
her coverage of the killing of the women students in Montreal (*Toronto Star*,
8 December 1989, A1, A16). Dorothy Smith also drew attention to the political nature of the incident in a radio interview on the same day.

5 E. Pleck, *Domestic Tyranny: The Making of American Social Policy against Family
Violence from Colonial Times to the Present*; L. Gordon, *Heroes of Their Own*

Lives: The Politics and History of Family Violence, Boston 1880–1960. Pleck introduces the useful notion of a virus-like organization of concepts such as child abuse and their function in obscuring significant aspects of the context of events.

6 Morgan, 'From Battered Wife to Program Client'
7 T. de Lauretis, *Technologies of Gender*, pp. 33–4
8 I thank Trudy Don, Colleen Lundy, and Cindy Player for accounts of this event. The interpretation put on it is my own. The remark about feminists not getting it all their own way is cited by Dorothy Smith in her forthcoming book *The Conceptual Practices of Power: A Feminist Sociology of Knowledge*.
9 J. Riddington, 'Providing Services the Feminist Way'

References

Abele, F. 'The Berger Inquiry and the Politics of Transformation in the MacKenzie Valley.' Unpublished doctoral dissertation, York University, Toronto 1983

Ahrens, L. 'Battered Women's Refuges: Feminist Cooperatives vs. Social Service Institutions.' *Radical America* Summer 1980, 41–9

Amir, M. *Pattern in Forcible Rape.* Chicago: University of Chicago Press 1971

Armstrong, P., and H. Armstrong. *The Double Ghetto: Canadian Women and Their Segregated Work.* Toronto: McClelland and Stewart 1984

Barnsley, J. *Feminist Action, Institutional Reaction: Responses to Wife Assault.* Vancouver: Women's Research Centre 1985

Barnsley, J., Vancouver Women's Research Centre, and Vancouver Transition House. *Battered and Blamed.* Vancouver 1980

Barrett, M. *Women's Oppression Today: Problems in Marxist Feminist Analysis.* London: Verso Editions 1980

Barrett, M., and M. McIntosh. *The Anti-Social Family.* London: Verso Editions 1982

Bauer, C., and L. Ritt. '"A Husband Is a Beating Animal": Frances Power Cobbe Confronts the Wife Abuse Problem in Victorian England.' *International Journal of Women's Studies*, 6/2 (1983a), 99–118

– 'Wife Abuse, Late Victorian English Feminists, and the Legacy of Frances Power Cobbe.' *International Journal of Women's Studies*, 6/3 (1983), 195–207

Bograd, M. 'Women and Family Therapy: Thoughts on Theory and Practice.' Paper presented at the Women's Institute of the Annual Meeting of the American Orthopsychiatric Association of Toronto, 1984

Breines, W., and L. Gordon. 'The New Scholarship on Family Violence.' *Signs*, 8/3 (1983), 490–531

Brown, C. 'Mothers, Fathers and Children: From Private to Pubic Patriarchy.' In

L. Sargent (ed.), *Women and Revolution: A Discussion of the Unhappy Marriage of Marxism and Feminism*, pp. 239–67. Montreal: Black Rose Books 1981

Burton, F. and P. Carlen. *Official Discourse*. London: Routledge & Kegan Paul 1979

Campbell, M. 'Sexism in British Columbia Trade Unions, 1900–1920.' In B. Lathan and C. Kess (eds.), *In Her Own Right: Selected Essays on Women's History in B.C.* pp. 167–86. Victoria: Camosen College 1980

Campbell, M.L. 'Information Systems and Management of Hospital Nursing: A Study in Social Organization of Knowledge.' Unpublished doctoral dissertation, University of Toronto 1984

Canada. Parliament. House of Commons. Standing Committee on Health, Welfare and Social Affairs. *Debates and Proceedings (Hansard)*. Issues 24, 27, 29. Ottawa: Queen's Printer 1982

– Standing Committee on Health, Welfare and Social Affairs. *Report on Violence in the Family: Wife Battering*. Ottawa, May 1982

Canadian Women's Educational Press. *Women Unite*. Toronto 1972

Crowe, T. 'Stealing the Fire.' Unpublished paper, School of Social Work, Carleton University, Ottawa, December 1986

Davin, A. Imperialism and Motherhood. *History Workshop*, 5 (1978), 9–65

de Lauretis, T. *Technologies of Gender*. Bloomington and Indianapolis: Indiana University Press 1987

Dickinson, J., and B. Russell 'Introduction: The Structure of Reproduction in Capitalist Culture.' In J. Dickinson and B. Russell (eds.), *Family, Economy and State: The Social Reproductive Process under Capitalism*, pp. 1–20. Toronto: Garamond Press 1986

Dobash, R.E., and R.P. Dobash *Violence against Wives: A Case against the Patriarchy*. New York: Free Press 1979

Dobash, R.P., and R.E. Dobash 'The Context Specific Approach.' In A. Finkelhor, R. Gelles and G. Hotaling (eds.), *The Dark Side of Families*, pp. 261–76. Beverly Hills, CA: Sage Publications 1983

Downey, J., and J. Howell. *Wife Battering: A Review and Preliminary Enquiry into Local Incidence, Needs, and Resources*. Vancouver: United Way of Greater Vancouver 1976

Dutton, Donald G. 'An Ecologically Nested Theory of Male Violence toward Intimates.' *International Journal of Women's Studies*, 8/4 (1985), 404–13

Dutton, D., and S.L. Painter with D. Patterson and C. Taylor. *Male Domestic Violence and Its Effects on the Victim*. Report to the Health Promotions Directorate, Health and Welfare Canada, 1980

Ehrenreich, B., and D. English. *For Her Own Good: 150 Years of the Experts' Advise to Women*. New York: Anchor Press 1979

Eisenstein, Z. *The Radical Future of Liberal Feminism*. New York: Longman Inc. 1981

Epstein, R., R. Ng, and M. Trebble. *The Social Organization of Family Violence: The Ethnography of Immigrant Experience in Vancouver*. Vancouver: Non-Medical Use of Drugs Directorate 1978

Errington, G. 'Family Violence – Is It a Women's Problem?' In Press Gang and the B.C. Association of Social Workers (eds.), *Counterpoint: Women's Perspectives and Social Work*, pp. 20–3. Vancouver 1978

Findlay, S. 'The Politics of the Women's Movement: Lobbying Our Way to the Revolution.' Unpublished paper, Carleton University, May 1982

– 'Struggles within the State: The Feminist Challenge to Hegemony.' Unpublished paper, Carleton University, December 1982

– 'Defining the Political: Creeping Pluralism and the Decline of the State/Capital Imperative.' Unpublished paper, University of Toronto, 1986

– 'Facing the State: The Politics of the Women's Movement Reconsidered.' In H.J. Maroney and M. Luxton (eds.), *Feminism and Political Economy: Women's Work, Women's Struggles*, pp. 31–50. Toronto: Methuen 1987

Finkelhor, A., R. Gelles and G. Hotaling (eds.). *The Dark Side of Families*. Beverly Hills, CA: Sage Publications 1983

Fleming, J.B. *Stopping Wife Abuse: A Guide to the Emotional, Psychological, and Legal Implications for the Abused Woman and Those Helping Her*. Garden City, NY: Anchor Press/Doubleday 1979

Gayford, J.J. 'Battered Wives.' *Medicine, Science, and the Law*, 15/4 (1975), 237–45

Geller, G. 'A Feminist Case against Patriarchal "Justice" for Women Victims of Abuse.' Paper presented at the Canadian Sociology and Anthropology Association Sessions, Learned Society Meetings, Quebec City, 1989

Gelles, R.J. *The Violent Home: A Study of Physical Aggression between Husbands and Wives*. Beverly Hills, CA: Sage Publications 1972

– 'The Myth of Battered Husbands.' *Ms Magazine*, October 1979, 69–73

Giles-Sims, J. *Wife Battering: A Systems Theory Approach*. New York: The Guilford Press 1983

Gillman, I. 'An Object-Relations Approach to the Phenomenon and Treatment of Battered Wives.' *Psychiatry*, 43 (November 1980), 346–56

Goode, W.J. 'Force and Violence in the Family.' *Journal of Marriage and the Family*, 33/4 (1971) 624–36

Goodrich, T.J., C. Rampage, B. Ellman, and K. Halstead. *Feminist Family Therapy*. New York: Norton 1988

Goodstein, R., and A. Rage. 'Battered Wife Syndrome: Overview of Dynamics and Treatment.' *American Journal of Psychiatry*, 138/8 (1981), 1036–44

Gordon, L. *Heroes of Their Own Lives: The Politics and History of Family Violence, Boston 1880–1960*. New York: Viking Press 1988

Gramsci, A. *Prison Note Books*. London: Lawrence & Wishart 1971

Grayson, L. *Final Summary of Recommendations re: Family Violence*. Toronto:

Legislative Research Service. Prepared for Standing Committee on Social Development 30 July 1982

Griffith, A. 'Single Parent Families: The Category as Ideology.' Paper presented to the Political Economy of Gender Relations in Education Conference, University of Toronto 1981

– 'Ideology, Education and Single Parent Families: The Normative Ordering of Families through Schooling.' Unpublished doctoral dissertation, University of Toronto 1984

Hamilton, R., and M. Barrett. *The Politics of Diversity: Feminism, Marxism and Nationalism*. Montreal: Book Centre Inc. 1986

Hanmer, J. and D. Leonard 'Negotiating the Problem: The DHHS and Research on Violence in Marriage.' In C. Bell and H. Roberts (eds.), *Social Researching*, pp. 32–53. London: Routledge & Kegan Paul 1984

Hilberman, E., and K. Munson 'Sixty Battered Women.' *Victimology: An International Journal*, 3–4 (1978), 460–70

Jaffe, P., and C.A. Burris. 'Wife Abuse as a Crime: The Impact of Police Laying Charges.' *Canadian Journal of Criminology*, 25/3 (1983), 309–18

Jenson, J. 'Gender and Reproduction: Or, Babies and the State.' *Studies in Political Economy*, 20 (Summer 1986), 9–46

Johnston, P. 'Abused Wives: Their Perceptions of the Help Offered by Mental Health Professionals.' Unpublished Independent Enquiry Project, School of Social Work, Carleton University, Ottawa 1984

Kelly-Gadol, J. 'The Social Relations of the Sexes: Methodological Implications of Women's History.' *Signs*, 1/4 (1976), 809–23

Kincaid, P.J. 'The Omitted Reality: Husband-Wife Violence in Ontario and Policy Implications for Education.' Unpublished doctoral dissertation, University of Toronto 1981

Levine, H., and A. Estable. *The Power Politics of Motherhood* (Monograph). Ottawa: Centre for Welfare Studies, Carleton University 1981

Lunbeck, E. 'Centuries of Cruelty.' *The Women's Review of Books*, 5/12 (1988), 1–3

MacKinnon, C.A. 'Feminism, Marxism, Method, and the State: An Agenda for Theory.' *Signs*, 7/3 (1982), 515–44

– 'Feminism, Marxism, Method, and the State: Toward Feminist Jurisprudence.' *Signs*, 8/4 (1983), 635–58

MacLeod, F. (ed.). *Report of the Task Force on Family Violence*. Vancouver: United Way of the Lower Mainland 1979

MacLeod, L. *Wife Battering in Canada: The Vicious Circle*. Quebec: Supply & Services Canada 1980

– *Wife Battering Is Everywoman's Issue: A Summary Report of the CACSW Consulta-*

tion on Wife Battering. Ottawa: Canadian Advisory Council on the Status of Women 1980

Madisso, M. Letter, 7 June 1982, from Merike Madisso, Research Officer, Legislative Research Service, to Richard Johnston, MPP, Committee Member; List of bibliographies supplied by witness to preliminary hearings.

– Memorandum, 17 June 1982, from Merike Madisso, Research Officer, Legislative Research Service, to Members of the Sub-Committee of the Standing Committee on Social Development, re. Witnesses to appear before the committee

Maroney, H.J., and M. Luxton. *Feminism and Political Economy: Women's Work, Women's Struggle*. Toronto: Methuen 1987

Martin, D. *Battered Wives*. San Francisco: New Glide Publications 1976; 2d. ed. San Francisco: Volcano Press 1981

Martin, N. 'Wife Beating Study Called Great Disappointment.' *London Free Press*, 18 December 1982

Marx, K., and F. Engels. *The German Ideology*. New York: International Publishers 1970

Matheson, G. (ed.). *Women in the Canadian Mosaic*. Toronto: Peter Martin Associates 1976

McIntosh, M. 'The State and the Oppression of Women.' In A. Kuhn and A.M. Wolpe (eds.), *Feminism and Materialism: Women and Modes of Production*, pp. 254–89. London: Routledge & Kegan Paul 1978

McNeely, R.L., and G. Robinson-Simpson. 'The Truth about Domestic Violence: A Falsely Framed Issue.' *Social Work*, November–December 1987, 485–90

Meade-Ramrattan, J., M. Cerre, and M. Porto. 'Physically Abused Women: Satisfaction with Sources of Help.' *The Social Worker*, 48/4 (1980), 162–6

Mies, M. 'Toward a Methodology for Feminist Research.' In G. Bowles and R. Duelli-Klein (eds.), *Theories of Women's Studies*, pp. 117–39. London: Routledge & Kegan Paul 1983

Morgan, P. 'From Battered Wife to Program Client: The State's Shaping of Social Problems.' *Kapitalistate*, 9 (1981), 17–39

Mueller, A. 'Peasants and Professionals: The Social Organization of Women in Development Knowledge.' Unpublished doctoral dissertation, University of Toronto 1987

National Film Board of Canada. *Loved, Honoured and Bruised*. Film, made in Manitoba, 1979

Newberger, E.H., and R. Bourne. 'The Medicalization and Legalization of Child Abuse.' In A. Skolnick and J.H. Skolnick (eds.), *Family in Transition*, 5th ed., pp. 440–55. Boston: Little, Brown 1986

Ng, R. 'Immigrant Women and the State: Toward an Analytic Framework.' Unpublished paper, Department of Sociology of Education, OISE 1982
- 'Immigrant Women and the State: A Study in the Social Organization of Knowledge.' Unpublished doctoral dissertation, University of Toronto 1984
- *The Politics of Community Services.* Toronto: Garamond Press 1988
Oakley, A., and J. Mitchell (eds.). *What Is Feminism?: A Re-examination.* New York: Pantheon Books 1986
Olsen, F.E. 'The Family and the Market: A Study of Ideology and Legal Reform.' *Harvard Law Review,* 96/7 (1983), 1497–1578
Ontario. Legislature of Ontario. *Family Violence: Wife Battering. Ontario Government Initiatives.* Toronto: Office of the Deputy Premier (Minister Responsible for Women's Issues) and Provincial Secretary for Justice, October 1983
- Standing Committee on Social Development. *First Report on Family Violence: Wife Battering.* Toronto: Queen's Park, December 1982
Ontario Association of Interval and Transition Houses. *Brief to the Committee of Social Development in Ontario: Battered Women's Emergency Housing in Ontario.* Trudy Don, co-ordinator. Toronto, July 1982
- *Response to the Standing Committee on Social Development on 'Wife Battering Report'.* Toronto, March 1983
- *Family Resource Centres in Northern Ontario: Response.* Toronto, September 1983
- *Presentation to the Provincial Consultation: Secretary for Justice.* Toronto, January 1984
- *Report on the Hearings of the Standing Committee on Social Development, 'Family Violence,'* Toronto, July 19–July 30, 1982, Queen's Park. Toronto, n.d.
- Press release no. 16, April 1987
Pagelow, M.D. *Woman-Battering: Victims and Their Experiences.* Beverly Hills, CA: Sage Publications 1981
- *Family Violence.* New York: Praeger 1984
Painter, S.L., and D. Dutton. 'Patterns of Emotional Bonding in Battered Women: Traumatic Bonding.' *International Journal of Women's Studies,* 8/4 (1985), 363–75
Penfold, P.S., and G.A. Walker. *Women and the Psychiatric Paradox.* Montreal: Eden Press 1983
Peterson, R. 'Social Class, Social Learning and Wife Abuse.' *Social Service Review,* 54/3 (1980), 390–406
Pizzey, E. *Scream Quietly or the Neighbours Will Hear.* London: Penguin Books 1974
Pizzey, E., and J. Shapiro. 'Choosing a Violent Relationship.' *New Society,* 56/962 (1981), 133–5
Pleck, E. 'Feminist Response to "Crimes against Women", 1868–1896.' *Signs,* 8/3 (1983), 451–70

– *Domestic Tyranny: The Making of American Social Policy against Family Violence from Colonial Times to the Present.* New York: Oxford University Press 1987

Pleck, E., J. Pleck, M. Grossman, and P. Bart. 'The Battered Data Syndrome: A Comment on Steinmetz' Article.' *Victimology*, 2/3–4 (1977–8), 680–3

Rapp, R. 'Family and Class in Contemporary America: Notes towards an Understanding of Ideology.' In B. Thorne with M. Yalom (eds.), *Rethinking the Family: Some Feminist Questions*, pp. 168–87. New York: Longman 1982

Riddington, J. 'The Transition House Process: A Feminist Environment as Reconstructive Milieu.' *Victimology*, 2 (1977–8), 563–75

– 'Providing Services the Feminist Way.' In M. Fitzgerald, C. Guberman, and M. Wolfe (eds.), *Still Ain't Satisfied: Canadian Feminism Today*, pp. 93–107. Toronto: Women's Press 1982

Roberts, H. (ed.). *Doing Feminist Research.* London: Routledge & Kegan Paul 1981

Roy, M. *Battered Women: A Psychosocial Study of Domestic Violence.* New York: Van Nostrand Reinhold 1982

– *The Abusive Partner: An Analysis of Domestic Battering.* New York: Van Nostrand Reinhold 1982

Schechter, S. *Women and Male Violence: The Visions and Struggles of the Battered Women's Movement.* Boston: South End Press 1982

Schreader, A. 'Professionalism and Its Implications for Women.' Unpublished paper, School of Social Work, Carleton University, Ottawa 1982

Segal, L. *Is the Future Female? Troubled Thoughts on Contemporary Feminism.* London: Virago Press 1987

– *What Is to be Done about the Family?* Harmondsworth: Penguin Books 1983

Selucky, M. 'Police Response to Wife Battering.' Unpublished Independent Enquiry Project, School of Social Work, Carleton University, Ottawa 1985

Shainess, N. 'Vulnerability to Violence: Masochism as Process.' *American Journal of Psychotherapy*, 33/2 (1979), 174–89

Small, S.E. *Wife Assault: An Overview of the Problem in Canada.* Toronto: Support Services for Assaulted Women 1980

Smith, D.E. 'Women, the Family and Corporate Capitalism.' In M. Stephenson (ed.), *Women in Canada*, pp. 2–35. Toronto: New Press 1973

– 'The Social Construction of Documentary Reality.' *Sociological Inquiry*, 44/1 (1974), 7–13

– 'The Ideological Practice of Sociology.' *Catalyst*, 8 (1974), 38–54

– 'Women and Psychiatry.' In D.E. Smith and S.J. David (eds.), *Women Look at Psychiatry*, pp. 1–19. Vancouver: Press Gang 1975

– *Feminism and Marxism – A Place to Begin, a Way to Go.* Vancouver: New Star Books 1977

- 'A Peculiar Eclipsing: Women's Exclusion from Men's Culture.' *Women's Studies International Quarterly*, 1/4 (1978), 281–95
- 'Women and the Politics of Professionalism.' Unpublished manuscript, Department of Sociology in Education, OISE 1979
- Where There Is Oppression There Is Resistance.' *Branching Out*, 6/1 (1979), 10–15
- 'Using the Oppressor's Language.' *Resources for Feminist Research, Special Issue on Feminist Theory*, Spring 1979
- 'Institutional Ethnography: A Method of Sociology for Women.' Paper presented to the Political Economy of Gender Relations in Education Conference, University of Toronto 1981
- *The Experienced World as Problematic: A Feminist Method* (Sorokin Lectures No. 12). Regina: University of Saskatchewan 1981
- 'Women's Inequality and the Family.' In A. Moscovitch and G. Drover (eds.). *Inequality: Essays on the Political Economy of Social Welfare*, pp. 156–95. Toronto: University of Toronto Press 1981
- 'The Active Text: A Textual Analysis of the Social Relations of Public Textual Discourse.' Paper presented at a meeting of the World Congress of Sociology, Mexico City, August 1982
- 'No One Commits Suicide: Textual Analysis of Ideological Practices.' *Human Studies*, 6 (1983), 309–59
- 'Femininity as Discourse: Notes toward a Materialist Analysis.' Unpublished manuscript. Department of Sociology in Education, OISE, April 1984
- 'Textually-Mediated Social Organization.' *International Social Science Journal*, 36/1 (1984), 59–75
- 'Women, Class and Family.' In V. Burstyn and D.E. Smith (eds.), *Women, Class, Family and the State*, pp. 1–44. Toronto: Garamond Press, Network Basic Books 1985
- 'Institutional Ethnography: A Feminist Method.' *Resources for Feminist Research/Documentation sur la recherche feministe*, 15/1 (1986), 6–13
- *The Everyday World as Problematic: A Feminist Sociology*. Toronto: University of Toronto Press 1987
- *The Conceptual Practices of Power: A Feminist Sociology of Knowledge*. Toronto: University of Toronto Press, forthcoming
Smith G. 'Policing the Gay Community: An Inquiry into Textually-Mediated Social Relations.' *International Journal of the Sociology of Law*, 16/2 (1988), 163–83
Snell, J., R. Rosenwald, and A. Robey. 'The Wife-Beater's Wife.' *Archives of General Psychiatry*, 11 (1964), 107–12
Stanley, L., and S. Wise. *Breaking Out: Feminist Consciousness and Feminist Research*. London: Routledge & Kegan Paul 1983

Stark, E., and A. Flitcraft. 'Social Knowledge, Social Policy, and the Abuse of Women: The Case against Patriarchal Benevolence.' In D. Finkelhor, R. Gelles and G.T. Hotaling (eds.), *The Dark Side of Families*, pp. 330–48. Beverly Hills, CA: Sage Publications 1983

Starr, B. 'Comparing Battered and Non-Battered Women.' *Victimology*, 3/1–2 (1978), 591–607

Steinmetz, S.K. and M.A. Straus. 'The Family as a Cradle of Violence.' *Society*, 10/6 (1973), 50–6

– (eds.). *Violence in the Family*. New York: Dodd, Mead 1974

Stephenson, M. (ed.). *Women in Canada*. Toronto: New Press 1973

Straus, M.A. 'A General Systems Theory Approach to a Theory of Violence between Family Members.' *Social Science Information*, 12/3 (1973), 105–25

– 'Leveling, Civility and Violence in the Family.' *Journal of Marriage and the Family*, 36 (1974), 13–29

– 'Sexual Inequality, Cultural Norms, and Wife Beating.' *Victimology*, 1 (1976), 54–70

– 'Ordinary Violence, Child Abuse, and Wife-Beating: What Do They Have in Common?' In D. Finkelhor, R. Gelles, and G.T. Hotaling (eds.), *The Dark Side of Families* pp. 197–212. Beverly Hills, CA: Sage Publications 1983

Straus, M.A. and G. Hotaling. *The Social Causes of Husband-Wife Violence*. Minneapolis: University of Minnesota Press 1980

Straus, M.A., R. Gelles, and S.K. Steinmetz. *Behind Closed Doors: Violence in the American Family*. Garden City, NY: Doubleday/Anchor Press 1980

Straus, M.A., and S.K. Steinmetz. 'Violence Research, Violence Control, and the Good Society.' In S.K. Steinmetz and M.A. Straus (eds.), *Violence in the Family*, pp. 321–4). New York: Dodd, Mead 1974

Teather, L. 'The Feminist Mosaic.' In G. Matheson (ed.), *Women in the Canadian Mosaic*, pp. 301–46. Toronto: Peter Martin Associates 1976

Thorne, B. 'Feminist Rethinking of the Family: An Overview.' In B. Thorne with M. Yalom (eds.), *Rethinking the Family: Some Feminist Questions*, pp. 1–24. New York: Longman 1982

Thorne, B., with M. Yalom (eds.). *Rethinking the Family: Some Feminist Questions*. New York: Longman 1982

Tierney, K.J. 'The Battered Woman Movement and the Creation of the Wife Beating Problem.' *Social Problems*, 29/3 (1982), 207–20

Ursel, J.E. 'Towards a Theory of Reproduction.' *Contemporary Crisis*, 8 (1984), 265–92

– 'The State and the Maintenance of Patriarchy: A Case Study of Family, Labour and Welfare Legislation in Canada.' In J. Dickinson and B. Russell (eds.),

Family, Economy and State: The Social Reproduction Process under Capitalism, pp. 150–91. Toronto: Garamond Press 1986

Vancouver Women's Research Centre. *Protection for Battered Women*. Vancouver: 1982

Vandepol, A. 'Dependent Children, Child Custody, and the Mother's Pensions: The Transformation of State-Family Relations in the Early 20th Century.' *Social Problems*, 29/3 (1982), 221–36

Walker, G.A. 'Doing It the United Way: A Preliminary Look at the Dilemma of Women and Professionalism in Action.' Unpublished manuscript, OISE 1981

– 'The Abuse of Male Authority: New Frameworks for Understanding Family Violence.' Paper presented at a meeting of the Canadian Sociology and Anthropology Associations, Guelph, Ontario, 1984

– 'Women's Work and the State: Professionalism and the Organization of Class Relations.' Paper presented at the Motherworks Workshop of the Simone de Beauvoir Institute, Montreal, Quebec, October 1985

Walker, L. *The Battered Woman*. New York: Harper and Row 1979

Warrior, B. *Wifebeating*. Somerville, MA: New England Free Press 1976

– *Working on Wife Abuse*, 7th Supplemented ed. Cambridge, MA, 1978

Wilson, E. *Women and the Welfare State*. London: Tavistock Publications 1977

– 'Feminism and Social Work.' In R. Bailey and M. Brake (eds.), *Radical Social Work and Practice*, pp. 26–42. London: E. Arnold 1980

Wilson, E., and A. Weir. *Hidden Agendas: Theory, Politics, and Experience in the Women's Movement*. London: Tavistock Publications 1986

Working Group on Sexual Violence. *Feminist Manifesto*. Vancouver: Press Gang 1984

Zaretsky, E. 'The Place of the Family in the Origins of the Welfare State.' In B. Thorne with M. Yalom (eds.), *Rethinking the Family: Some Feminist Questions*, pp. 188–224. New York: Longman 1982

– 'Rethinking the Welfare State: Dependence, Economic Individualism and the Family.' In J. Dickinson and B. Russell (eds.), *Family, Economy and State: The Social Reproduction Process under Capitalism*, pp. 85–109. Toronto: Garamond Press 1986

Index

abused husbands, 120, 128–9
Addiction Research Foundation, 115, 118, 120, 122–3, 164
alcohol, role in wife-battering, 122–3, 174
Anderson, Doris, 42
Attorney General (Ontario), 121–2

Bannon, James, 87, 162
Barnsley, Jan, 39, 41, 54–5, 85
battered babies, 96, 97
battered women: and murder, 155; as clients of social services, 192, 202; co-ordination of services to, 133–51; immigrants and the law, 190; percentage of in Canada, 50; protection by law, 190; support groups, 29–30
battered women's movement, 92, 113; and change, 92; lobbying, 41, 72–4, 192–3; professionalization of lobbyists for, 49; usurped by state, 192–3; see also Ontario Association of Interval and Transition Houses
battered women's syndrome, 89, 92, 108–9

battering men: as responsibility of courts, 202; causes, 146–8; clinical treatment focus on, 31–2, 210; cycle of violence and, 144; focus on, 29, 30; forced therapy for, 143; London Alternatives to Violence Project, 182, 210; recommendations regarding, 61; right to batter, 140–1; testimony from, 146–8; treatment, 28, 67, 92, 146; violence blamed on feminists, 31–2; within clinical conceptual framework, 77
battery, as defined in British Criminal Code, 97
Boudria, Don, 169
Brienes, W., 82, 83
Bryden, Marion, 114, 123, 164–5
Burris, Carol Ann, 145

Canada, Standing Committee on Health, Welfare and Social Affairs, 111; as mediator between women and the state, 52; 'family violence' conceptual framework, 52; legal framework, 52; terms of reference, 50

Canada, Standing Committee on
Health, Welfare and Social Affairs, *Report on Violence in the Family: Wife Battering*, 68–70; and
private nature of the family, 131;
assignment of responses to
state institutions, 70; recommendations, 69–70
Canadian Advisory Council on the
Status of Women, 13, 34, 38–44,
149, 201; report as appropriation of
wife-battering issue by state, 56;
role as mediators between women
and state, 209; *Wife Battering in
Canada: The Vicious Circle*, 38
Canadian Advisory Council on the
Status of Women, Consultation
on Wife-Battering proceedings:
*Wife Battering Is Everywoman's
Issue*, 39–44; and systemic violence
against women, 43; defining
wife-battering as crime, 44; divisions among participants, 41,
46; goals, 44; information sharing,
40; naming the phenomena of
wife-battering, 44
capitalism, 10
capitalist society: family organization
in, 205; patriarchy in, 205
class-action suits against the police
(u.s.), 47–8
Collett, Staff Sergeant, 153–4, 162
comsoc. *See* Ontario Ministry of
Community and Social Services
concepts: as organizers of social construction of knowledge, 101; negotiating 133–51: translated to the
state's domain, 36–56, 209
conceptual framework of ideology,
10–11

Conceptual Framework for Wife-beating
(text), 48
co-optation, 6–7
Copps, Sheila, 128, 129, 169
court procedures, 108
Criminal Code (Canada), 19, 42, 131;
interpretation, 141
Criminal Code (Great Britain), 97
criminal justice system: and family-
violence conceptual framework,
167; co-ordination with social services, 166; jurisdiction, 163;
need for improved response, 25–6,
152, 162; response to battered
women, 42, 53, 54, 92, 127; survey
of 'victims,' 145–6; withdrawal
of assault charges by battered women, 163, 165
*Criminal Justice System's Response to
Abused Women*, 53
cycle of violence, 88, 107, 144, 149;
statistics, 144

Dark Side of Families, 90
De Laurentis, T., 210
Department of Justice (Canada), 38
Detroit police department, 154–5
degendering. *See* language
depoliticizing transition houses,
203–4
discourse: absorption of feminist
framework, 89–92; as theory building, 73; psychodynamic formulations, 76–8; psychosocial formulations, 78–83; relations of, 89
Dobash, R.D., 80, 85–6, 92
Dobash, R.E., 80, 85–6, 92
documentation: as expression of
point of view, 57–72, 210; of
state agency responsibility, 210

Don, Trudy, 134, 150, 152; influence on report, 172, 174, 197; testimony, 137–8, 140–1
Drea, Frank, 200
Dutton, Donald, 52

economic dependence, 121; and the law, 121, 122, 155; and restriction of battered women's choices, 160; as cause of wife-battering, 137, 155
education: failure to acknowledge wife-battering, 156; recommendations for Ontario education system, 187–9
Engels, F., 8, 23
euphemisms: as the language of diplomacy, 97; obscuring violence, 82, 93, 97; see also language
experts: discourse of, 90–1; Ontario Committee Report and, 199

facts about wife-battering, 74
family: and traditional family values, 191; privacy and state, 105, 167, 205, 186; reluctance to interfere in, 161
family violence, 50–1, 64, 79, 96; as a private matter, 98; as degendered term, 64, 98, 130; as euphemism, 101; as ideology, 64; as social-services orientation, 110; defined, 48–9; defined by Ontario Standing Committee on Social Development, 131; Ontario division of responsibility for, 122; wife-battering as a feature of, 46, 172
family violence (social-service concept), 27, 98; and criminal-justice conceptual framework, 166–7;

and professional expertise, 62; as acceptable conceptual framework for wife-battering, 58–9, 124; as a concept, 103; as a conceptual practice, 100, 103; as ideology, 70–1, 216; as learned behaviour, 80–1; as organizing principle of state, 210–11, 212; as Ontario Standing Committee on Social Development conceptual framework, 116–32; criticism, 90–1; defined, 28, 80, 127; degendering of wife-battering, 216; division of government responses to, 132; education preventing, 187–9; expanded to include wife-battering, 58–9; resistance to by feminists, 102; United Way Symposium on Family Violence (Vancouver), 27–8; United Way Task Force on Family Violence (Vancouver), 14, 29–32
federal government, involvement with wife-battering, 38–44; Working Together: 1989 National Forum on Family Violence, 216
Federal Government Consultation 1980, 14; Toward Equality for Women, 38
Federal-Provincial Conference, 189–90
Federal Standing Committee on Health, Welfare and Social Affairs, 113; and experts 199; and health-care professions, 185–6; and laying charges, 162, 182; and traditional family values, 191; and violence against women, 192; co-ordinating committees on family violence, 186–7; depolitici-

zation of wife-battering, 197;
education, 187–9; family and criminal court, 182; family as legal
unit, 183; government initiative in
response, 201–2; immigrant
women, 190; judicial emphasis of,
191, 198; mandatory reporting
of family violence, 186, 187; services to children, 184, 185; transition houses, 183, 184–5, 203–4;
uniform sentencing, 190; within
legal discourse, 153–9
feminism: discrediting of, 215; state
and media response to, 215
feminist analysis of wife-battering,
25, 30, 33–4, 37–8; absorption
by academic discourse, 91–3; absorption by other analyses, 85,
89–93; and critique of psychosocial
conceptual framework of wife-
battering, 81–3, 84; and discourse
on wife-battering, 85–9; and
feminist literature on wife-
battering, 85–9; and psychodynamic conceptual framework of
wife-battering, 77–8, 86–7; as
process of politicizing battered
women, 37–8; defining wife-
battering, 95; development, 66–7;
influence on London Response
to Violence Project, 149; in the Ontario Standing Committee on
Social Development, 124–6, 127,
129; loss of political analysis in,
85; resistance to, 30; solution to
wife-battering, 37–8
feminist response to wife-battering,
95
Findlay, Sue, 39
Flitcraft, A., 91

Freudian analysis, 77, 84

Gelles, R., 81, 87
gendering of family violence. *See*
language
Gordon, L., 82, 83, 215
government funding, 14, 20; of transition houses, 15, 51, 196–8; of
women's movement, 3
government response to wife-
battering, 50; assignment of responsibilities to government agencies, 111; controlling the issue
of wife-battering, 195–200; emphasis of family unit, 194; Ontario
government initiatives, 201–2;
Standing Committee on Health,
Welfare and Social Affairs, 50,
68–70; *see also* Canada, Standing
Committee on Health, Welfare and
Social Affairs; jurisdictional difficulties; legislation; Ontario government; Ontario Standing
Committee on Social Development
Gramsci, A., 9
Greaves, Lorraine, 160
Guyatt, Doris, 124–6; as broker between women's movement and
the state, 127, 129; influence on
Ontario Standing Committee
Report, 131, 172, 174, 197

House of Commons, 115, 118
Howie, Hon. Robert, 50

ideology, 10–12, 65; defined, 101;
ideological features of the process
of social organization, 217; making
ideology, 62, 103; recognition of

change, 63; relationship to knowledge production, 62
immigration laws, 190
institutional ethnography, 11–12
institutional practices, co-ordination,
14
institutional relations defined, 12–13
institutional response to wife-
battering, 119–23
*Integrated Response to Wife Assault: A
Community Model*, 53

Jaffe, Peter, 53, 143, 145, 149–50, 187
Johnston, Pamela, 76–9, 83–5
Johnston, Richard, 114–15, 120, 123,
156, 203
jurisdictional difficulties, 71; and
comsoc, 200; and funding, 196;
as organizing principle for Ontario
government report, 170; between
federal and provincial governments, 189–90; co-ordination of
response to government initiatives,
186–7; difficulties created by,
160–1; institutional alignment,
113; legal jurisdiction, 179–80;
response to, 159–60; *see also*
Standing Committees; London Alternatives to Violence Project
justice system response to battered
women, 131–2, 162–6, 211–12

Killens, Thérèse, 52
knowledge: and the relations of ruling, 3–20; and the women's
movement, 4–6; making, process
of, 94; social construction of, 101

language: as ideology, 108–9; as in-
strument of ruling, 10; as reflection of conceptual framework, 10–
11; gendering/degendering of wife-
battering, 81, 82, 153–4, 161; of
'wife abuse,' 96–7, 138; of 'wife-
battering,' 26; language, 'violence'
as actorless, *individual euphemisms;* 'battered wife,' 96, 101–2,
207; 'conjugal crime,' 35; 'conjugal terrorism,' 93; 'conjugal violence,' 51, 64; 'domestic crisis,'
26; 'domestic dispute,' 64, 93;
'domestic violence,' 60, 79, 93,
96; 'domestic violence,' defined,
105; 'domestic violence' and
'wife assault,' 158; 'family abuse,'
90; 'husband-wife fights,' 26;
'interspousal (violent) episodes,'
64, 97; 'intrauterine child abuse,'
65; 'male violence,' 106–7;
'marital abuse,' 35; 'marital violence,' 60, 79; 'perpetrator,' 107,
137; 'relationship violence,' 82;
'spouse abuse,' 11, 35, 50, 79, 97,
116, 120, 172; 'victim,' 107, 108,
137, 153; 'victim' in Ontario Standing Committee report, 169; 'violence against women,' 210; 'wife
abuse,' 19, 47, 96; 'wife assault,'
49, 57, 70, 158, 205; 'wife assault,'
within legal conceptual framework, 47–51, 100, 158; 'wife-
battering' *see* wife-battering
(term)
legal conceptual framework, 154
legal response to wife-battering. *See*
justice system response to battered women
legislation: Canada Assistance Act,
119; Child Welfare Act, 119;
Michigan 1978, 155; Ontario

General Welfare Assistance Act,
119, 121, 140
legitimization of wife-battering issue,
41, 42
Lepine, Marc, 215
Lewis, Debra, 51
London Alternatives to Violence
Project, 134, 137, 138; and family
court, 180; and laying charges, 16,
139, 146; and public education,
146; clinical/criminal conceptual
framework of, 211–12; feminist
input, 149, 150–1; influence on
Ontario Standing Committee
report, 187; jurisdictional co-
ordination, 144–5, 146
London Battered Women's Advocacy Clinic, 159–61; and jurisdictional co-ordination, 159–60
London Family Court Clinic, 53
London Police Force, 53
Loved, Honoured and Bruised (National
Film Board), 42, 134

MacDonald, Flora, 52
McGuigan, Jim, 127, 169
MacLeod, Linda, 42, 88, 134
McMurtry, Roy, 162–6
male domination of women, 33, 93
male violence against women, 95; as
target for feminist action, 99
Martin, Del, 86–9, 90, 91–3, 97; use
of term 'wife-battering,' 98, 108
Martin, N., 85
media response to feminism, 215
medical profession: psychological
analysis, 77–8; response to
wife-battering, 25, 54, 127; tranquillizers, 139.
Mitchell, Margaret, 52, 55, 118

Morgan, P., 6–7, 18, 21; contradictions in women's movement,
206, 208; women's movement and
the state, 216
Mueller, A., 8

New Democratic Party (Ontario),
114–15
Ng, R., 7

Ontario Association of Interval and
Transition Houses, 13, 15, 113,
134, 137; influence on Ontario
Standing Committee report,
211; liaison with Richard Johnston,
170; participation in Ministry of
Community and Social Services
Consultation, 203; testimony at
Standing Committee on Social Development (Ontario), 137–41,
150, 152
Ontario Attorney General's Office,
164
Ontario government; 1987 initiatives,
15; funding of OAITH, 15
Ontario Ministry of Community and
Social Services (COMSOC), 114,
116; report, 134, 197
Ontario Standing Committee on Social Development, 12, 15, 168–
93, 209; as a public inquiry, 118;
assignment of government department responsibility, 119, 172;
attorney general's testimony,
164–6; committee structure, 114;
conceptual framework, 120–32,
133–51; discourse preparation,
134–6; focus on wife-battering,
136; hearings, 113–51; jurisdictional
differences, 139–40; legal con-

ceptual framework, 162–6; membership, 114; Ministry of Community and Social Services testimony, 121; 'referring out,' 114–15, 117; report, 168–93; research for, 115; role of opposition parties, 117–18; social problem conceptual framework, 149; spouse abuse as a conceptual framework, 120; witnesses, 115–18, 119

Ontario Standing Committee on Social Development, *First Report on Family Violence: Wife Battering*, 168–93
– areas of concern, 169
– areas of disagreement, 170
– criminality of wife-battering, 173
– definition of wife-battering, 173
– fundamental principles, 169
– recommendations, 174–93, 194–206; accessibility of services, 175–6; and immigrant women, 175; Family Consultant Programs, 177–8; family/criminal courts, 180; federal/provincial liaison, 189–90; police liaison with other agencies, 177; police record-keeping, 177, 178; police training, 177–8; rural women, 178; sentencing, 181; services to rural women, 175; transition houses, 179

Pagelow, M.D., 92
patriarchal structure of society, 31, 43, 44, 87, 93
patriarchal structure of the family, 91, 105
Pépin, Lucie, 51–2
Pizzey, E., 25, 83, 86, 87, 102

Pleck, E., 215, 85
police: and budget cuts, 157; and gender in assault cases, 154; and services to battered women, 69, 92; and the laying of charges, 165; as law enforcers, 61; as personification of violence, 156; as providers of legal protection, 157; as therapists, 155; attitude to wife-battering, 140: neglect of battered women, 25; practices, 26; referral to transition houses, 179; response to domestic violence, 26, 53, 127, 144, 178; social service/legal conceptual framework, 26, 155; survey (London, 1979), 145–6; use of legal/social-science terms, 26
policy on wife-battering, 19
professional intervention: as remedy to wife-battering, 31; recommended by United Way Survey, 61–2
professionalization: and institutionalization of social movements, 213; and psychodynamic conceptual framework, 77–83; of services to battered women, 178, 202, 213
professionals: and women's position in society, 67–8; authority, 66; ideology, 5; intervention, 31, 61–2; status, 30; within feminist analysis, 76–83; within the women's movement, 218
Protection for Battered Women, 54
Pyymaki, Joy, 142

Report on Violence in the Family: Wife Battering. *See* Canada, Standing

Committee on Health, Welfare and
Social Affairs, *Report on Violence
in the Family: Wife Battering*
restraining orders, 139
Riddington, J., 218
Robertson, Joann, 29
Robinson, Alan, 128, 164, 170
Roy, Maria, 89–90
Royal Commission on the Status of
Women, 36–8
ruling ideas, and ideological hegemony, 9; as expression of dominant material relationships, 8–9;
conceptual practice in political
process, 10
ruling institutions, absorption of
battered women's movement,
17–20, 45–6
ruling process, 204; and feminist
strategy, 205
ruling relations, 8–10, 13, 130, 207–8;
and analysis of wife-battering,
83; defined, 4; exclusion of wom-
en, 43, 71, 83: location of wife-
battering within, 218–19

Schechter, S., 85–6
Schreader, A., 9
*Scream Quietly or the Neighbours Will
Hear You*, 25
semantic differences. *See* language
sentencing, 140; *see also* justice system
Shymko, Yuri, 130
Small, S., 85
Smith, Dorothy, 8; and economic dependence of women, 33; and
family-violence conceptual framework, 102; and Federal Government Consultation, 40–1, 43, 45,
99; and ideology, 10–11, 14

social construction of knowledge, 91,
101
social problem analysis, 78–81
social reality, 9
social services: absorption of battered
women's movement, 58; extension
of mandate to include battered
women, 56; inadequacy of social-
service solution, 54; neglect of
battered women, 25; recognition of
wife-battering as a problem, 156
Social Services for Assaulted Women
(Toronto), *Conceptual Framework for
Wife-Beating*, 48
Solicitor-General (Canada), 38
Standing Committees. *See* Ontario
Stark, E., 91
state: absorption of feminist issues,
17–20; and battered women's
movement, 5–6, 41–2; as set of apparatuses, 6–7; control of wife-
battering issue, 195; depoliticizing
wife-battering issue, 213; existing institutions and wife-battering,
82; funding of battered wom-
en's movement, 26, 201; funding
of transition houses, 139–40;
funding of women's movement, 3,
15; influence of Standing Committee witnesses on, 16; institutional framework and wife-
battering, 82; jurisdictions as organizing principle, 159, 170–1,
174–6; relation to family, 105, 141,
172; reproduction of class relations, 7, 213–14; response to concept of violence, 150–1; violence
as organizing concept, 169
Steinmetz, S., 81, 87
Strauss, Murray, 27, 64, 79–80, 81, 87

Support Services for Battered
Women, 189

Themes of Dialogue, 143–4
Toward Equality for Women, 38
transition houses, 15, 22, 37; as the
new poorhouses, 214; children in,
188; funding formula, 139–40; mar-
ginalization by Ontario Report,
185, 202, 213; perceived as hostile
to men, 61; relation to Children's
Aid Society, 140

United Way of Vancouver, 34, 37, 43,
209; Survey (1976), 58
United Way of Vancouver Task Force
on Family Violence, 14, 58; as
knowledge production, 62–4;
focus on battering men, 31; institutional orientation of, 58; legitimizing wife-battering issue, 64;
role of professionals, 31; social-
problem conceptual framework,
64
United Way of Vancouver Task Force
on Family Violence report: *Wife Battering: A Review and Preliminary
Enquiry into Local Incidence, Needs
and Resources*, 59; family-violence
conceptual framework, 60–2; feminist response to, 26; recommendations, 60–1
University of Montreal, 215
University of New Hampshire Family
Violence Research Programme, 79

Vancouver Transition House, 22–3
Vancouver Women's Research
Centre, 39, 86
victim blaming, 53; and masochism,

125, 129, 215–16; and role of
women, 147; in systems theory
analysis, 67
violence, 95–110; and breakdown of
social order, 78–81; and clinical
conceptual framework of wife-
battering, 214–15; and maintenance of social order, 82; and the
state, 104–5, 151; as conceptual
practice, 100–3, 108–9; concept of,
103–4, 169, 214–15; concept of as
strategy, 150; defining, 95; deindividuated, 106; *see also* language
violence against women, 99–100; as a
conceptual framework, 161–2; as
cause of wife-battering, 156; as
context for wife-battering, 43, 49,
50, 67; concept of, 96

Walker, Gillian, 84; and establishment of battered women's support
group, 29–30; involvement with
Vancouver Transition House, 23–4;
participation in Status of Women
Consultation, 40, 41
Walker, Lenore, 86–7, 88–9, 92, 109
wife-battering (term), 15; as used by
CAC spokeswomen, 24; conceptual
alignment of synonyms, 47; jurisdictional divisions, 42, 54; on title
of Ontario Standing Committee
report, 172; origin of term, 6–7,
9; redefined as 'wife assault,'
57
wife-battering: and child abuse protection 127; and the state 149,
156; as a developing issue, 21–35;
as expression of male violence,
48; as a gender-neutral problem,
83; as a problem of individuals,

207; as a psychosocial problem, 78–81, 153; as a social problem, 149; as a welfare problem, 197; as a 'women's issue,' 96; as 'family violence,' 58, 172; as pathology, 77–8; as permission to control women, 84; as violence against women, 149; causes of 141–2, 173; clinical-criminal conceptual framework, 159–60; co-ordination of services to, 137–8, 152–3; cultural acceptance of, 125–6; cultural variation of, 125–6; definition, 141, 173; degendering, 26, 64, 98; in public arena, 25, 37; legislative questions, 51; prevention and cure, 139; professionalization of, 85; role of alcohol and drug abuse, 141–2; statistics, 60; as a crime, 44, 46–8, 121–2, 144–5; as assault, 150, 156, 165–6; as a crime against the state, 52; as stranger-to-stranger crime, 166–7

Wife Battering in Canada: The Vicious Circle, 134

Wife Battering Is Everywoman's Issue, 34–40

women's movement: and the state, 3–8, 17, 132; as creator of wife-battering issue, 17–18, 132; contradictions in, 208; control of wife-battering issue, 20–35, 45, 195–206; history of, 36–7; influence, 202; political position on wife-battering, 32–3, 37–8